SUPER HOROSCOPE
TAURUS

2013

APRIL 21 – MAY 20

B

BERKLEY BOOKS, NEW YORK

THE BERKLEY PUBLISHING GROUP
Published by the Penguin Group
Penguin Group (USA) Inc.
375 Hudson Street, New York, New York 10014, USA
Penguin Group (Canada), 90 Eglinton Avenue East, Suite 700, Toronto, Ontario M4P 2Y3, Canada
(a division of Pearson Penguin Canada Inc.) • Penguin Books Ltd., 80 Strand, London WC2R 0RL,
England • Penguin Group Ireland, 25 St. Stephen's Green, Dublin 2, Ireland (a division of Penguin
Books Ltd.) • Penguin Group (Australia), 250 Camberwell Road, Camberwell, Victoria 3124, Australia
(a division of Pearson Australia Group Pty. Ltd.) • Penguin Books India Pvt. Ltd., 11 Community
Centre, Panchsheel Park, New Delhi—110 017, India • Penguin Group (NZ), 67 Apollo Drive,
Rosedale, Auckland 0632, New Zealand (a division of Pearson New Zealand Ltd.) • Penguin Books
(South Africa) (Pty.) Ltd., 24 Sturdee Avenue, Rosebank, Johannesburg 2196, South Africa

Penguin Books Ltd., Registered Offices: 80 Strand, London WC2R 0RL, England

The publishers regret that they cannot answer individual letters requesting personal horoscope information.

2013 SUPER HOROSCOPE TAURUS

PUBLISHING HISTORY
Berkley trade paperback edition / July 2012

Berkley trade paperback ISBN: 978-0-425-24634-4

Library of Congress Cataloging-in-Publication Data

ISSN: 1535-0509

PRINTED IN THE UNITED STATES OF AMERICA

10 9 8 7 6 5 4 3 2 1

ALWAYS LEARNING   PEARSON

Contents

THE CUSP-BORN TAURUS

Are you *really* a Taurus? If your birthday falls during the fourth week of April, at the beginning of Taurus, will you still retain the traits of Aries, the sign of the Zodiac before Taurus? And what if you were born late in May—are you more Gemini than Taurus? Many people born at the edge, or cusp, of a sign have difficulty determining exactly what sign they are. If you are one of these people, here's how you can figure it out, once and for all.

Consult the cusp table on the facing page, then locate the year of your birth. The table will tell you the precise days on which the Sun entered and left your sign for the year of your birth. In that way you can determine if you are a true Taurus—or whether you are an Aries or a Gemini—according to the variations in cusp dates from year to year (see also page 17).

If you were born at the beginning or end of Taurus, yours is a lifetime reflecting a process of subtle transformation. Your life on Earth will symbolize a significant change in consciousness, for you are either about to enter a whole new way of living or are leaving one behind.

If you were born toward the end of April, you may want to read the horoscope book for Aries as well as for Taurus. The investment might be strangely revealing, for Aries contains the secret to many of your complexities and unexpressed assets and liabilities.

But this is the very irony of an Aries-Taurus cusp. The more fixed you become, the less able you are to seek out adventure, take chances, gamble—and win. Your natural tendency is to acquire, build, and collect. The more you possess, the more permanent your status in life; thus, the less able you are to simply pick up and go back to zero. Fulfillment comes through loyalty, constancy, and success in the material world.

If you were born during the third week of May, you may want to see the Gemini horoscope book as well as Taurus, for without Gemini your assets are often too stable, too fixed. Gemini provides you with fluidity and gets you moving.

You are a blend of stability and mobility—rich, raw material—with a dexterity of mind and body. Even around a fixed and constant center, change is always taking place. No matter how you hang on, there will be a series of changes, experiences, new people, new faces, places, facts, and events.

You are conservative with the very definite hint of an open mind, the blend of hardheaded realism and freewheeling experimentalism, earthy, tactile sensuality, and bold participation in life's joys.

THE CUSPS OF TAURUS

DATES SUN ENTERS TAURUS (LEAVES ARIES)

April 20 every year from 1900 to 2015, except for the following:

April 19

1948	1972	1988	2000	2012
52	76	89	2001	2013
56	80	92	2004	
60	81	93	2005	
64	84	96	2008	
68	85	97	2009	

DATES SUN LEAVES TAURUS (ENTERS GEMINI)

May 21 every year from 1900 to 2015, except for the following:

May 20

1948	1972	1988	2000	2012
52	76	89	2001	2013
56	80	92	2004	
60	81	93	2005	
64	84	96	2008	
68	85	97	2009	

THE ASCENDANT: TAURUS RISING

Could you be a "double" Taurus? That is, could you have Taurus as your Rising sign as well as your Sun sign? The tables on pages 8–9 will tell you Taurus what your Rising sign happens to be. Just find the hour of your birth, then find the day of your birth, and you will see which sign of the Zodiac is your Ascendant, as the Rising sign is called. The Ascendant is called that because it is the sign rising on the eastern horizon at the time of your birth. For a more detailed discussion of the Rising sign and the twelve houses of the Zodiac, see pages 17–20.

The Ascendant, or Rising sign, is placed on the 1st house in a horoscope, of which there are twelve houses. The 1st house represents your response to the environment—your unique response. Call it identity, personality, ego, self-image, facade, come-on, body-mind-spirit—whatever term best conveys to you the meaning of the you that acts and reacts in the world. It is a you that is always changing, discovering a new you. Your identity started with birth and early environment, over which you had little conscious control, and continues to experience, to adjust, to express itself. The 1st house also represents how others see you. Has anyone ever guessed your sign to be your Rising sign? People may respond to that personality, that facade, that body type governed by your Rising sign.

Your Ascendant, or Rising sign, modifies your basic Sun sign personality, and it affects the way you act out the daily predictions for your Sun sign. If your Rising sign is indeed Taurus, what follows is a description of its effects on your horoscope. If your Rising sign is not Taurus, but some other sign of the Zodiac, you may wish to read the horoscope book for that sign as well.

With Taurus on the Ascendant, that is, in your 1st house, the planet rising in the 1st house is Venus, ruler of Taurus. Venus confers an intuitive, creative mind, and a liking for ease and luxury. Venus here gives you a sociable nature—loyal, lovable, and loving. But there are contradictions! Like the Bull, the zodiacal symbol of Taurus, you strike contrasting poses. In repose, you can be seen sweetly, peaceably smelling the flowers. Enraged, you trample the very turf that supports you. A passionate, selfish, demanding streak overcomes the mild, gentle, docile mood.

You have a well-developed need for people. Personal relationships are important to you, often centering around your love life. Bestowed with ample good looks and sensual appeal, you do not lack for admirers. In fact, you are sought after, often chased. Though generally loyal and steadfast, and capable of success in marriage, you may, however, have an irresistible urge for secret affairs, which arouse other people's jealousy and antagonism. There is also the danger that you can be caught between a fierce possessiveness and a thoughtless desire to acquire popularity in an indiscriminating way.

You have an even greater need for money. For you with Taurus Rising, money symbolizes the successful self. You intend to earn money in a steady, practical way, especially one that is time-honored and contains few risks. But you tend to spend money lavishly, when your comfort and edification demand it. You like sparkle and glitter, ornamentation, and nourishment. Food, clothes, "things" can become extravagances you cannot afford. Only when threats to your personal security loom do you jealously guard your money. You may also confuse money and love, using the one to get the other and vice versa.

You have a strong creative drive, tending toward the arts and crafts. Your self-expression is best achieved by creating sensations that are pleasing to the eye and to the body in general. You are, however, capable of sustained efforts of the mind, for you are both patient and intuitive. For you, the creator, one problem lies in being too fixed in your vision, too proud to ask for help, and too self-centered to think you need it. If you get bogged down, you abandon your undertakings for a lazy, self-indulgent spell. You also keep a too tenacious hold on your creations.

Because you are basically cautious, what you create or build is usually very sound. Success through stability is your motto. Your efforts, focused in a relationship or in a product, have a tempering, personalizing influence. Sometimes you shy away from group efforts if they stress generalities or nonpersonal goals. In a setting where intimacy is discouraged, your drive is inhibited. On the other hand, you have deep compassion and an unselfish need to serve others. When an activity or cause sponsors both personal satisfaction and kindly justice, you will work for it laboriously. Otherwise, you prefer the pursuit of heady living, sometimes alone, sometimes with a partner.

For Taurus Rising, two key words are sense and sensibility. Weave them together into a rich, thick tapestry, rather than raveling them in bits and pieces of pleasure.

RISING SIGNS FOR TAURUS

Hour of Birth*	Date of Birth		
	April 20–25	April 26–29	April 30–May 4
Midnight	Capricorn	Capricorn	Capricorn
1 AM	Capricorn	Aquarius	Aquarius
2 AM	Aquarius	Aquarius	Aquarius; Pisces 5/4
3 AM	Pisces	Pisces	Pisces
4 AM	Pisces; Aries 4/22	Aries	Aries
5 AM	Aries	Taurus	Taurus
6 AM	Taurus	Taurus	Taurus; Gemini 5/4
7 AM	Gemini	Gemini	Gemini
8 AM	Gemini	Gemini	Gemini; Cancer 5/2
9 AM	Cancer	Cancer	Cancer
10 AM	Cancer	Cancer	Cancer
11 AM	Cancer; Leo 4/22	Leo	Leo
Noon	Leo	Leo	Leo
1 PM	Leo	Leo	Virgo
2 PM	Virgo	Virgo	Virgo
3 PM	Virgo	Virgo	Virgo
4 PM	Virgo; Libra 4/23	Libra	Libra
5 PM	Libra	Libra	Libra
6 PM	Libra	Libra; Scorpio 4/29	Scorpio
7 PM	Scorpio	Scorpio	Scorpio
8 PM	Scorpio	Scorpio	Scorpio
9 PM	Scorpio; Sagittarius 4/23	Sagittarius	Sagittarius
10 PM	Sagittarius	Sagittarius	Sagittarius
11 PM	Sagittarius	Sagittarius; Capricorn 4/27	Capricorn

*Hour of birth given here is for Standard Time in any time zone. If your hour of birth was recorded in Daylight Saving Time, subtract one hour from it and consult that hour in the table above. For example, if you were born at 6 AM D.S.T., see 5 AM above.

Hour of Birth*	Date of Birth		
	May 5–10	May 11–15	May 16–21
Midnight	Capricorn	Aquarius	Aquarius
1 AM	Aquarius	Aquarius	Aquarius; Pisces 5/18
2 AM	Pisces	Pisces	Pisces
3 AM	Pisces; Aries 5/6	Aries	Aries
4 AM	Aries	Taurus	Taurus
5 AM	Taurus	Taurus	Taurus; Gemini 5/19
6 AM	Gemini	Gemini	Gemini
7 AM	Gemini	Gemini	Gemini; Cancer 5/18
8 AM	Cancer	Cancer	Cancer
9 AM	Cancer	Cancer	Cancer
10 AM	Cancer; Leo 5/8	Leo	Leo
11 AM	Leo	Leo	Leo
Noon	Leo	Leo	Virgo
1 PM	Virgo	Virgo	Virgo
2 PM	Virgo	Virgo	Virgo
3 PM	Virgo; Libra 5/8	Libra	Libra
4 PM	Libra	Libra	Libra
5 PM	Libra	Scorpio	Scorpio
6 PM	Scorpio	Scorpio	Scorpio
7 PM	Scorpio	Scorpio	Scorpio
8 PM	Scorpio; Sagittarius 5/8	Sagittarius	Sagittarius
9 PM	Sagittarius	Sagittarius	Sagittarius
10 PM	Sagittarius	Sagittarius; Capricorn 5/12	Capricorn
11 PM	Capricorn	Capricorn	Capricorn

* See note on facing page.

THE PLACE OF ASTROLOGY IN TODAY'S WORLD

Does astrology have a place in the fast-moving, ultra-scientific world we live in today? Can it be justified in a sophisticated society whose outriders are already preparing to step off the moon into the deep space of the planets themselves? Or is it just a hangover of ancient superstition, a psychological dummy for neurotics and dreamers of every historical age?

These are the kind of questions that any inquiring person can be expected to ask when they approach a subject like astrology which goes beyond, but never excludes, the materialistic side of life.

The simple, single answer is that astrology works. It works for many millions of people in the western world alone. In the United States there are 10 million followers and in Europe, an estimated 25 million. America has more than 4000 practicing astrologers, Europe nearly three times as many. Even down-under Australia has its hundreds of thousands of adherents. In the eastern countries, astrology has enormous followings, again, because it has been proved to work. In India, for example, brides and grooms for centuries have been chosen on the basis of their astrological compatibility.

Astrology today is more vital than ever before, more practicable because all over the world the media devotes much space and time to it, more valid because science itself is confirming the precepts of astrological knowledge with every new exciting step. The ordinary person who daily applies astrology intelligently does not have to wonder whether it is true nor believe in it blindly. He can see it working for himself. And, if he can use it—and this book is designed to help the reader to do just that—he can make living a far richer experience, and become a more developed personality and a better person.

Astrology and Relationships

Astrology is the science of relationships. It is not just a study of planetary influences on man and his environment. It is the study of man himself.

We are at the center of our personal universe, of all our relationships. And our happiness or sadness depends on how we act, how we relate to the people and things that surround us. The emotions that we generate have a distinct effect—for better or worse—on the world around us. Our friends and our enemies will confirm this. Just look in the mirror the next time you are angry. In other words, each of us is a kind of sun or planet or star radiating our feelings on the environment around us. Our influence on our personal universe, whether loving, helpful, or destructive, varies with our changing moods, expressed through our individual character.

Our personal "radiations" are potent in the way they affect our moods and our ability to control them. But we usually are able to throw off our emotion in some sort of action—we have a good cry, walk it off, or tell someone our troubles—before it can build up too far and make us physically ill. Astrology helps us to understand the universal forces working on us, and through this understanding, we can become more properly adjusted to our surroundings so that we find ourselves coping where others may flounder.

The Challenge of Love

The challenge of love lies in recognizing the difference between infatuation, emotion, sex, and, sometimes, the intentional deceit of the other person. Mankind, with its record of broken marriages, despair, and disillusionment, is obviously not very good at making these distinctions.

Can astrology help?

Yes. In the same way that advance knowledge can usually help in any human situation. And there is probably no situation as human, as poignant, as pathetic and universal, as the failure of man's love.

Love, of course, is not just between man and woman. It involves love of children, parents, home, and friends. But the big problems usually involve the choice of partner.

Astrology has established degrees of compatibility that exist between people born under the various signs of the Zodiac. Because people are individuals, there are numerous variations and modifications. So the astrologer, when approached on mate and marriage matters, makes allowances for them. But the fact remains that some groups of people are suited for each other and some are not, and astrology has expressed this in terms of characteristics we all can study and use as a personal guide.

No matter how much enjoyment and pleasure we find in the different aspects of each other's character, if it is not an overall compatibility, the chances of our finding fulfillment or enduring happiness in each other are pretty hopeless. And astrology can help us to find someone compatible.

Astrology and Science

Closely related to our emotions is the "other side" of our personal universe, our physical welfare. Our body, of course, is largely influenced by things around us over which we have very little control. The phone rings, we hear it. The train runs late. We snag our stocking or cut our face shaving. Our body is under a constant bombardment of events that influence our daily lives to varying degrees.

The question that arises from all this is, what makes each of us act so that we have to involve other people and keep the ball of activity and evolution rolling? This is the question that both science and astrology are involved with. The scientists have attacked it from different angles: anthropology, the study of human evolution as body, mind and response to environment; anatomy, the study of bodily structure; psychology, the science of the human mind; and so on. These studies have produced very impressive classifications and valuable information, but because the approach to the problem is fragmented, so is the result. They remain "branches" of science. Science generally studies effects. It keeps turning up wonderful answers but no lasting solutions. Astrology, on the other hand, approaches the question from the broader viewpoint. Astrology began its inquiry with the totality of human experience and saw it as an effect. It then looked to find the cause, or at least the prime movers, and during thousands of years of observation of man and his *universal* environment came up with the extraordinary principle of planetary influence—or astrology, which, from the Greek, means the science of the stars.

Modern science, as we shall see, has confirmed much of astrology's foundations—most of it unintentionally, some of it reluctantly, but still, indisputably.

It is not difficult to imagine that there must be a connection between outer space and Earth. Even today, scientists are not too sure how our Earth was created, but it is generally agreed that it is only a tiny part of the universe. And as a part of the universe, people on Earth see and feel the influence of heavenly bodies in almost every aspect of our existence. There is no doubt that the Sun has the greatest influence on life on this planet. Without it there would be no life, for without it there would be no warmth, no division into day and night, no cycles of time or season at all. This is clear and easy to see. The influence of the Moon, on the other hand, is more subtle, though no less definite.

There are many ways in which the influence of the Moon manifests itself here on Earth, both on human and animal life. It is a well-known fact, for instance, that the large movements of water on our planet—that is the ebb and flow of the tides—are caused by the Moon's gravitational pull. Since this is so, it follows that these water movements do not occur only in the oceans, but that all bodies of water are affected, even down to the tiniest puddle.

The human body, too, which consists of about 70 percent water, falls within the scope of this lunar influence. For example the menstrual cycle of most women corresponds to the 28-day lunar month; the period of pregnancy in humans is 273 days, or equal to nine lunar months. Similarly, many illnesses reach a crisis at the change of the Moon, and statistics in many countries have shown that the crime rate is highest at the time of the Full Moon. Even human sexual desire has been associated with the phases of the Moon. But it is in the movement of the tides that we get the clearest demonstration of planetary influence, which leads to the irresistible correspondence between the so-called metaphysical and the physical.

Tide tables are prepared years in advance by calculating the future positions of the Moon. Science has known for a long time that the Moon is the main cause of tidal action. But only in the last few years has it begun to realize the possible extent of this influence on mankind. To begin with, the ocean tides do not rise and fall as we might imagine from our personal observations of them. The Moon as it orbits around Earth sets up a circular wave of attraction which pulls the oceans of the world after it, broadly in an east to west direction. This influence is like a phantom wave crest, a loop of power stretching from pole to pole which passes over and around the Earth like an invisible shadow. It travels with equal effect across the land masses and, as scientists were recently amazed to observe, caused oysters placed in the dark in the middle of the United States where there is no sea to open their shells to receive the nonexistent tide. If the land-locked oysters react to this invisible signal, what effect does it have on us who not so long ago in evolutionary time came out of the sea and still have its salt in our blood and sweat?

Less well known is the fact that the Moon is also the primary force behind the circulation of blood in human beings and animals, and the movement of sap in trees and plants. Agriculturists have established that the Moon has a distinct influence on crops, which explains why for centuries people have planted according to Moon cycles. The habits of many animals, too, are directed by the movement of the Moon. Migratory birds, for instance, depart only at or near the time of the Full Moon. And certain sea creatures, eels in particular, move only in accordance with certain phases of the Moon.

Know Thyself—Why?

In today's fast-changing world, everyone still longs to know what the future holds. It is the one thing that everyone has in common: rich and poor, famous and infamous, all are deeply concerned about tomorrow.

But the key to the future, as every historian knows, lies in the past. This is as true of individual people as it is of nations. You cannot understand your future without first understanding your past, which is simply another way of saying that you must first of all know yourself.

The motto "know thyself" seems obvious enough nowadays, but it was originally put forward as the foundation of wisdom by the ancient Greek philosophers. It was then adopted by the "mystery religions" of the ancient Middle East, Greece, Rome, and is still used in all genuine schools of mind training or mystical discipline, both in those of the East, based on yoga, and those of the West. So it is universally accepted now, and has been through the ages.

But how do you go about discovering what sort of person you are? The first step is usually classification into some sort of system of types. Astrology did this long before the birth of Christ. Psychology has also done it. So has modern medicine, in its way.

One system classifies people according to the source of the impulses they respond to most readily: the muscles, leading to direct bodily action; the digestive organs, resulting in emotion; or the brain and nerves, giving rise to thinking. Another such system says that character is determined by the endocrine glands, and gives us such labels as "pituitary," "thyroid," and "hyperthyroid" types. These different systems are neither contradictory nor mutually exclusive. In fact, they are very often different ways of saying the same thing.

Very popular, useful classifications were devised by Carl Jung, the eminent disciple of Freud. Jung observed among the different faculties of the mind, four which have a predominant influence on character. These four faculties exist in all of us without exception, but not in perfect balance. So when we say, for instance, that someone is a "thinking type," it means that in any situation he or she tries to be rational. Emotion, which may be the opposite of thinking, will be his or her weakest function. This thinking type can be sensible and reasonable, or calculating and unsympathetic. The emotional type, on the other hand, can often be recognized by exaggerated language—everything is either marvelous or terrible—and in extreme cases they even invent dramas and quarrels out of nothing just to make life more interesting.

The other two faculties are intuition and physical sensation. The sensation type does not only care for food and drink, nice clothes and furniture; he or she is also interested in all forms of physical experience. Many scientists are sensation types as are athletes and nature-lovers. Like sensation, intuition is a form of perception and we all possess it. But it works through that part of the mind which is not under conscious control—consequently it sees meanings and connections which are not obvious to thought or emotion. Inventors and original thinkers are always intuitive, but so, too, are superstitious people who see meanings where none exist.

Thus, sensation tells us what is going on in the world, feeling (that is, emotion) tells us how important it is to ourselves, thinking enables us to interpret it and work out what we should do about it, and intuition tells us what it means to ourselves and others. All four faculties are essential, and all are present in every one of us. But some people are guided chiefly by one, others by another. In addition, Jung also observed a division of the human personality into the extrovert and the introvert, which cuts across these four types.

A disadvantage of all these systems of classification is that one cannot tell very easily where to place oneself. Some people are reluctant to admit that they act to please their emotions. So they deceive themselves for years by trying to belong to whichever type they think is the "best." Of course, there is no best; each has its faults and each has its good points.

The advantage of the signs of the Zodiac is that they simplify classification. Not only that, but your date of birth is personal—it is unarguably yours. What better way to know yourself than by going back as far as possible to the very moment of your birth? And this is precisely what your horoscope is all about, as we shall see in the next section.

WHAT IS A HOROSCOPE?

If you had been able to take a picture of the skies at the moment of your birth, that photograph would be your horoscope. Lacking such a snapshot, it is still possible to recreate the picture—and this is at the basis of the astrologer's art. In other words, your horoscope is a representation of the skies with the planets in the exact positions they occupied at the time you were born.

The year of birth tells an astrologer the positions of the distant, slow-moving planets Jupiter, Saturn, Uranus, Neptune, and Pluto. The month of birth indicates the Sun sign, or birth sign as it is commonly called, as well as indicating the positions of the rapidly moving planets Venus, Mercury, and Mars. The day and time of birth will locate the position of our Moon. And the moment—the exact hour and minute—of birth determines the houses through what is called the Ascendant, or Rising sign.

With this information the astrologer consults various tables to calculate the specific positions of the Sun, Moon, and other planets relative to your birthplace at the moment you were born. Then he or she locates them by means of the Zodiac.

The Zodiac

The Zodiac is a band of stars (constellations) in the skies, centered on the Sun's apparent path around the Earth, and is divided into twelve equal segments, or signs. What we are actually dividing up is the Earth's path around the Sun. But from our point of view here on Earth, it seems as if the Sun is making a great circle around our planet in the sky, so we say it is the Sun's apparent path. This twelve-fold division, the Zodiac, is a reference system for the astrologer. At any given moment the planets—and in astrology both the Sun and Moon are considered to be planets—can all be located at a specific point along this path.

Now where in all this are you, the subject of the horoscope? Your character is largely determined by the sign the Sun is in. So that is where the astrologer looks first in your horoscope, at your Sun sign.

The Sun Sign and the Cusp

There are twelve signs in the Zodiac, and the Sun spends approximately one month in each sign. But because of the motion of the Earth around the Sun—the Sun's apparent motion—the dates when the Sun enters and leaves each sign may change from year to year. Some people born near the cusp, or edge, of a sign have difficulty determining which is their Sun sign. But in this book a Table of Cusps is provided for the years 1900 to 2015 (page 5) so you can find out what your true Sun sign is.

Here are the twelve signs of the Zodiac, their ancient zodiacal symbol, and the dates when the Sun enters and leaves each sign for the year 2013. Remember, these dates may change from year to year.

ARIES	Ram	March 20–April 19
TAURUS	Bull	April 19–May 20
GEMINI	Twins	May 20–June 21
CANCER	Crab	June 21–July 22
LEO	Lion	July 22–August 22
VIRGO	Virgin	August 22–September 22
LIBRA	Scales	September 22–October 23
SCORPIO	Scorpion	October 23–November 22
SAGITTARIUS	Archer	November 22–December 21
CAPRICORN	Sea Goat	December 21–January 19
AQUARIUS	Water Bearer	January 19–February 18
PISCES	Fish	February 18–March 20

It is possible to draw significant conclusions and make meaningful predictions based simply on the Sun sign of a person. There are many people who have been amazed at the accuracy of the description of their own character based only on the Sun sign. But an astrologer needs more information than just your Sun sign to interpret the photograph that is your horoscope.

The Rising Sign and the Zodiacal Houses

An astrologer needs the exact time and place of your birth in order to construct and interpret your horoscope. The illustration on the next page shows the flat chart, or natural wheel, an astrologer uses. Note the inner circle of the wheel labeled 1 through 12. These 12 divisions are known as the houses of the Zodiac.

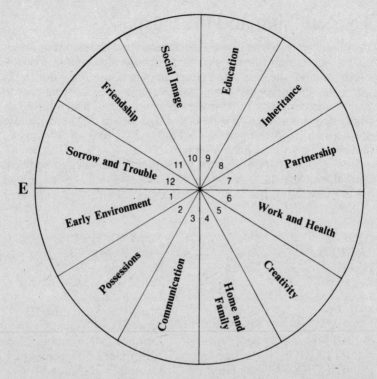

The 1st house always starts from the position marked E, which corresponds to the eastern horizon. The rest of the houses 2 through 12 follow around in a "counterclockwise" direction. The point where each house starts is known as a cusp, or edge.

The cusp, or edge, of the 1st house (point E) is where an astrologer would place your Rising sign, the Ascendant. And, as already noted, the exact time of your birth determines your Rising sign. Let's see how this works.

As the Earth rotates on its axis once every 24 hours, each one of the twelve signs of the Zodiac appears to be "rising" on the horizon, with a new one appearing about every 2 hours. Actually it is the turning of the Earth that exposes each sign to view, but in our astrological work we are discussing apparent motion. This Rising sign marks the Ascendant, and it colors the whole orientation of a horoscope. It indicates the sign governing the 1st house of the chart, and will thus determine which signs will govern all the other houses.

To visualize this idea, imagine two color wheels with twelve divisions superimposed upon each other. For just as the Zodiac is divided into twelve constellations that we identify as the signs, another twelvefold division is used to denote the houses. Now imagine one wheel (the signs) moving slowly while the other wheel (the houses) remains still. This analogy may help you see how the signs keep shifting the "color" of the houses as the Rising sign continues to change every two hours. To simplify things, a Table of Rising Signs has been provided (pages 8–9) for your specific Sun sign.

Once your Rising sign has been placed on the cusp of the 1st house, the signs that govern the rest of the 11 houses can be placed on the chart. In any individual's horoscope the signs do not necessarily correspond with the houses. For example, it could be that a sign covers part of two adjacent houses. It is the interpretation of such variations in an individual's horoscope that marks the professional astrologer.

But to gain a workable understanding of astrology, it is not necessary to go into great detail. In fact, we just need a description of the houses and their meanings, as is shown in the illustration above and in the table below.

THE 12 HOUSES OF THE ZODIAC

1st	Individuality, body appearance, general outlook on life	Personality house
2nd	Finance, possessions, ethical principles, gain or loss	Money house
3rd	Relatives, communication, short journeys, writing, education	Relatives house
4th	Family and home, parental ties, land and property, security	Home house
5th	Pleasure, children, creativity, entertainment, risk	Pleasure house
6th	Health, harvest, hygiene, work and service, employees	Health house
7th	Marriage and divorce, the law, partnerships and alliances	Marriage house
8th	Inheritance, secret deals, sex, death, regeneration	Inheritance house
9th	Travel, sports, study, philosophy, religion	Travel house
10th	Career, social standing, success and honor	Business house
11th	Friendship, social life, hopes and wishes	Friends house
12th	Troubles, illness, secret enemies, hidden agendas	Trouble house

The Planets in the Houses

An astrologer, knowing the exact time and place of your birth, will use tables of planetary motion in order to locate the planets in your horoscope chart. He or she will determine which planet or planets are in which sign and in which house. It is not uncommon, in an individual's horoscope, for there to be two or more planets in the same sign and in the same house.

The characteristics of the planets modify the influence of the Sun according to their natures and strengths.

Sun: Source of life. Basic temperament according to the Sun sign. The conscious will. Human potential.

Moon: Emotions. Moods. Customs. Habits. Changeable. Adaptive. Nurturing.

Mercury: Communication. Intellect. Reasoning power. Curiosity. Short travels.

Venus: Love. Delight. Charm. Harmony. Balance. Art. Beautiful possessions.

Mars: Energy. Initiative. War. Anger. Adventure. Courage. Daring. Impulse.

Jupiter: Luck. Optimism. Generous. Expansive. Opportunities. Protection.

Saturn: Pessimism. Privation. Obstacles. Delay. Hard work. Research. Lasting rewards after long struggle.

Uranus: Fashion. Electricity. Revolution. Independence. Freedom. Sudden changes. Modern science.

Neptune: Sensationalism. Theater. Dreams. Inspiration. Illusion. Deception.

Pluto: Creation and destruction. Total transformation. Lust for power. Strong obsessions.

Superimpose the characteristics of the planets on the functions of the house in which they appear. Express the result through the character of the Sun sign, and you will get the basic idea.

Of course, many other considerations have been taken into account in producing the carefully worked out predictions in this book: the aspects of the planets to each other; their strength according to position and sign; whether they are in a house of exaltation or decline; whether they are natural enemies or not; whether a planet occupies its own sign; the position of a planet in relation to its own house or sign; whether the sign is male or female; whether the sign is a fire, earth, water, or air sign. These are only a few of the colors on the astrologer's pallet which he or she must mix with the inspiration of the artist and the accuracy of the mathematician.

How To Use These Predictions

A person reading the predictions in this book should understand that they are produced from the daily position of the planets for a group of people and are not, of course, individually specialized. To get the full benefit of them our readers should relate the predictions to their own character and circumstances, coordinate them, and draw their own conclusions from them.

If you are a serious observer of your own life, you should find a definite pattern emerging that will be a helpful and reliable guide.

The point is that we always retain our free will. The stars indicate certain directional tendencies but we are not compelled to follow. We can do or not do, and wisdom must make the choice.

We all have our good and bad days. Sometimes they extend into cycles of weeks. It is therefore advisable to study daily predictions in a span ranging from the day before to several days ahead.

Daily predictions should be taken very generally. The word "difficult" does not necessarily indicate a whole day of obstruction or inconvenience. It is a warning to you to be cautious. Your caution will often see you around the difficulty before you are involved. This is the correct use of astrology.

In another section (pages 78–84), detailed information is given about the influence of the Moon as it passes through each of the twelve signs of the Zodiac. There are instructions on how to use the Moon Tables (pages 85–92), which provide Moon Sign Dates throughout the year as well as the Moon's role in health and daily affairs. This information should be used in conjunction with the daily forecasts to give a fuller picture of the astrological trends.

HISTORY OF ASTROLOGY

The origins of astrology have been lost far back in history, but we do know that reference is made to it as far back as the first written records of the human race. It is not hard to see why. Even in primitive times, people must have looked for an explanation for the various happenings in their lives. They must have wanted to know why people were different from one another. And in their search they turned to the regular movements of the Sun, Moon, and stars to see if they could provide an answer.

It is interesting to note that as soon as man learned to use his tools in any type of design, or his mind in any kind of calculation, he turned his attention to the heavens. Ancient cave dwellings reveal dim crescents and circles representative of the Sun and Moon, rulers of day and night. Mesopotamia and the civilization of Chaldea, in itself the foundation of those of Babylonia and Assyria, show a complete picture of astronomical observation and well-developed astrological interpretation.

Humanity has a natural instinct for order. The study of anthropology reveals that primitive people—even as far back as prehistoric times—were striving to achieve a certain order in their lives. They tried to organize the apparent chaos of the universe. They had the desire to attach meaning to things. This demand for order has persisted throughout the history of man. So that observing the regularity of the heavenly bodies made it logical that primitive peoples should turn heavenward in their search for an understanding of the world in which they found themselves so random and alone.

And they did find a significance in the movements of the stars. Shepherds tending their flocks, for instance, observed that when the cluster of stars now known as the constellation Aries was in sight, it was the time of fertility and they associated it with the Ram. And they noticed that the growth of plants and plant life corresponded with different phases of the Moon, so that certain times were favorable for the planting of crops, and other times were not. In this way, there grew up a tradition of seasons and causes connected with the passage of the Sun through the twelve signs of the Zodiac.

Astrology was valued so highly that the king was kept informed of the daily and monthly changes in the heavenly bodies, and the results of astrological studies regarding events of the future. Head astrologers were clearly men of great rank and position, and the office was said to be a hereditary one.

Omens were taken, not only from eclipses and conjunctions of the Moon or Sun with one of the planets, but also from storms and earthquakes. In the eastern civilizations, particularly, the reverence inspired by astrology appears to have remained unbroken since the very earliest days. In ancient China, astrology, astronomy, and religion went hand in hand. The astrologer, who was also an astronomer, was part of the official government service and had his own corner in the Imperial Palace. The duties of the Imperial astrologer, whose office was one of the most important in the land, were clearly defined, as this extract from early records shows:

> This exalted gentleman must concern himself with the stars in the heavens, keeping a record of the changes and movements of the Planets, the Sun and the Moon, in order to examine the movements of the terrestrial world with the object of prognosticating good and bad fortune. He divides the territories of the nine regions of the empire in accordance with their dependence on particular celestial bodies. All the fiefs and principalities are connected with the stars and from this their prosperity or misfortune should be ascertained. He makes prognostications according to the twelve years of the Jupiter cycle of good and evil of the terrestrial world. From the colors of the five kinds of clouds, he determines the coming of floods or droughts, abundance or famine. From the twelve winds, he draws conclusions about the state of harmony of heaven and earth, and takes note of good and bad signs that result from their accord or disaccord. In general, he concerns himself with five kinds of phenomena so as to warn the Emperor to come to the aid of the government and to allow for variations in the ceremonies according to their circumstances.

The Chinese were also keen observers of the fixed stars, giving them such unusual names as Ghost Vehicle, Sun of Imperial Concubine, Imperial Prince, Pivot of Heaven, Twinkling Brilliance, Weaving Girl. But, great astrologers though they may have been, the Chinese lacked one aspect of mathematics that the Greeks applied to astrology—deductive geometry. Deductive geometry was the basis of much classical astrology in and after the time of the Greeks, and this explains the different methods of prognostication used in the East and West.

Down through the ages the astrologer's art has depended, not so much on the uncovering of new facts, though this is important, as on the interpretation of the facts already known. This is the essence of the astrologer's skill.

But why should the signs of the Zodiac have any effect at all on the formation of human character? It is easy to see why people thought they did, and even now we constantly use astrological expressions in our everyday speech. The thoughts of "lucky star," "ill-fated," "star-crossed," "mooning around," are interwoven into the very structure of our language.

Wherever the concept of the Zodiac is understood and used, it could well appear to have an influence on the human character. Does this mean, then, that the human race, in whose civilization the idea of the twelve signs of the Zodiac has long been embedded, is divided into only twelve types? Can we honestly believe that it is really as simple as that? If so, there must be pretty wide ranges of variation within each type. And if, to explain the variation, we call in heredity and environment, experiences in early childhood, the thyroid and other glands, and also the four functions of the mind together with extroversion and introversion, then one begins to wonder if the original classification was worth making at all. No sensible person believes that his favorite system explains everything. But even so, he will not find the system much use at all if it does not even save him the trouble of bothering with the others.

In the same way, if we were to put every person under only one sign of the Zodiac, the system becomes too rigid and unlike life. Besides, it was never intended to be used like that. It may be convenient to have only twelve types, but we know that in practice there is every possible gradation between aggressiveness and timidity, or between conscientiousness and laziness. How, then, do we account for this?

A person born under any given Sun sign can be mainly influenced by one or two of the other signs that appear in their individual horoscope. For instance, famous persons born under the sign of Gemini include Henry VIII, whom nothing and no one could have induced to abdicate, and Edward VIII, who did just that. Obviously, then, the sign Gemini does not fully explain the complete character of either of them.

Again, under the opposite sign, Sagittarius, were both Stalin, who was totally consumed with the notion of power, and Charles V, who freely gave up an empire because he preferred to go into a monastery. And we find under Scorpio many uncompromising characters such as Luther, de Gaulle, Indira Gandhi, and Montgomery, but also Petain, a successful commander whose name later became synonymous with collaboration.

A single sign is therefore obviously inadequate to explain the differences between people; it can only explain resemblances, such as the combativeness of the Scorpio group, or the far-reaching devotion of Charles V and Stalin to their respective ideals—the Christian heaven and the Communist utopia.

But very few people have only one sign in their horoscope chart. In addition to the month of birth, the day and, even more, the hour to the nearest minute if possible, ought to be considered. Without this, it is impossible to have an actual horoscope, for the word horoscope literally means "a consideration of the hour."

The month of birth tells you only which sign of the Zodiac was occupied by the Sun. The day and hour tell you what sign was occupied by the Moon. And the minute tells you which sign was rising on the eastern horizon. This is called the Ascendant, and, as some astrologers believe, it is supposed to be the most important thing in the whole horoscope.

The Sun is said to signify one's heart, that is to say, one's deepest desires and inmost nature. This is quite different from the Moon, which signifies one's superficial way of behaving. When the ancient Romans referred to the Emperor Augustus as a Capricorn, they meant that he had the Moon in Capricorn. Or, to take another example, a modern astrologer would call Disraeli a Scorpion because he had Scorpio Rising, but most people would call him Sagittarius because he had the Sun there. The Romans would have called him Leo because his Moon was in Leo.

So if one does not seem to fit one's birth month, it is always worthwhile reading the other signs, for one may have been born at a time when any of them were rising or occupied by the Moon. It also seems to be the case that the influence of the Sun develops as life goes on, so that the month of birth is easier to guess in people over the age of forty. The young are supposed to be influenced mainly by their Ascendant, the Rising sign, which characterizes the body and physical personality as a whole.

It is nonsense to assume that all people born at a certain time will exhibit the same characteristics, or that they will even behave in the same manner. It is quite obvious that, from the very moment of its birth, a child is subject to the effects of its environment, and that this in turn will influence its character and heritage to a decisive extent. Also to be taken into account are education and economic conditions, which play a very important part in the formation of one's character as well.

People have, in general, certain character traits and qualities which, according to their environment, develop in either a positive or a negative manner. Therefore, selfishness (inherent selfishness, that is) might emerge as unselfishness; kindness and consideration as cruelty and lack of consideration toward others. In the same way, a naturally constructive person may, through frustration, become destructive, and so on. The latent characteristics with which people are born can, therefore, through environment and good or bad training, become something that would appear to be its opposite, and so give the lie to the astrologer's description of their character. But this is not the case. The true character is still there, but it is buried deep beneath these external superficialities.

Careful study of the character traits of various signs of the Zodiac are of immeasurable help, and can render beneficial service to the intelligent person. Undoubtedly, the reader will already have discovered that, while he is able to get on very well with some people, he just "cannot stand" others. The causes sometimes seem inexplicable. At times there is intense dislike, at other times immediate sympathy. And there is, too, the phenomenon of love at first sight, which is also apparently inexplicable. People appear to be either sympathetic or unsympathetic toward each other for no apparent reason.

Now if we look at this in the light of the Zodiac, we find that people born under different signs are either compatible or incompatible with each other. In other words, there are good and bad interrelating factors among the various signs. This does not, of course, mean that humanity can be divided into groups of hostile camps. It would be quite wrong to be hostile or indifferent toward people who happen to be born under an incompatible sign. There is no reason why everybody should not, or cannot, learn to control and adjust their feelings and actions, especially after they are aware of the positive qualities of other people by studying their character analyses, among other things.

Every person born under a certain sign has both positive and negative qualities, which are developed more or less according to our free will. Nobody is entirely good or entirely bad, and it is up to each of us to learn to control ourselves on the one hand and at the same time to endeavor to learn about ourselves and others.

It cannot be emphasized often enough that it is free will that determines whether we will make really good use of our talents and abilities. Using our free will, we can either overcome our failings or allow them to rule us. Our free will enables us to exert sufficient willpower to control our failings so that they do not harm ourselves or others.

Astrology can reveal our inclinations and tendencies. Astrology can tell us about ourselves so that we are able to use our free will to overcome our shortcomings. In this way astrology helps us do our best to become needed and valuable members of society as well as helpmates to our family and our friends. Astrology also can save us a great deal of unhappiness and remorse.

Yet it may seem absurd that an ancient philosophy could be a prop to modern men and women. But below the materialistic surface of modern life, there are hidden streams of feeling and thought. Symbology is reappearing as a study worthy of the scholar; the psychosomatic factor in illness has passed from the writings of the crank to those of the specialist; spiritual healing in all its forms is no longer a pious hope but an accepted phenomenon. And it is into this context that we consider astrology, in the sense that it is an analysis of human types.

Astrology and medicine had a long journey together, and only parted company a couple of centuries ago. There still remain in medical language such astrological terms as "saturnine," "choleric," and "mercurial," used in the diagnosis of physical tendencies. The herbalist, for long the handyman of the medical profession, has been dominated by astrology since the days of the Greeks. Certain herbs traditionally respond to certain planetary influences, and diseases must therefore be treated to ensure harmony between the medicine and the disease.

But the stars are expected to foretell and not only to diagnose.

Astrological forecasting has been remarkably accurate, but often it is wide of the mark. The brave person who cares to predict world events takes dangerous chances. Individual forecasting is less clear cut; it can be a help or a disillusionment. Then we come to the nagging question: if it is possible to foreknow, is it right to foretell? This is a point of ethics on which it is hard to pronounce judgment. The doctor faces the same dilemma if he finds that symptoms of a mortal disease are present in his patient and that he can only prognosticate a steady decline. How much to tell an individual in a crisis is a problem that has perplexed many distinguished scholars. Honest and conscientious astrologers in this modern world, where so many people are seeking guidance, face the same problem.

Five hundred years ago it was customary to call in a learned man who was an astrologer who was probably also a doctor and a philosopher. By his knowledge of astrology, his study of planetary influences, he felt himself qualified to guide those in distress. The world has moved forward at a fantastic rate since then, and yet people are still uncertain of themselves. At first sight it seems fantastic in the light of modern thinking that they turn to the most ancient of all studies, and get someone to calculate a horoscope for them. But is it really so fantastic if you take a second look? For astrology is concerned with tomorrow, with survival. And in a world such as ours, tomorrow and survival are the keywords for the twenty-first century.

SPECIAL OVERVIEW 2011–2020

The second decade of the twenty-first century opens on major planetary shifts that set the stage for challenge, opportunity, and change. The personal planets—notably Jupiter and Saturn—and the generational planets—Uranus, Neptune, and Pluto—have all moved forward into new signs of the zodiac. These fresh planetary influences act to shape unfolding events and illuminate pathways to the future.

Jupiter, the big planet that attracts luck, spends about one year in each zodiacal sign. It takes approximately twelve years for Jupiter to travel through all twelve signs of the zodiac in order to complete a cycle. In 2011 a new Jupiter cycle is initiated with Jupiter transiting Aries, the first sign of the zodiac. As each year progresses over the course of the decade, Jupiter moves forward into the next sign, following the natural progression of the zodiac. Jupiter visits Taurus in 2012, Gemini in 2013, Cancer in 2014, Leo in 2015, Virgo in 2016, Libra in 2017, Scorpio in 2018, Sagittarius in 2019, Capricorn in 2020. Then in late December 2020 Jupiter enters Aquarius just two weeks before the decade closes. Jupiter's vibrations are helpful and fruitful, a source of good luck and a protection against bad luck. Opportunity swells under Jupiter's powerful rays. Learning takes leaps of faith.

Saturn, the beautiful planet of reason and responsibility, spends about two and a half years in each zodiacal sign. A complete Saturn cycle through all twelve signs of the zodiac takes about twenty-nine to thirty years. Saturn is known as the lawgiver: setting boundaries and codes of conduct, urging self-discipline and structure within a creative framework. The rule of law, the role of government, the responsibility of the individual are all sourced from Saturn. Saturn gives as it takes. Once a lesson is learned, Saturn's reward is just and full.

Saturn transits Libra throughout 2011 until early autumn of 2012. Here Saturn seeks to harmonize, to balance, to bring order out of chaos. Saturn in Libra ennobles the artist, the judge, the high-minded, the honest. Saturn next visits Scorpio from autumn 2012 until late December 2014. With Saturn in Scorpio, tactic and strategy combine to get workable solutions and desired results. Saturn's problem-solving tools here can harness dynamic energy for the common good. Saturn in Sagittarius, an idealistic and humanistic transit that stretches from December 2014 into the last day of autumn 2017, promotes activism over mere dogma and debate. Saturn in Sagittarius can be a driving force for good. Saturn tours Capricorn, the sign that Saturn rules, from the first day of winter 2017 into early spring 2020. Saturn in Capricorn is a consolidating transit, bringing things forth and into fruition. Here a plan can be made right, made whole, then launched for success. Saturn starts to visit Aquarius, a sign that Saturn corules and a very good sign for Saturn to visit, in the very last year of the decade. Saturn in Aquarius fosters team spirit, the unity of effort amid diversity. The transit of Saturn in Aquarius until early 2023 represents a period of enlightened activism and unprecedented growth.

Uranus, Neptune, and Pluto spend more than several years in each sign. They produce the differences in attitude, belief, behavior, and taste that distinguish one generation from another—and so are called the generational planets.

Uranus, planet of innovation and surprise, is known as the awakener. Uranus spends seven to eight years in each sign. Uranus started a new cycle when it entered Aries, the first sign of the zodiac, in May 2010. Uranus tours Aries until May 2018. Uranus in Aries accents originality, freedom, independence, unpredictability. There can be a start-stop quality to undertakings given this transit. Despite contradiction and confrontation, significant invention and productivity mark this transit. Uranus next visits Taurus through the end of the decade into 2026. Strategic thinking and timely action characterize the transit of Uranus in Taurus. Here intuition is backed up by common sense, leading to fresh discoveries upon which new industries can be built.

Neptune spends about fourteen years in each sign. Neptune, the visionary planet, enters Pisces, the sign Neptune rules and the final sign of the zodiac, in early April 2011. Neptune journeys through Pisces until 2026 to complete the Neptune cycle of visiting all twelve zodiacal signs. Neptune's tour of Pisces ushers in a long period of great potentiality: universal understanding, universal good, universal love, universal generosity, universal forgiveness—the universal spirit affects all. Neptune in Pisces can oversee the fruition of such noble aims as human rights for all and liberation from all forms of tyranny. Neptune in Pisces is a pervasive influence that changes concepts, consciences, attitudes, actions. The impact of Neptune in Pisces is to illuminate and to inspire.

Pluto, dwarf planet of beginnings and endings, entered the earthy sign of Capricorn in 2008 and journeys there for sixteen years into late 2024. Pluto in Capricorn over the course of this extensive visit has the capacity to change the landscape as well as the humanscape. The transforming energy of Pluto combines with the persevering power of Capricorn to give depth and character to potential change. Pluto in Capricorn brings focus and cohesion to disparate, diverse creativities. As new forms arise and take root, Pluto in Capricorn organizes the rebuilding process. Freedom versus limitation, freedom versus authority is in the framework during this transit. Reasonableness struggles with recklessness to solve divisive issues. Pluto in Capricorn teaches important lessons about adversity, and the lessons will be learned.

THE SIGNS OF THE ZODIAC

Dominant Characteristics

Aries: March 21–April 20

The Positive Side of Aries

The Aries has many positive points to his character. People born under this first sign of the Zodiac are often quite strong and enthusiastic. On the whole, they are forward-looking people who are not easily discouraged by temporary setbacks. They know what they want out of life and they go out after it. Their personalities are strong. Others are usually quite impressed by the Ram's way of doing things. Quite often they are sources of inspiration for others traveling the same route. Aries men and women have a special zest for life that can be contagious; for others, they are a fine example of how life should be lived.

The Aries person usually has a quick and active mind. He is imaginative and inventive. He enjoys keeping busy and active. He generally gets along well with all kinds of people. He is interested in mankind, as a whole. He likes to be challenged. Some would say he thrives on opposition, for it is when he is set against that he often does his best. Getting over or around obstacles is a challenge he generally enjoys. All in all, Aries is quite positive and young-thinking. He likes to keep abreast of new things that are happening in the world. Aries are often fond of speed. They like things to be done quickly, and this sometimes aggravates their slower colleagues and associates.

The Aries man or woman always seems to remain young. Their whole approach to life is youthful and optimistic. They never say

die, no matter what the odds. They may have an occasional setback, but it is not long before they are back on their feet again.

The Negative Side of Aries

Everybody has his less positive qualities—and Aries is no exception. Sometimes the Aries man or woman is not very tactful in communicating with others; in his hurry to get things done he is apt to be a little callous or inconsiderate. Sensitive people are likely to find him somewhat sharp-tongued in some situations. Often in his eagerness to get the show on the road, he misses the mark altogether and cannot achieve his aims.

At times Aries can be too impulsive. He can occasionally be stubborn and refuse to listen to reason. If things do not move quickly enough to suit the Aries man or woman, he or she is apt to become rather nervous or irritable. The uncultivated Aries is not unfamiliar with moments of doubt and fear. He is capable of being destructive if he does not get his way. He can overcome some of his emotional problems by steadily trying to express himself as he really is, but this requires effort.

Taurus: April 21–May 20

The Positive Side of Taurus

The Taurus person is known for his ability to concentrate and for his tenacity. These are perhaps his strongest qualities. The Taurus man or woman generally has very little trouble in getting along with others; it's his nature to be helpful toward people in need. He can always be depended on by his friends, especially those in trouble.

Taurus generally achieves what he wants through his ability to persevere. He never leaves anything unfinished but works on something until it has been completed. People can usually take him at his word; he is honest and forthright in most of his dealings. The Taurus person has a good chance to make a success of his life because of his many positive qualities. The Taurus who aims high seldom falls short of his mark. He learns well by experience. He is thorough and does not believe in shortcuts of any kind. The Bull's thoroughness pays off in the end, for through his deliberateness he learns how to rely on himself and what he has learned. The Taurus person tries to get along with others, as a rule.

He is not overly critical and likes people to be themselves. He is a tolerant person and enjoys peace and harmony—especially in his home life.

Taurus is usually cautious in all that he does. He is not a person who believes in taking unnecessary risks. Before adopting any one line of action, he will weigh all of the pros and cons. The Taurus person is steadfast. Once his mind is made up it seldom changes. The person born under this sign usually is a good family person—reliable and loving.

The Negative Side of Taurus

Sometimes the Taurus man or woman is a bit too stubborn. He won't listen to other points of view if his mind is set on something. To others, this can be quite annoying. Taurus also does not like to be told what to do. He becomes rather angry if others think him not too bright. He does not like to be told he is wrong, even when he is. He dislikes being contradicted.

Some people who are born under this sign are very suspicious of others—even of those persons close to them. They find it difficult to trust people fully. They are often afraid of being deceived or taken advantage of. The Bull often finds it difficult to forget or forgive. His love of material things sometimes makes him rather avaricious and petty.

Gemini: May 21–June 20

The Positive Side of Gemini

The person born under this sign of the Heavenly Twins is usually quite bright and quick-witted. Some of them are capable of doing many different things. The Gemini person very often has many different interests. He keeps an open mind and is always anxious to learn new things.

Gemini is often an analytical person. He is a person who enjoys making use of his intellect. He is governed more by his mind than by his emotions. He is a person who is not confined to one view; he can often understand both sides to a problem or question. He knows how to reason, how to make rapid decisions if need be.

He is an adaptable person and can make himself at home almost anywhere. There are all kinds of situations he can adapt to. He is a person who seldom doubts himself; he is sure of his talents and his ability to think and reason. Gemini is generally most satisfied when he is in a situation where he can make use of his intellect. Never short of imagination, he often has strong talents for invention. He is rather a modern person when it comes to life; Gemini almost always moves along with the times—perhaps that is why he remains so youthful throughout most of his life.

Literature and art appeal to the person born under this sign. Creativity in almost any form will interest and intrigue the Gemini man or woman.

The Gemini is often quite charming. A good talker, he often is the center of attraction at any gathering. People find it easy to like a person born under this sign because he can appear easygoing and usually has a good sense of humor.

The Negative Side of Gemini

Sometimes the Gemini person tries to do too many things at one time—and as a result, winds up finishing nothing. Some Twins are easily distracted and find it rather difficult to concentrate on one thing for too long a time. Sometimes they give in to trifling fancies and find it rather boring to become too serious about any one thing. Some of them are never dependable, no matter what they promise.

Although the Gemini man or woman often appears to be well-versed on many subjects, this is sometimes just a veneer. His knowledge may be only superficial, but because he speaks so well he gives people the impression of erudition. Some Geminis are sharp-tongued and inconsiderate; they think only of themselves and their own pleasure.

Cancer: June 21–July 20

The Positive Side of Cancer

The Moon Child's most positive point is his understanding nature. On the whole, he is a loving and sympathetic person. He would never go out of his way to hurt anyone. The Cancer man or woman is often very kind and tender; they give what they can to others. They hate to see others suffering and will do what they can to help someone in less fortunate circumstances than themselves. They are often very concerned about the world. Their interest in people generally goes beyond that of just their own families and close friends; they have a deep sense of community and respect humanitarian values. The Moon Child means what he says, as a rule; he is honest about his feelings.

The Cancer man or woman is a person who knows the art of patience. When something seems difficult, he is willing to wait until the situation becomes manageable again. He is a person who knows how to bide his time. Cancer knows how to concentrate on one thing at a time. When he has made his mind up he generally sticks with what he does, seeing it through to the end.

Cancer is a person who loves his home. He enjoys being surrounded by familiar things and the people he loves. Of all the signs, Cancer is the most maternal. Even the men born under this sign often have a motherly or protective quality about them. They like to take care of people in their family—to see that they are well loved and well provided for. They are usually loyal and faithful. Family ties mean a lot to the Cancer man or woman. Parents and in-laws are respected and loved. Young Cancer responds very well to adults who show faith in him. The Moon Child has a strong sense of tradition. He is very sensitive to the moods of others.

The Negative Side of Cancer

Sometimes Cancer finds it rather hard to face life. It becomes too much for him. He can be a little timid and retiring, when things don't go too well. When unfortunate things happen, he is apt to just shrug and say, "Whatever will be will be." He can be fatalistic to a fault. The uncultivated Cancer is a bit lazy. He doesn't have very much ambition. Anything that seems a bit difficult he'll gladly leave to others. He may be lacking in initiative. Too sensitive, when he feels he's been injured, he'll crawl back into his shell and nurse his imaginary wounds. The immature Moon Child often is given to crying when the smallest thing goes wrong.

Some Cancers find it difficult to enjoy themselves in environments outside their homes. They make heavy demands on others, and need to be constantly reassured that they are loved. Lacking such reassurance, they may resort to sulking in silence.

Leo: July 21–August 21

The Positive Side of Leo

Often Leos make good leaders. They seem to be good organizers and administrators. Usually they are quite popular with others. Whatever group it is that they belong to, the Leo man or woman is almost sure to be or become the leader. Loyalty, one of the Lion's noblest traits, enables him or her to maintain this leadership position.

Leo is generous most of the time. It is his best characteristic. He or she likes to give gifts and presents. In making others happy, the Leo person becomes happy himself. He likes to splurge when spending money on others. In some instances it may seem that the Lion's generosity knows no boundaries. A hospitable person, the Leo man or woman is very fond of welcoming people to his house and entertaining them. He is never short of company.

Leo has plenty of energy and drive. He enjoys working toward some specific goal. When he applies himself correctly, he gets what he wants most often. The Leo person is almost never unsure of himself. He has plenty of confidence and aplomb. He is a person who is direct in almost everything he does. He has a quick mind and can make a decision in a very short time.

He usually sets a good example for others because of his ambitious manner and positive ways. He knows how to stick to something once he's started. Although Leo may be good at making a joke, he is not superficial or glib. He is a loving person, kind and thoughtful.

There is generally nothing small or petty about the Leo man or woman. He does what he can for those who are deserving. He is a person others can rely upon at all times. He means what he says. An honest person, generally speaking, he is a friend who is valued and sought out.

The Negative Side of Leo

Leo, however, does have his faults. At times, he can be just a bit too arrogant. He thinks that no one deserves a leadership position except him. Only he is capable of doing things well. His opinion of himself is often much too high. Because of his conceit, he is sometimes rather unpopular with a good many people. Some Leos are too materialistic; they can only think in terms of money and profit.

Some Leos enjoy lording it over others—at home or at their place of business. What is more, they feel they have the right to. Egocentric to an impossible degree, this sort of Leo cares little about how others think or feel. He can be rude and cutting.

Virgo: August 22–September 22

The Positive Side of Virgo

The person born under the sign of Virgo is generally a busy person. He knows how to arrange and organize things. He is a good planner. Above all, he is practical and is not afraid of hard work.

Often called the sign of the Harvester, Virgo knows how to attain what he desires. He sticks with something until it is finished. He never shirks his duties, and can always be depended upon. The Virgo person can be thoroughly trusted at all times.

The man or woman born under this sign tries to do everything to perfection. He doesn't believe in doing anything halfway. He always aims for the top. He is the sort of a person who is always learning and constantly striving to better himself—not because he wants more money or glory, but because it gives him a feeling of accomplishment.

The Virgo man or woman is a very observant person. He is sensitive to how others feel, and can see things below the surface of a situation. He usually puts this talent to constructive use.

It is not difficult for the Virgo to be open and earnest. He believes in putting his cards on the table. He is never secretive or underhanded. He's as good as his word. The Virgo person is generally plainspoken and down to earth. He has no trouble in expressing himself.

The Virgo person likes to keep up to date on new developments in his particular field. Well-informed, generally, he sometimes has a keen interest in the arts or literature. What he knows, he knows well. His ability to use his critical faculties is well-developed and sometimes startles others because of its accuracy.

Virgos adhere to a moderate way of life; they avoid excesses. Virgo is a responsible person and enjoys being of service.

The Negative Side of Virgo

Sometimes a Virgo person is too critical. He thinks that only he can do something the way it should be done. Whatever anyone else does is inferior. He can be rather annoying in the way he quibbles over insignificant details. In telling others how things should be done, he can be rather tactless and mean.

Some Virgos seem rather emotionless and cool. They feel emotional involvement is beneath them. They are sometimes too tidy, too neat. With money they can be rather miserly. Some Virgos try to force their opinions and ideas on others.

Libra: September 23–October 22

The Positive Side of Libra

Libras love harmony. It is one of their most outstanding character traits. They are interested in achieving balance; they admire beauty and grace in things as well as in people. Generally speaking, they are kind and considerate people. Libras are usually very sympathetic. They go out of their way not to hurt another person's feelings. They are outgoing and do what they can to help those in need.

People born under the sign of Libra almost always make good friends. They are loyal and amiable. They enjoy the company of others. Many of them are rather moderate in their views; they believe in keeping an open mind, however, and weighing both sides of an issue fairly before making a decision.

Alert and intelligent, Libra, often known as the Lawgiver, is always fair-minded and tries to put himself in the position of the other person. They are against injustice; quite often they take up for the underdog. In most of their social dealings, they try to be tactful and kind. They dislike discord and bickering, and most Libras strive for peace and harmony in all their relationships.

The Libra man or woman has a keen sense of beauty. They appreciate handsome furnishings and clothes. Many of them are artistically inclined. Their taste is usually impeccable. They know how to use color. Their homes are almost always attractively arranged and inviting. They enjoy entertaining people and see to it that their guests always feel at home and welcome.

Libra gets along with almost everyone. He is well-liked and socially much in demand.

The Negative Side of Libra

Some people born under this sign tend to be rather insincere. So eager are they to achieve harmony in all relationships that they will even go so far as to lie. Many of them are escapists. They find facing the truth an ordeal and prefer living in a world of make-believe.

In a serious argument, some Libras give in rather easily even when they know they are right. Arguing, even about something they believe in, is too unsettling for some of them.

Libras sometimes care too much for material things. They enjoy possessions and luxuries. Some are vain and tend to be jealous.

Scorpio: October 23–November 22

The Positive Side of Scorpio

The Scorpio man or woman generally knows what he or she wants out of life. He is a determined person. He sees something through to the end. Scorpio is quite sincere, and seldom says anything he doesn't mean. When he sets a goal for himself he tries to go about achieving it in a very direct way.

The Scorpion is brave and courageous. They are not afraid of hard work. Obstacles do not frighten them. They forge ahead until they achieve what they set out for. The Scorpio man or woman has a strong will.

Although Scorpio may seem rather fixed and determined, inside he is often quite tender and loving. He can care very much for others. He believes in sincerity in all relationships. His feelings about someone tend to last; they are profound and not superficial.

The Scorpio person is someone who adheres to his principles no matter what happens. He will not be deterred from a path he believes to be right.

Because of his many positive strengths, the Scorpion can often achieve happiness for himself and for those that he loves.

He is a constructive person by nature. He often has a deep understanding of people and of life, in general. He is perceptive and unafraid. Obstacles often seem to spur him on. He is a positive person who enjoys winning. He has many strengths and resources; challenge of any sort often brings out the best in him.

The Negative Side of Scorpio

The Scorpio person is sometimes hypersensitive. Often he imagines injury when there is none. He feels that others do not bother to recognize him for his true worth. Sometimes he is given to excessive boasting in order to compensate for what he feels is neglect.

Scorpio can be proud, arrogant, and competitive. They can be sly when they put their minds to it and they enjoy outwitting persons or institutions noted for their cleverness.

Their tactics for getting what they want are sometimes devious and ruthless. They don't care too much about what others may think. If they feel others have done them an injustice, they will do their best to seek revenge. The Scorpion often has a sudden, violent temper; and this person's interest in sex is sometimes quite unbalanced or excessive.

Sagittarius: November 23–December 20

The Positive Side of Sagittarius

People born under this sign are honest and forthright. Their approach to life is earnest and open. Sagittarius is often quite adult in his way of seeing things. They are broad-minded and tolerant people. When dealing with others the person born under the sign of the Archer is almost always open and forthright. He doesn't believe in deceit or pretension. His standards are high. People who associate with Sagittarius generally admire and respect his tolerant viewpoint.

The Archer trusts others easily and expects them to trust him. He is never suspicious or envious and almost always thinks well of others. People always enjoy his company because he is so friendly and easygoing. The Sagittarius man or woman is often good-humored. He can always be depended upon by his friends, family, and coworkers.

The person born under this sign of the Zodiac likes a good joke every now and then. Sagittarius is eager for fun and laughs, which makes him very popular with others.

A lively person, he enjoys sports and outdoor life. The Archer is fond of animals. Intelligent and interesting, he can begin an ani-

mated conversation with ease. He likes exchanging ideas and discussing various views.

He is not selfish or proud. If someone proposes an idea or plan that is better than his, he will immediately adopt it. Imaginative yet practical, he knows how to put ideas into practice.

The Archer enjoys sport and games, and it doesn't matter if he wins or loses. He is a forgiving person, and never sulks over something that has not worked out in his favor.

He is seldom critical, and is almost always generous.

The Negative Side of Sagittarius

Some Sagittarius are restless. They take foolish risks and seldom learn from the mistakes they make. They don't have heads for money and are often mismanaging their finances. Some of them devote much of their time to gambling.

Some are too outspoken and tactless, always putting their feet in their mouths. They hurt others carelessly by being honest at the wrong time. Sometimes they make promises which they don't keep. They don't stick close enough to their plans and go from one failure to another. They are undisciplined and waste a lot of energy.

Capricorn: December 21–January 19

The Positive Side of Capricorn

The person born under the sign of Capricorn, known variously as the Mountain Goat or Sea Goat, is usually very stable and patient. He sticks to whatever tasks he has and sees them through. He can always be relied upon and he is not averse to work.

An honest person, Capricorn is generally serious about whatever he does. He does not take his duties lightly. He is a practical person and believes in keeping his feet on the ground.

Quite often the person born under this sign is ambitious and knows how to get what he wants out of life. The Goat forges ahead and never gives up his goal. When he is determined about something, he almost always wins. He is a good worker—a hard worker. Although things may not come easy to him, he will not complain, but continue working until his chores are finished.

He is usually good at business matters and knows the value of money. He is not a spendthrift and knows how to put something away for a rainy day; he dislikes waste and unnecessary loss.

Capricorn knows how to make use of his self-control. He can apply himself to almost anything once he puts his mind to it. His ability to concentrate sometimes astounds others. He is diligent and does well when involved in detail work.

The Capricorn man or woman is charitable, generally speaking, and will do what is possible to help others less fortunate. As a friend, he is loyal and trustworthy. He never shirks his duties or responsibilities. He is self-reliant and never expects too much of the other fellow. He does what he can on his own. If someone does him a good turn, then he will do his best to return the favor.

The Negative Side of Capricorn

Like everyone, Capricorn, too, has faults. At times, the Goat can be overcritical of others. He expects others to live up to his own high standards. He thinks highly of himself and tends to look down on others.

His interest in material things may be exaggerated. The Capricorn man or woman thinks too much about getting on in the world and having something to show for it. He may even be a little greedy.

He sometimes thinks he knows what's best for everyone. He is too bossy. He is always trying to organize and correct others. He may be a little narrow in his thinking.

Aquarius: January 20–February 18

The Positive Side of Aquarius

The Aquarius man or woman is usually very honest and forthright. These are his two greatest qualities. His standards for himself are generally very high. He can always be relied upon by others. His word is his bond.

Aquarius is perhaps the most tolerant of all the Zodiac personalities. He respects other people's beliefs and feels that everyone is entitled to his own approach to life.

He would never do anything to injure another's feelings. He is never unkind or cruel. Always considerate of others, the Water

Bearer is always willing to help a person in need. He feels a very strong tie between himself and all the other members of mankind.

The person born under this sign, called the Water Bearer, is almost always an individualist. He does not believe in teaming up with the masses, but prefers going his own way. His ideas about life and mankind are often quite advanced. There is a saying to the effect that the average Aquarius is fifty years ahead of his time.

Aquarius is community-minded. The problems of the world concern him greatly. He is interested in helping others no matter what part of the globe they live in. He is truly a humanitarian sort. He likes to be of service to others.

Giving, considerate, and without prejudice, Aquarius have no trouble getting along with others.

The Negative Side of Aquarius

Aquarius may be too much of a dreamer. He makes plans but seldom carries them out. He is rather unrealistic. His imagination has a tendency to run away with him. Because many of his plans are impractical, he is always in some sort of a dither.

Others may not approve of him at all times because of his unconventional behavior. He may be a bit eccentric. Sometimes he is so busy with his own thoughts that he loses touch with the realities of existence.

Some Aquarius feel they are more clever and intelligent than others. They seldom admit to their own faults, even when they are quite apparent. Some become rather fanatic in their views. Their criticism of others is sometimes destructive and negative.

Pisces: February 19–March 20

The Positive Side of Pisces

Known as the sign of the Fishes, Pisces has a sympathetic nature. Kindly, he is often dedicated in the way he goes about helping others. The sick and the troubled often turn to him for advice and assistance. Possessing keen intuition, Pisces can easily understand people's deepest problems.

He is very broad-minded and does not criticize others for their faults. He knows how to accept people for what they are. On the whole, he is a trustworthy and earnest person. He is loyal to his friends and will do what he can to help them in time of need. Generous and good-natured, he is a lover of peace; he is often willing to help others solve their differences. People who have taken a wrong turn in life often interest him and he will do what he can to persuade them to rehabilitate themselves.

He has a strong intuitive sense and most of the time he knows how to make it work for him. Pisces is unusually perceptive and often knows what is bothering someone before that person, himself, is aware of it. The Pisces man or woman is an idealistic person, basically, and is interested in making the world a better place in which to live. Pisces believes that everyone should help each other. He is willing to do more than his share in order to achieve cooperation with others.

The person born under this sign often is talented in music or art. He is a receptive person; he is able to take the ups and downs of life with philosophic calm.

The Negative Side of Pisces

Some Pisces are often depressed; their outlook on life is rather glum. They may feel that they have been given a bad deal in life and that others are always taking unfair advantage of them. Pisces sometimes feel that the world is a cold and cruel place. The Fishes can be easily discouraged. The Pisces man or woman may even withdraw from the harshness of reality into a secret shell of his own where he dreams and idles away a good deal of his time.

Pisces can be lazy. He lets things happen without giving the least bit of resistance. He drifts along, whether on the high road or on the low. He can be lacking in willpower.

Some Pisces people seek escape through drugs or alcohol. When temptation comes along they find it hard to resist. In matters of sex, they can be rather permissive.

Sun Sign Personalities

ARIES: Hans Christian Andersen, Pearl Bailey, Marlon Brando, Wernher Von Braun, Charlie Chaplin, Joan Crawford, Da Vinci, Bette Davis, Doris Day, W.C. Fields, Alec Guinness, Adolf Hitler, William Holden, Thomas Jefferson, Nikita Khrushchev, Elton John, Arturo Toscanini, J.P. Morgan, Paul Robeson, Gloria Steinem, Sarah Vaughn, Vincent van Gogh, Tennessee Williams

TAURUS: Fred Astaire, Charlotte Brontë, Carol Burnett, Irving Berlin, Bing Crosby, Salvador Dali, Tchaikovsky, Queen Elizabeth II, Duke Ellington, Ella Fitzgerald, Henry Fonda, Sigmund Freud, Orson Welles, Joe Louis, Lenin, Karl Marx, Golda Meir, Eva Peron, Bertrand Russell, Shakespeare, Kate Smith, Benjamin Spock, Barbra Streisand, Shirley Temple, Harry Truman

GEMINI: Ruth Benedict, Josephine Baker, Rachel Carson, Carlos Chavez, Walt Whitman, Bob Dylan, Ralph Waldo Emerson, Judy Garland, Paul Gauguin, Allen Ginsberg, Benny Goodman, Bob Hope, Burl Ives, John F. Kennedy, Peggy Lee, Marilyn Monroe, Joe Namath, Cole Porter, Laurence Olivier, Harriet Beecher Stowe, Queen Victoria, John Wayne, Frank Lloyd Wright

CANCER: "Dear Abby," Lizzie Borden, David Brinkley, Yul Brynner, Pearl Buck, Marc Chagall, Princess Diana, Babe Didrikson, Mary Baker Eddy, Henry VIII, John Glenn, Ernest Hemingway, Lena Horne, Oscar Hammerstein, Helen Keller, Ann Landers, George Orwell, Nancy Reagan, Rembrandt, Richard Rodgers, Ginger Rogers, Rubens, Jean-Paul Sartre, O.J. Simpson

LEO: Neil Armstrong, James Baldwin, Lucille Ball, Emily Brontë, Wilt Chamberlain, Julia Child, William J. Clinton, Cecil B. De Mille, Ogden Nash, Amelia Earhart, Edna Ferber, Arthur Goldberg, Alfred Hitchcock, Mick Jagger, George Meany, Annie Oakley, George Bernard Shaw, Napoleon, Jacqueline Onassis, Henry Ford, Francis Scott Key, Andy Warhol, Mae West, Orville Wright

VIRGO: Ingrid Bergman, Warren Burger, Maurice Chevalier, Agatha Christie, Sean Connery, Lafayette, Peter Falk, Greta Garbo, Althea Gibson, Arthur Godfrey, Goethe, Buddy Hackett, Michael Jackson, Lyndon Johnson, D.H. Lawrence, Sophia Loren, Grandma Moses, Arnold Palmer, Queen Elizabeth I, Walter Reuther, Peter Sellers, Lily Tomlin, George Wallace

LIBRA: Brigitte Bardot, Art Buchwald, Truman Capote, Dwight D. Eisenhower, William Faulkner, F. Scott Fitzgerald, Gandhi, George Gershwin, Micky Mantle, Helen Hayes, Vladimir Horowitz, Doris Lessing, Martina Navratalova, Eugene O'Neill, Luciano Pavarotti, Emily Post, Eleanor Roosevelt, Bruce Springsteen, Margaret Thatcher, Gore Vidal, Barbara Walters, Oscar Wilde

SCORPIO: Vivien Leigh, Richard Burton, Art Carney, Johnny Carson, Billy Graham, Grace Kelly, Walter Cronkite, Marie Curie, Charles de Gaulle, Linda Evans, Indira Gandhi, Theodore Roosevelt, Rock Hudson, Katherine Hepburn, Robert F. Kennedy, Billie Jean King, Martin Luther, Georgia O'Keeffe, Pablo Picasso, Jonas Salk, Alan Shepard, Robert Louis Stevenson

SAGITTARIUS: Jane Austen, Louisa May Alcott, Woody Allen, Beethoven, Willy Brandt, Mary Martin, William F. Buckley, Maria Callas, Winston Churchill, Noel Coward, Emily Dickinson, Walt Disney, Benjamin Disraeli, James Doolittle, Kirk Douglas, Chet Huntley, Jane Fonda, Chris Evert Lloyd, Margaret Mead, Charles Schulz, John Milton, Frank Sinatra, Steven Spielberg

CAPRICORN: Muhammad Ali, Isaac Asimov, Pablo Casals, Dizzy Dean, Marlene Dietrich, James Farmer, Ava Gardner, Barry Goldwater, Cary Grant, J. Edgar Hoover, Howard Hughes, Joan of Arc, Gypsy Rose Lee, Martin Luther King, Jr., Rudyard Kipling, Mao Tse-tung, Richard Nixon, Gamal Nasser, Louis Pasteur, Albert Schweitzer, Stalin, Benjamin Franklin, Elvis Presley

AQUARIUS: Marian Anderson, Susan B. Anthony, Jack Benny, John Barrymore, Mikhail Baryshnikov, Charles Darwin, Charles Dickens, Thomas Edison, Clark Gable, Jascha Heifetz, Abraham Lincoln, Yehudi Menuhin, Mozart, Jack Nicklaus, Ronald Reagan, Jackie Robinson, Norman Rockwell, Franklin D. Roosevelt, Gertrude Stein, Charles Lindbergh, Margaret Truman

PISCES: Edward Albee, Harry Belafonte, Alexander Graham Bell, Chopin, Adelle Davis, Albert Einstein, Golda Meir, Jackie Gleason, Winslow Homer, Edward M. Kennedy, Victor Hugo, Mike Mansfield, Michelangelo, Edna St. Vincent Millay, Liza Minelli, John Steinbeck, Linus Pauling, Ravel, Renoir, Diana Ross, William Shirer, Elizabeth Taylor, George Washington

The Signs and Their Key Words

		POSITIVE	NEGATIVE
ARIES	self	courage, initiative, pioneer instinct	brash rudeness, selfish impetuosity
TAURUS	money	endurance, loyalty, wealth	obstinacy, gluttony
GEMINI	mind	versatility	capriciousness, unreliability
CANCER	family	sympathy, homing instinct	clannishness, childishness
LEO	children	love, authority, integrity	egotism, force
VIRGO	work	purity, industry, analysis	faultfinding, cynicism
LIBRA	marriage	harmony, justice	vacillation, superficiality
SCORPIO	sex	survival, regeneration	vengeance, discord
SAGITTARIUS	travel	optimism, higher learning	lawlessness
CAPRICORN	career	depth	narrowness, gloom
AQUARIUS	friends	human fellowship, genius	perverse unpredictability
PISCES	confine-ment	spiritual love, universality	diffusion, escapism

The Elements and Qualities of The Signs

Every sign has both an *element* and a *quality* associated with it. The element indicates the basic makeup of the sign, and the quality describes the kind of activity associated with each.

Element	Sign	Quality	Sign
FIRE............	ARIES	CARDINAL	ARIES
	LEO		LIBRA
	SAGITTARIUS		CANCER
			CAPRICORN
EARTH	TAURUS		
	VIRGO		
	CAPRICORN	FIXED	TAURUS
			LEO
			SCORPIO
AIR..............	GEMINI		AQUARIUS
	LIBRA		
	AQUARIUS		
		MUTABLE	GEMINI
WATER	CANCER		VIRGO
	SCORPIO		SAGITTARIUS
	PISCES		PISCES

Signs can be grouped together according to their element and quality. Signs of the same element share many basic traits in common. They tend to form stable configurations and ultimately harmonious relationships. Signs of the same quality are often less harmonious, but they share many dynamic potentials for growth as well as profound fulfillment.

Further discussion of each of these sign groupings is provided on the following pages.

The Fire Signs

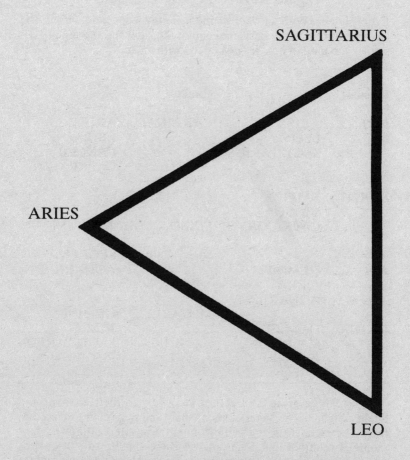

This is the fire group. On the whole these are emotional, volatile types, quick to anger, quick to forgive. They are adventurous, powerful people and act as a source of inspiration for everyone. They spark into action with immediate exuberant impulses. They are intelligent, self-involved, creative, and idealistic. They all share a certain vibrancy and glow that outwardly reflects an inner flame and passion for living.

The Earth Signs

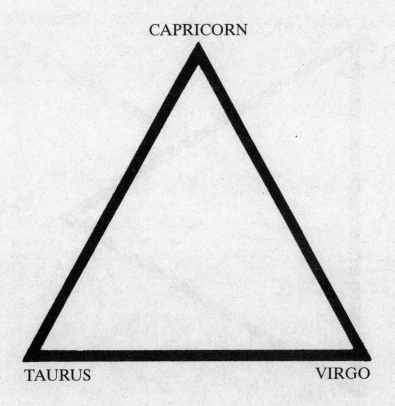

CAPRICORN

TAURUS

VIRGO

This is the earth group. They are in constant touch with the material world and tend to be conservative. Although they are all capable of spartan self-discipline, they are earthy, sensual people who are stimulated by the tangible, elegant, and luxurious. The thread of their lives is always practical, but they do fantasize and are often attracted to dark, mysterious, emotional people. They are like great cliffs overhanging the sea, forever married to the ocean but always resisting erosion from the dark, emotional forces that thunder at their feet.

The Air Signs

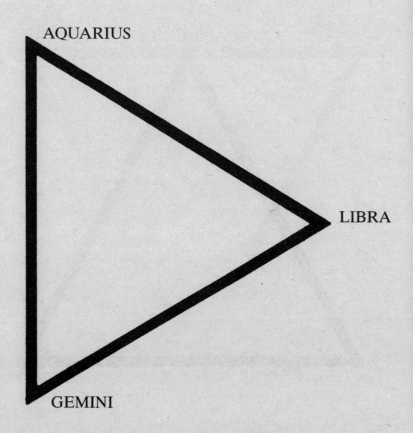

This is the air group. They are light, mental creatures desirous of contact, communication, and relationship. They are involved with people and the forming of ties on many levels. Original thinkers, they are the bearers of human news. Their language is their sense of word, color, style, and beauty. They provide an atmosphere suitable and pleasant for living. They add change and versatility to the scene, and it is through them that we can explore new territory of human intelligence and experience.

The Water Signs

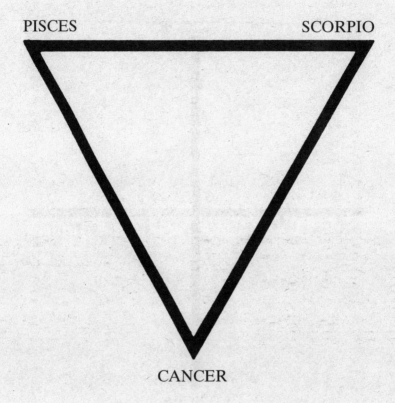

PISCES   SCORPIO

CANCER

This is the water group. Through the water people, we are all joined together on emotional, nonverbal levels. They are silent, mysterious types whose magic hypnotizes even the most determined realist. They have uncanny perceptions about people and are as rich as the oceans when it comes to feeling, emotion, or imagination. They are sensitive, mystical creatures with memories that go back beyond time. Through water, life is sustained. These people have the potential for the depths of darkness or the heights of mysticism and art.

The Cardinal Signs

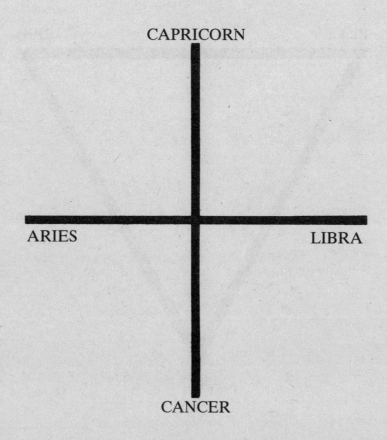

CAPRICORN

ARIES

LIBRA

CANCER

Put together, this is a clear-cut picture of dynamism, activity, tremendous stress, and remarkable achievement. These people know the meaning of great change since their lives are often characterized by significant crises and major successes. This combination is like a simultaneous storm of summer, fall, winter, and spring. The danger is chaotic diffusion of energy; the potential is irrepressible growth and victory.

The Fixed Signs

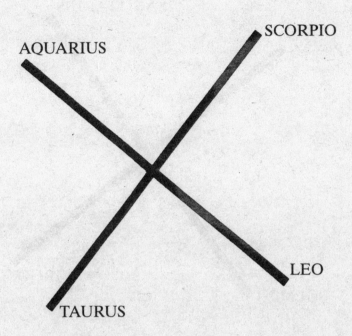

Fixed signs are always establishing themselves in a given place or area of experience. Like explorers who arrive and plant a flag, these people claim a position from which they do not enjoy being deposed. They are staunch, stalwart, upright, trusty, honorable people, although their obstinacy is well-known. Their contribution is fixity, and they are the angels who support our visible world.

The Mutable Signs

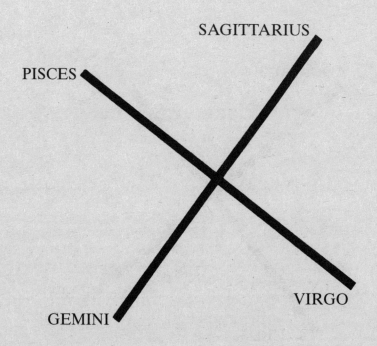

Mutable people are versatile, sensitive, intelligent, ner vous, and deeply curious about life. They are the translators of all energy. They often carry out or complete tasks initiated by others. Combinations of these signs have highly developed minds; they are imaginative and jumpy and think and talk a lot. At worst their lives are a Tower of Babel. At best they are adaptable and ready creatures who can assimilate one kind of experience and enjoy it while anticipating coming changes.

THE PLANETS
OF THE SOLAR SYSTEM

This section describes the planets of the solar system. In astrology, both the Sun and the Moon are considered to be planets. Because of the Moon's influence in our day-to-day lives, the Moon is described in a separate section following this one.

The Planets and the Signs They Rule

The signs of the Zodiac are linked to the planets in the following way. Each sign is governed or ruled by one or more planets. No matter where the planets are located in the sky at any given moment, they still rule their respective signs, and when they travel through the signs they rule, they have special dignity and their effects are stronger.

Following is a list of the planets and the signs they rule. After looking at the list, read the definitions of the planets and see if you can determine how the planet ruling *your* Sun sign has affected your life.

SIGNS	RULING PLANETS
Aries	Mars, Pluto
Taurus	Venus
Gemini	Mercury
Cancer	Moon
Leo	Sun
Virgo	Mercury
Libra	Venus
Scorpio	Mars, Pluto
Sagittarius	Jupiter
Capricorn	Saturn
Aquarius	Saturn, Uranus
Pisces	Jupiter, Neptune

Characteristics of the Planets

The following pages give the meaning and characteristics of the planets of the solar system. They all travel around the Sun at different speeds and different distances. Taken with the Sun, they all distribute individual intelligence and ability throughout the entire chart.

The planets modify the influence of the Sun in a chart according to their own particular natures, strengths, and positions. Their positions must be calculated for each year and day, and their function and expression in a horoscope will change as they move from one area of the Zodiac to another.

We start with a description of the sun.

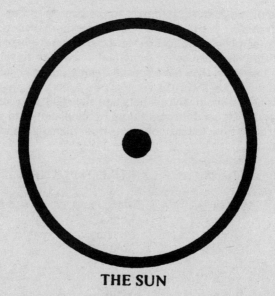

THE SUN

SUN

This is the center of existence. Around this flaming sphere all the planets revolve in endless orbits. Our star is constantly sending out its beams of light and energy without which no life on Earth would be possible. In astrology it symbolizes everything we are trying to become, the center around which all of our activity in life will always revolve. It is the symbol of our basic nature and describes the natural and constant thread that runs through everything that we do from birth to death on this planet.

To early astrologers, the Sun seemed to be another planet because it crossed the heavens every day, just like the rest of the bodies in the sky.

It is the only star near enough to be seen well—it is, in fact, a dwarf star. Approximately 860,000 miles in diameter, it is about ten times as wide as the giant planet Jupiter. The next nearest star is nearly 300,000 times as far away, and if the Sun were located as far away as most of the bright stars, it would be too faint to be seen without a telescope.

Everything in the horoscope ultimately revolves around this singular body. Although other forces may be prominent in the charts of some individuals, still the Sun is the total nucleus of being and symbolizes the complete potential of every human being alive. It is vitality and the life force. Your whole essence comes from the position of the Sun.

You are always trying to express the Sun according to its position by house and sign. Possibility for all development is found in the Sun, and it marks the fundamental character of your personal radiations all around you.

It is the symbol of strength, vigor, wisdom, dignity, ardor, and generosity, and the ability for a person to function as a mature individual. It is also a creative force in society. It is consciousness of the gift of life.

The underdeveloped solar nature is arrogant, pushy, undependable, and proud, and is constantly using force.

MERCURY

Mercury is the planet closest to the Sun. It races around our star, gathering information and translating it to the rest of the system. Mercury represents your capacity to understand the desires of your own will and to translate those desires into action.

In other words it is the planet of mind and the power of communication. Through Mercury we develop an ability to think, write, speak, and observe—to become aware of the world around us. It colors our attitudes and vision of the world, as well as our capacity to communicate our inner responses to the outside world. Some people who have serious disabilities in their power of verbal communication have often wrongly been described as people lacking intelligence.

Although this planet (and its position in the horoscope) indicates your power to communicate your thoughts and perceptions to the world, intelligence is something deeper. Intelligence is distributed throughout all the planets. It is the relationship of the planets to each other that truly describes what we call intelligence. Mercury rules speaking, language, mathematics, draft and design, students, messengers, young people, offices, teachers, and any pursuits where the mind of man has wings.

VENUS

Venus is beauty. It symbolizes the harmony and radiance of a rare and elusive quality: beauty itself. It is refinement and delicacy, softness and charm. In astrology it indicates grace, balance, and the aesthetic sense. Where Venus is we see beauty, a gentle drawing in of energy and the need for satisfaction and completion. It is a special touch that finishes off rough edges. It is sensitivity, and affection, and it is always the place for that other elusive phenomenon: love. Venus describes our sense of what is beautiful and loving. Poorly developed, it is vulgar, tasteless, and self-indulgent. But its ideal is the flame of spiritual love — Aphrodite, goddess of love, and the sweetness and power of personal beauty.

MARS

Mars is raw, crude energy. The planet next to Earth but outward from the Sun is a fiery red sphere that charges through the horoscope with force and fury. It represents the way you reach out for new adventure and new experience. It is energy and drive, initiative, courage, and daring. It is the power to start something and see it through. It can be thoughtless, cruel and wild, angry and hostile, causing cuts, burns, scalds, and wounds. It can stab its way through a chart, or it can be the symbol of healthy spirited adventure, well-channeled constructive power to begin and keep up the drive. If you have trouble starting things, if you lack the get-up-and-go to start the ball rolling, if you lack aggressiveness and self-confidence, chances are there's another planet influencing your Mars. Mars rules soldiers, butchers, surgeons, salesmen—any field that requires daring, bold skill, operational technique, or self-promotion.

JUPITER

This is the largest planet of the solar system. Scientists have recently learned that Jupiter reflects more light than it receives from the Sun. In a sense it is like a star itself. In astrology it rules good luck and good cheer, health, wealth, optimism, happiness, success, and joy. It is the symbol of opportunity and always opens the way for new possibilities in your life. It rules exuberance, enthusiasm, wisdom, knowledge, generosity, and all forms of expansion in general. It rules actors, statesmen, clerics, professional people, religion, publishing, and the distribution of many people over large areas.

Sometimes Jupiter makes you think you deserve everything, and you become sloppy, wasteful, careless and rude, prodigal and lawless, in the illusion that nothing can ever go wrong. Then there is the danger of overconfidence, exaggeration, undependability, and overindulgence.

Jupiter is the minimization of limitation and the emphasis on spirituality and potential. It is the thirst for knowledge and higher learning.

SATURN

Saturn circles our system in dark splendor with its mysterious rings, forcing us to be awakened to what ever we have neglected in the past. It will present real puzzles and problems to be solved, causing delays, obstacles, and hindrances. By doing so, Saturn stirs our own sensitivity to those areas where we are laziest.

Here we must patiently develop *method*, and only through painstaking effort can our ends be achieved. It brings order to a horoscope and imposes reason just where we are feeling least reasonable. By creating limitations and boundary, Saturn shows the consequences of being human and demands that we accept the changing cycles inevitable in human life. Saturn rules time, old age, and sobriety. It can bring depression, gloom, jealousy, and greed, or serious acceptance of responsibilities out of which success will develop. With Saturn there is nothing to do but face facts. It rules laborers, stones, granite, rocks, and crystals of all kinds.

THE OUTER PLANETS:
URANUS, NEPTUNE, PLUTO

Uranus, Neptune, Pluto are the outer planets. They liberate human beings from cultural conditioning, and in that sense are the lawbreakers. In early times it was thought that Saturn was the last planet of the system—the outer limit beyond which we could never go. The discovery of the next three planets ushered in new phases of human history, revolution, and technology.

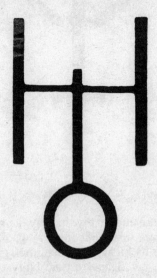

URANUS

Uranus rules unexpected change, upheaval, revolution. It is the symbol of total independence and asserts the freedom of an individual from all restriction and restraint. It is a breakthrough planet and indicates talent, originality, and genius in a horoscope. It usually causes last-minute reversals and changes of plan, unwanted separations, accidents, catastrophes, and eccentric behavior. It can add irrational rebelliousness and perverse bohemianism to a personality or a streak of unaffected brilliance in science and art. It rules technology, aviation, and all forms of electrical and electronic advancement. It governs great leaps forward and topsy-turvy situations, and *always* turns things around at the last minute. Its effects are difficult to predict, since it rules sudden last-minute decisions and events that come like lightning out of the blue.

NEPTUNE

Neptune dissolves existing reality the way the sea erodes the cliffs beside it. Its effects are subtle like the ringing of a buoy's bell in the fog. It suggests a reality higher than definition can usually describe. It awakens a sense of higher responsibility often causing guilt, worry, anxieties, or delusions. Neptune is associated with all forms of escape and can make things seem a certain way so convincingly that you are absolutely sure of something that eventually turns out to be quite different.

It is the planet of illusion and therefore governs the invisible realms that lie beyond our ordinary minds, beyond our simple factual ability to prove what is "real." Treachery, deceit, disillusionment, and disappointment are linked to Neptune. It describes a vague reality that promises eternity and the divine, yet in a manner so complex that we cannot really fathom it at all. At its worst Neptune is a cheap intoxicant; at its best it is the poetry, music, and inspiration of the higher planes of spiritual love. It has dominion over movies, photographs, and much of the arts.

PLUTO

Pluto lies at the outpost of our system and therefore rules finality in a horoscope—the final closing of chapters in your life, the passing of major milestones and points of development from which there is no return. It is a final wipeout, a closeout, an evacuation. It is a distant, subtle but powerful catalyst in all transformations that occur. It creates, destroys, then re creates. Sometimes Pluto starts its influence with a minor event or insignificant incident that might even go unnoticed. Slowly but surely, little by little, everything changes, until at last there has been a total transformation in the area of your life where Pluto has been operating. It rules mass thinking and the trends that society first rejects, then adopts, and finally outgrows.

Pluto rules the dead and the underworld—all the powerful forces of creation and destruction that go on all the time beneath, around, and above us. It can bring a lust for power with strong obsessions.

It is the planet that rules the metamorphosis of the caterpillar into a butterfly, for it symbolizes the capacity to change totally and forever a person's lifestyle, way of thought, and behavior.

THE MOON IN EACH SIGN

The Moon is the nearest planet to the Earth. It exerts more observable influence on us from day to day than any other planet. The effect is very personal, very intimate, and if we are not aware of how it works it can make us quite unstable in our ideas. And the annoying thing is that at these times we often see our own instability but can do nothing about it. A knowledge of what can be expected may help considerably. We can then be prepared to stand strong against the Moon's negative influences and use its positive ones to help us to get ahead. Who has not heard of going with the tide?

The Moon reflects, has no light of its own. It reflects the Sun—the life giver—in the form of vital movement. The Moon controls the tides, the blood rhythm, the movement of sap in trees and plants. Its nature is inconstancy and change so it signifies our moods, our superficial behavior—walking, talking, and especially thinking. Being a true reflector of other forces, the Moon is cold, watery like the surface of a still lake, brilliant and scintillating at times, but easily ruffled and disturbed by the winds of change.

The Moon takes about 27⅓ days to make a complete transit of the Zodiac. It spends just over 2¼ days in each sign. During that time it reflects the qualities, energies, and characteristics of the sign and, to a degree, the planet which rules the sign. When the Moon in its transit occupies a sign incompatible with our own birth sign, we can expect to feel a vague uneasiness, perhaps a touch of irritableness. We should not be discouraged nor let the feeling get us down, or, worse still, allow ourselves to take the discomfort out on others. Try to remember that the Moon has to change signs within 55 hours and, provided you are not physically ill, your mood will probably change with it. It is amazing how frequently depression lifts with the shift in the Moon's position. And, of course, when the Moon is transiting a sign compatible or sympathetic to yours, you will probably feel some sort of stimulation or just be plain happy to be alive.

In the horoscope, the Moon is such a powerful indicator that competent astrologers often use the sign it occupied at birth as the birth sign of the person. This is done particularly when the Sun is on the cusp, or edge, of two signs. Most experienced astrologers, however, coordinate both Sun and Moon signs by reading and confirming from one to the other and secure a far more accurate and personalized analysis.

For these reasons, the Moon tables which follow this section (see pages 86–92) are of great importance to the individual. They show the days and the exact times the Moon will enter each sign of the Zodiac for the year. Remember, you have to adjust the indicated times to local time. The corrections, already calculated for most of the main cities, are at the beginning of the tables. What follows now is a guide to the influences that will be reflected to the Earth by the Moon while it transits each of the twelve signs. The influence is at its peak about 26 hours after the Moon enters a sign. As you read the daily forecast, check the Moon sign for any given day and glance back at this guide.

MOON IN ARIES
This is a time for action, for reaching out beyond the usual self-imposed limitations and faint-hearted cautions. If you have plans in your head or on your desk, put them into practice. New ventures, applications, new jobs, new starts of any kind—all have a good chance of success. This is the period when original and dynamic impulses are being reflected onto Earth. Such energies are extremely vital and favor the pursuit of pleasure and adventure in practically every form. Sick people should feel an improvement. Those who are well will probably find themselves exuding confidence and optimism. People fond of physical exercise should find their bodies growing with tone and well-being. Boldness, strength, determination should characterize most of your activities with a readiness to face up to old challenges. Yesterday's problems may seem petty and exaggerated—so deal with them. Strike out alone. Self-reliance will attract others to you. This is a good time for making friends. Business and marriage partners are more likely to be impressed with the man and woman of action. Opposition will be overcome or thrown aside with much less effort than usual. CAUTION: Be dominant but not domineering.

MOON IN TAURUS
The spontaneous, action-packed person of yesterday gives way to the cautious, diligent, hardworking "thinker." In this period ideas will probably be concentrated on ways of improving finances. A great deal of time may be spent figuring out and going over schemes and plans. It is the right time to be careful with detail.

People will find themselves working longer than usual at their desks. Or devoting more time to serious thought about the future. A strong desire to put order into business and financial arrangements may cause extra work. Loved ones may complain of being neglected and may fail to appreciate that your efforts are for their ultimate benefit. Your desire for system may extend to criticism of arrangements in the home and lead to minor upsets. Health may be affected through overwork. Try to secure a reasonable amount of rest and relaxation, although the tendency will be to "keep going" despite good advice. Work done conscientiously in this period should result in a solid contribution to your future security. CAUTION: Try not to be as serious with people as the work you are engaged in.

MOON IN GEMINI

The humdrum of routine and too much work should suddenly end. You are likely to find yourself in an expansive, quicksilver world of change and self-expression. Urges to write, to paint, to experience the freedom of some sort of artistic outpouring, may be very strong. Take full advantage of them. You may find yourself finishing something you began and put aside long ago. Or embarking on something new which could easily be prompted by a chance meeting, a new acquaintance, or even an advertisement. There may be a yearning for a change of scenery, the feeling to visit another country (not too far away), or at least to get away for a few days. This may result in short, quick journeys. Or, if you are planning a single visit, there may be some unexpected changes or detours on the way. Familiar activities will seem to give little satisfaction unless they contain a fresh element of excitement or expectation. The inclination will be toward untried pursuits, particularly those that allow you to express your inner nature. The accent is on new faces, new places. CAUTION: Do not be too quick to commit yourself emotionally.

MOON IN CANCER

Feelings of uncertainty and vague insecurity are likely to cause problems while the Moon is in Cancer. Thoughts may turn frequently to the warmth of the home and the comfort of loved ones. Nostalgic impulses could cause you to bring out old photographs and letters and reflect on the days when your life seemed to be much more rewarding and less demanding. The love and understanding of parents and family may be important, and, if it is not forthcoming, you may have to fight against bouts of self-pity. The cordiality of friends and the thought of good times with them that are sure to be repeated will help to restore you to a happier frame of mind. The desire to be alone may follow minor setbacks or re-buffs at this time, but solitude is unlikely to help. Better to get on the telephone or visit someone. This period often causes peculiar dreams and upsurges of imaginative thinking which can be helpful to authors of occult and mystical works. Preoccupation with the personal world of simple human needs can overshadow any material strivings. CAUTION: Do not spend too much time thinking—seek the company of loved ones or close friends.

MOON IN LEO

New horizons of exciting and rather extravagant activity open up. This is the time for exhilarating entertainment, glamorous and lavish parties, and expensive shopping sprees. Any merrymaking that relies upon your generosity as a host has every chance of being a spectacular success. You should find yourself right in the center of the fun, either as the life of the party or simply as a person whom happy people like to be with. Romance thrives in this heady atmosphere and friendships are likely to explode unexpectedly into serious attachments. Children and younger people should be attracted to you and you may find yourself organizing a picnic or a visit to a fun-fair, the movies, or the beach. The sunny company and vitality of youthful companions should help you to find some unsuspected energy. In career, you could find an opening for promotion or advancement. This should be the time to make a direct approach. The period favors those engaged in original research. CAUTION: Bask in popularity, not in flattery.

MOON IN VIRGO

Off comes the party cap and out steps the busy, practical worker. He wants to get his personal affairs straight, to rearrange them, if necessary, for more efficiency, so he will have more time for more work. He clears up his correspondence, pays outstanding bills, makes numerous phone calls. He is likely to make inquiries, or sign up for some new insurance and put money into gilt-edged investment. Thoughts probably revolve around the need for future security—to tie up loose ends and clear the decks. There may be a tendency to be "finicky," to interfere in the routine of others, particularly friends and family members. The motive may be a genuine desire to help with suggestions for updating or streamlining their affairs, but these will probably not be welcomed. Sympathy may be felt for less fortunate sections of the community and a flurry of some sort of voluntary service is likely. This may be accompanied by strong feelings of responsibility on several fronts and health may suffer from extra efforts made. CAUTION: Everyone may not want your help or advice.

MOON IN LIBRA

These are days of harmony and agreement and you should find yourself at peace with most others. Relationships tend to be smooth and sweet-flowing. Friends may become closer and bonds deepen in mutual understanding. Hopes will be shared. Progress by cooperation could be the secret of success in every sphere. In business, established partnerships may flourish and new ones get off to a good start. Acquaintances could discover similar interests that lead to congenial discussions and rewarding exchanges of some sort. Love, as a unifying force, reaches its optimum. Marriage partners should find accord. Those who wed at this time face the prospect of a happy union. Cooperation and tolerance are felt to be stronger than dissension and impatience. The argumentative are not quite so loud in their bellowings, nor as inflexible in their attitudes. In the home, there should be a greater recognition of the other point of view and a readiness to put the wishes of the group before selfish insistence. This is a favorable time to join an art group. CAUTION: Do not be too independent—let others help you if they want to.

MOON IN SCORPIO

Driving impulses to make money and to economize are likely to cause upsets all around. No area of expenditure is likely to be spared the ax, including the household budget. This is a time when the desire to cut down on extravagance can become near fanatical. Care must be exercised to try to keep the aim in reasonable perspective. Others may not feel the same urgent need to save and may retaliate. There is a danger that possessions of sentimental value will be sold to realize cash for investment. Buying and selling of stock for quick profit is also likely. The attention turns to organizing, reorganizing, tidying up at home and at work. Neglected jobs could suddenly be done with great bursts of energy. The desire for solitude may intervene. Self-searching thoughts could disturb. The sense of invisible and mysterious energies in play could cause some excitability. The reassurance of loves ones may help. CAUTION: Be kind to the people you love.

MOON IN SAGITTARIUS

These are days when you are likely to be stirred and elevated by discussions and reflections of a religious and philosophical nature. Ideas of faraway places may cause unusual response and excitement. A decision may be made to visit someone overseas, perhaps a person whose influence was important to your earlier character development. There could be a strong resolution to get away from present intellectual patterns, to learn new subjects, and to meet more interesting people. The superficial may be rejected in all its forms. An impatience with old ideas and unimaginative contacts could lead to a change of companions and interests. There may be an upsurge of religious feeling and metaphysical inquiry. Even a new insight into the significance of astrology and other occult studies is likely under the curious stimulus of the Moon in Sagittarius. Physically, you may express this need for fundamental change by spending more time outdoors: sports, gardening, long walks appeal. CAUTION: Try to channel any restlessness into worthwhile study.

MOON IN CAPRICORN

Life in these hours may seem to pivot around the importance of gaining prestige and honor in the career, as well as maintaining a spotless reputation. Ambitious urges may be excessive and could be accompanied by quite acquisitive drives for money. Effort should be directed along strictly ethical lines where there is no possibility of reproach or scandal. All endeavors are likely to be characterized by great earnestness, and an air of authority and purpose which should impress those who are looking for leadership or reliability. The desire to conform to accepted standards may extend to sharp criticism of family members. Frivolity and unconventional actions are unlikely to amuse while the Moon is in Capricorn. Moderation and seriousness are the orders of the day. Achievement and recognition in this period could come through community work or organizing for the benefit of some amateur group. CAUTION: Dignity and esteem are not always self-awarded.

MOON IN AQUARIUS

Moon in Aquarius is in the second last sign of the Zodiac where ideas can become disturbingly fine and subtle. The result is often a mental "no-man's land" where imagination cannot be trusted with the same certitude as other times. The dangers for the individual are the extremes of optimism and pessimism. Unless the imagination is held in check, situations are likely to be misread, and rosy conclusions drawn where they do not exist. Consequences for the unwary can be costly in career and business. Best to think twice and not speak or act until you think again. Pessimism can be a cruel self-inflicted penalty for delusion at this time. Between the two extremes are strange areas of self-deception which, for example, can make the selfish person think he is actually being generous. Eerie dreams which resemble the reality and even seem to continue into the waking state are also possible. CAUTION: Look for the fact and not just for the image in your mind.

MOON IN PISCES

Everything seems to come to the surface now. Memory may be crystal clear, throwing up long-forgotten information which could be valuable in the career or business. Flashes of clairvoyance and intuition are possible along with sudden realizations of one's own nature, which may be used for self-improvement. A talent, never before suspected, may be discovered. Qualities not evident before in friends and marriage partners are likely to be noticed. As this is a period in which the truth seems to emerge, the discovery of false characteristics is likely to lead to disenchantment or a shift in attachments. However, when qualities are accepted, it should lead to happiness and deeper feeling. Surprise solutions could bob up for old problems. There may be a public announcement of the solving of a crime or mystery. People with secrets may find someone has "guessed" correctly. The secrets of the soul or the inner self also tend to reveal themselves. Religious and philosophical groups may make some interesting discoveries. CAUTION: Not a time for activities that depend on secrecy.

NOTE: When you read your daily forecasts, use the Moon Sign Dates that are provided in the following section of Moon Tables. Then you may want to glance back here for the Moon's influence in a given sign.

MOON TABLES

Atlanta, Boston, Detroit, Miami, Washington, Montreal,
 Ottawa, Quebec, Bogota, Havana, Lima, Santiago...... Same time
Chicago, New Orleans, Houston, Winnipeg, Churchill,
 Mexico City .... Deduct 1 hour
Albuquerque, Denver, Phoenix, El Paso, Edmonton,
 Helena .... Deduct 2 hours
Los Angeles, San Francisco, Reno, Portland,
 Seattle, Vancouver.. Deduct 3 hours
Honolulu, Anchorage, Fairbanks, Kodiak .... Deduct 5 hours
Nome, Samoa, Tonga, Midway .... Deduct 6 hours
Halifax, Bermuda, San Juan, Caracas, La Paz,
 Barbados.. Add 1 hour
St. John's, Brasilia, Rio de Janeiro, Sao Paulo,
 Buenos Aires, Montevideo .... Add 2 hours
Azores, Cape Verde Islands.. Add 3 hours
Canary Islands, Madeira, Reykjavik .... Add 4 hours
London, Paris, Amsterdam, Madrid, Lisbon,
 Gibraltar, Belfast, Raba .... Add 5 hours
Frankfurt, Rome, Oslo, Stockholm, Prague,
 Belgrade.. Add 6 hours
Bucharest, Beirut, Tel Aviv, Athens, Istanbul, Cairo,
 Alexandria, Cape Town, Johannesburg...................... Add 7 hours
Moscow, Leningrad, Baghdad, Dhahran,
 Addis Ababa, Nairobi, Teheran, Zanzibar .... Add 8 hours
Bombay, Calcutta, Sri Lanka .... Add $10\frac{1}{2}$
Hong Kong, Shanghai, Manila, Peking, Perth............. Add 13 hours
Tokyo, Okinawa, Darwin, Pusan .... Add 14 hours
Sydney, Melbourne, Port Moresby, Guam.................... Add 15 hours
Auckland, Wellington, Suva, Wake .... Add 17 hours

2013 MOON SIGN DATES — NEW YORK TIME

JANUARY Day Moon Enters		FEBRUARY Day Moon Enters		MARCH Day Moon Enters	
1. Virgo	12.36 pm	1. Libra		1. Scorp.	12.35 pm
2. Virgo		2. Scorp.	7:03 am	2. Scorp	
3. Libra	8:12 pm	3. Scorp.		3. Sagitt.	4:12 pm
4. Libra		4. Sagitt.	10:46 am	4. Sagitt.	
5. Libra		5. Sagitt.		5. Capric.	7:15 pm
6. Scorp.	1:10 am	6. Capric.	12:56 pm	6. Capric.	
7. Scorp.		7. Capric.		7. Aquar.	10:03 pm
8. Sagitt.	3:29 am	8. Aquar.	1:18 pm	8. Aquar.	
9. Sagitt.		9. Aquar.		9. Aquar.	
10. Capric.	3:55 am	10. Pisces	4:21 pm	10. Pisces	1:20 am
11. Capric.		11. Pisces		11. Pisces	
12. Aquar.	4:02 am	12. Aries	8:52 pm	12. Aries	6:18 am
13. Aquar.		13. Aries		13. Aries	
14. Pisces	5:50 am	14. Aries		14. Taurus	2:09 pm
15. Pisces		15. Taurus	5:09 am	15. Taurus	
16. Aries	11:08 am	16. Taurus		16. Taurus	
17. Aries		17. Gemini	4:51 pm	17. Gemini	1:10 am
18. Taurus	8:37 pm	18. Gemini		18. Gemini	
19. Taurus		19. Gemini		19. Cancer	1:56 pm
20. Taurus		20. Cancer	5:46 am	20. Cancer	
21. Gemini	9:05 am	21. Cancer		21. Cancer	
22. Gemini		22. Leo	5:13 pm	22. Leo	1:51 am
23. Cancer	10:01 pm	23. Leo		23. Leo	
24. Cancer		24. Leo		24. Virgo	10:50 am
25. Cancer		25. Virgo	1:54 am	25. Virgo	
26. Leo	9:21 am	26. Virgo		26. Libra	4:33 pm
27. Leo		27. Libra	8:03 am	27. Libra	
28. Virgo	6:28 pm	28. Libra		28. Scorp.	7:55 pm
29. Virgo				29. Scorp.	
30. Virgo				30. Sagitt.	10:14 pm
31. Libra	1:37 am			31. Sagitt.	

Daylight saving time to be considered where applicable.

2013 MOON SIGN DATES —
NEW YORK TIME

APRIL		MAY		JUNE	
Day Moon Enters		**Day Moon Enters**		**Day Moon Enters**	
1. Sagitt.		1. Aquar.	9:21 am	1. Pisces	
2. Capric.	12:36 am	2. Aquar.		2. Aries	1:34 am
3. Capric.		3. Pisces	1:26 pm	3. Aries	
4. Aquar.	3:43 am	4. Pisces		4. Taurus	10:55 am
5. Aquar.		5. Aries	8:04 pm	5. Taurus	
6. Pisces	8:01 am	6. Aries		6. Gemini	10:33 pm
7. Pisces		7. Aries		7. Gemini	
8. Aries	2:03 pm	8. Taurus	5:10 am	8. Gemini	
9. Aries		9. Taurus		9. Cancer	11:17 am
10. Taurus	10:23 pm	10. Gemini	4:22 pm	10. Cancer	
11. Taurus		11. Gemini		11. Leo	11:59 pm
12. Taurus		12. Gemini		12. Leo	
13. Gemini	9:14 am	13. Cancer	4:58 am	13. Leo	
14. Gemini		14. Cancer		14. Virgo	11:27 am
15. Cancer	9:50 pm	15. Leo	5:39 pm	15. Virgo	
16. Cancer		16. Leo		16. Libra	8:20 pm
17. Cancer		17. Leo		17. Libra	
18. Leo	10:15 am	18. Virgo	4:34 am	18. Libra	
19. Leo		19. Virgo		19. Scorp.	1:40 am
20. Virgo	8:10 pm	20. Libra	12:08 pm	20. Scorp.	
21. Virgo		21. Libra		21. Sagitt.	3:32 am
22. Virgo		22. Scorp.	3:56 pm	22. Sagitt.	
23. Libra	2:26 am	23. Scorp.		23. Capric.	3:09 am
24. Libra		24. Sagitt.	4:50 pm	24. Capric.	
25. Scorp.	5:26 am	25. Sagitt.		25. Aquar.	2:28 am
26. Scorp.		26. Capric.	4:30 pm	26. Aquar.	
27. Sagitt.	6:33 am	27. Capric.		27. Pisces	3:33 am
28. Sagitt.		28. Aquar.	4:49 pm	28. Pisces	
29. Capric.	7:22 am	29. Aquar.		29. Aries	8:08 am
30. Capric.		30. Pisces	7:31 pm	30. Aries	
		31. Pisces			

Daylight saving time to be considered where applicable.

2013 MOON SIGN DATES —
NEW YORK TIME

JULY		AUGUST		SEPTEMBER	
Day Moon Enters		**Day Moon Enters**		**Day Moon Enters**	
1. Taurus	4:44 pm	1. Gemini		1. Leo	7:02 pm
2. Taurus		2. Cancer	11:31 pm	2. Leo	
3. Taurus		3. Cancer		3. Leo	
4. Gemini	4:23 am	4. Cancer		4. Virgo	5:45 am
5. Gemini		5. Leo	11:59 am	5. Virgo	
6. Cancer	5:15 pm	6. Leo		6. Libra	2:14pm
7. Cancer		7. Virgo	10:58 pm	7. Libra	
8. Cancer		8. Virgo		8. Scorp.	8:45 pm
9. Leo	5:49 am	9. Virgo		9. Scorp.	
10. Leo		10. Libra	8:09 am	10. Scorp.	
11. Virgo	5:13 pm	11. Libra		11. Sagitt.	1:37 am
12. Virgo		12. Scorp.	3:19 pm	12. Sagitt.	
13. Virgo		13. Scorp.		13. Capric.	4:57 am
14. Libra	2:42 am	14. Sagitt.	8:05 pm	14. Capric.	
15. Libra		15. Sagitt.		15. Aquar.	7:06 am
16. Scorp.	9:25 am	16. Capric.	10:26 pm	16. Aquar.	
17. Scorp.		17. Capric.		17. Pisces	8:59 am
18. Sagitt.	12:55 pm	18. Aquar.	11:08 pm	18. Pisces	
19. Sagitt.		19. Aquar.		19. Aries	11:59 am
20. Capric.	1:40 pm	20. Pisces	11:44 pm	20. Aries	
21. Capric.		21. Pisces		21. Taurus	5:34 pm
22. Aquar.	1:06 pm	22. Pisces		22. Taurus	
23. Aquar.		23. Aries	2:14 am	23. Taurus	
24. Pisces	1:23 pm	24. Aries		24. Gemini	2:35 am
25. Pisces		25. Taurus	8:14 am	25. Gemini	
26. Aries	4:30 pm	26. Taurus		26. Cancer	2:26 pm
27. Aries		27. Gemini	6:09 pm	27. Cancer	
28. Taurus	11:44 pm	28. Gemini		28. Cancer	
29. Taurus		29. Gemini		29. Leo	2:58 am
30. Taurus		30. Cancer	6:34 am	30. Leo	
31. Gemini	10:43 am	31. Cancer			

Daylight saving time to be considered where applicable.

2013 MOON SIGN DATES— NEW YORK TIME

OCTOBER
Day Moon Enters
1. Virgo   1:53 pm
2. Virgo
3. Libra   10:01 pm
4. Libra
5. Libra
6. Scorp.   3:34 am
7. Scorp.
8. Sagitt.   7:23 am
9. Sagitt.
10. Capric. 10:18 am
11. Capric.
12. Aquar.   1:01 pm
13. Aquar.
14. Pisces   4:07 pm
15. Pisces
16. Aries   8:19 pm
17. Aries
18. Aries
19. Taurus   2:28 am
20. Taurus
21. Gemini 11:15 am
22. Gemini
23. Cancer 10:39 am
24. Cancer
25. Cancer
26. Leo   11:13 am
27. Leo
28. Virgo   10:46 pm
29. Virgo
30. Virgo
31. Libra   7:23 am

NOVEMBER
Day Moon Enters
1. Libra
2. Scorp.   12:36 pm
3. Scorp.
4. Sagitt.   3:15 pm
5. Sagitt.
6. Capric.   4:45 pm
7. Capric.
8. Aquar.   6:31 pm
9. Aquar.
10. Pisces   9:37 pm
11. Pisces
12. Pisces
13. Aries   2:40 am
14. Aries
15. Taurus   9:50 am
16. Taurus
17. Gemini 7:08 pm
18. Gemini
19. Gemini
20. Cancer   6:24 am
21. Cancer
22. Leo   6:58 pm
23. Leo
24. Leo
25. Virgo   7:12 am
26. Virgo
27. Libra   5:01 pm
28. Libra
29. Scorp.   11:04 pm
30. Scorp.

DECEMBER
Day Moon Enters
1. Scorp.
2. Sagitt.   1:32 am
3. Sagitt.
4. Capric.   1:50 am
5. Capric.
6. Aquar.   1:54 am
7. Aquar.
8. Pisces   3:35 am
9. Pisces
10. Aries   8:07 am
11. Aries
12. Taurus   3:41 pm
13. Taurus
14. Taurus
15. Gemini 1:42 am
16. Gemini
17. Cancer   1:18 pm
18. Cancer
19. Cancer
20. Leo   1:49 am
21. Leo
22. Virgo   2:20 pm
23. Virgo
24. Virgo
25. Libra   1:18 am
26. Libra
27. Scorp.   8:59 am
28. Scorp.
29. Sagitt.   12:38 pm
30. Sagitt.
31. Capric.   1:02 pm

Daylight saving time to be considered where applicable.

2013 PHASES OF THE MOON—
NEW YORK TIME

New Moon	First Quarter	Full Moon	Last Quarter
Dec. 13 ('12)	Dec. 20	Dec. 28	Jan. 4
Jan. 11	Jan. 18	Jan. 27	Feb. 4
Feb. 10	Feb. 17	Feb. 25	March 4
March 11	March 19	March 27	April 3
April 10	April 18	April 25	May 2
May 9	May 17	May 25	May 31
June 8	June 16	June 23	June 30
July 8	July 15	July 22	July 29
August 6	August 14	August 20	August 28
Sept. 5	Sept. 12	Sept. 19	Sept. 27
Oct. 4	Oct. 11	Oct. 18	Oct. 26
Nov. 3	Nov. 10	Nov. 17	Nov. 25
Dec. 2	Dec. 9	Dec. 17	Dec. 25

Each phase of the Moon lasts approximately seven to eight days, during which the Moon's shape gradually changes as it comes out of one phase and goes into the next.

There will be a solar eclipse during the New Moon phase on May 9 and November 3.

There will be a lunar eclipse during the Full Moon phase on April 25, May 25, and October 18.

2013 FISHING GUIDE

	Good	Best
January	4-5-9-13-29-23	6-15-25
February	2-11-16-17-21-22	3-12-19-28
March	2-3-11-12-21-22	4-13-19-20-27
April	5-7-8-9-17-23	4-15-24-28
May	4-9-14-15-21-23-24	2-5-12-21
June	1-10-19-21-26-27-28	3-11-17-20-22
July	8-8-16-23-25-26	7-15-17-21
August	5-10-11-14-22-23	4-13-19-27
September	1-8-9-10-19-28-29	7-9-16-18-20
October	8-16-18-20-22-27	6-15-19-24-26
November	2-3-13-18-23-30	4-12-15-18-21
December	3-12-13-14-18-30	5-9-19-28

2013 PLANTING GUIDE

	Aboveground Crops	Root Crops
January	2-6-15-25-29	4-11-20-25
February	3-12-14-21-26	7-19-24-28
March	4-6-21-25-29	2-6-18-29
April	7-17-22-26	2-12-24
May	4-14-19-23-31	9-10-21-27
June	1-11-15-20-28	6-17-20-24
July	8-12-17-25	3-15-21-30
August	4-9-13-22	11-17-27
September	1-5-9-18-28	7-14-23
October	3-7-15-25-30	4-5-11-20
November	3-12-21-26	1-7-16-29
December	1-9-19-24-28	5-14-26

	Pruning	Weeds and Pests
January	9-18-20	13-18-23-27
February	5-14-15	9-14-19-24
March	4-13-14	8-18-23
April	9-10-28	5-15-20
May	6-7-25	2-12-17-29
June	3-4-21-22	8-13-26
July	1-19-27-28	5-10-23
August	15-16-24-25	2-19-30
September	11-12-20-21	3-16-25-30
October	9-18-19	1-13-23-28
November	5-14-15	9-19-24
December	3-11-12-30	7-16-21

MOON'S INFLUENCE OVER PLANTS

Centuries ago it was established that seeds planted when the Moon is in signs and phases called Fruitful will produce more growth than seeds planed when the Moon is in a Barren sign.

Fruitful Signs: Taurus, Cancer, Libra, Scorpio, Capricorn, Pisces
Barren Signs: Aries, Gemini, Leo, Virgo, Sagittarius, Aquarius
Dry Signs: Aries, Gemini, Sagittarius, Aquarius

Activity	Moon In
Mow lawn; trim plants	**Fruitful sign:** 1st & 2nd quarter
Plant flowers	**Fruitful sign:** 2nd quarter; best in Cancer and Libra
Prune	**Fruitful sign:** 3rd & 4th quarter
Destroy pests; spray	**Barren sign:** 4th quarter
Harvest potatoes, root crops	**Dry sign:** 3rd & 4th quarter; Taurus, Leo, and Aquarius

MOON'S INFLUENCE OVER YOUR HEALTH

ARIES	Head, brain, face, upper jaw
TAURUS	Throat, neck, lower jaw
GEMINI	Hands, arms, lungs, shoulders, ner vous system
CANCER	Esophagus, stomach, breasts, womb, liver
LEO	Heart, spine
VIRGO	Intestines, liver
LIBRA	Kidneys, lower back
SCORPIO	Sex and eliminative organs
SAGITTARIUS	Hips, thighs, liver
CAPRICORN	Skin, bones, teeth, knees
AQUARIUS	Circulatory system, lower legs
PISCES	Feet, tone of being

Try to avoid work being done on that part of the body when the Moon is in the sign governing that part.

MOON'S INFLUENCE OVER DAILY AFFAIRS

The Moon makes a complete transit of the Zodiac every 27 days 7 hours and 43 minutes. In making this transit the Moon forms different aspects with the planets and consequently has favorable or unfavorable bearings on affairs and events for persons according to the sign of the Zodiac under which they were born.

When the Moon is in conjunction with the Sun it is called a New Moon; when the Moon and Sun are in opposition it is called a Full Moon. From New Moon to Full Moon, first and second quarter—which takes about two weeks—the Moon is increasing or waxing. From Full Moon to New Moon, third and fourth quarter, the Moon is decreasing or waning.

Activity	Moon In
Business: buying and selling new, requiring public support	Sagittarius, Aries, Gemini, Virgo 1st and 2nd quarter
meant to be kept quiet	3rd and 4th quarter
Investigation	3rd and 4th quarter
Signing documents	1st & 2nd quarter, Cancer, Scorpio, Pisces
Advertising	2nd quarter, Sagittarius
Journeys and trips	1st & 2nd quarter, Gemini, Virgo
Renting offices, etc.	Taurus, Leo, Scorpio, Aquarius
Painting of house/apartment	3rd & 4th quarter, Taurus, Scorpio, Aquarius
Decorating	Gemini, Libra, Aquarius
Buying clothes and accessories	Taurus, Virgo
Beauty salon or barber shop visit	1st & 2nd quarter, Taurus, Leo, Libra, Scorpio, Aquarius
Weddings	1st & 2nd quarter

Taurus

TAURUS

Character Analysis

Of all the signs of the Zodiac, Taurus is perhaps the most diligent and determined. Taurus are hard workers and stick with something once it's begun. They are thorough people and are careful to avoid making mistakes. Patient, the Bull knows how to bide his time. If something doesn't work out as scheduled, he or she will wait until the appropriate moment comes along, then forge ahead.

The person born under this sign is far from lazy. He will work hard to achieve whatever it is he desires. He is so determined that others often think of him as being unreasonably stubborn. He'll stick to a point he believes is right—nothing can force him to give up his chosen path once his mind is made up.

Taurus takes his time in whatever he does. He wants to make sure everything is done right. At times this may exasperate people who are quick about things. Still and all, a job done by a Taurus is generally a job well done. Careful, steady, and reliable, Taurus is just the opposite of high-strung. This person can take a lot upon himself. Sometimes his burdens or worries are of such proportions that others would find them impossible to carry, but somehow Taurus manages in his silent way.

Taurus may be even-tempered, but he puts up with nonsense from no one. Others had better not take advantage of his balanced disposition. If they do, they are apt to rue the day.

The Taurus man or woman plans well before taking any one line of action. He believes in being well-prepared before embarking on any one project. Others may see him as a sort of slowpoke, but he is not being slow—just sure. He is not the sort of person who would act on a whim or fancy. He wants to be certain of the ground he is standing on.

Material things make him feel comfortable and successful. Some have a definite love of luxury and the like. This may be the result of a slight feeling of inferiority. Material goods make him feel that he is doing well and that he is just as good as the next person.

Taurus is someone who can be trusted at all times. Once he has declared himself a friend, he remains so. He is loyal and considerate of others. In his circle of friends he is quite apt to be one of the successful people. Taurus admires success; he looks up to people who have made something of themselves.

On the whole, Taurus is a down-to-earth person. He is not pretentious or lofty, but direct and earnest. Things that are a bit abstract or far-fetched may not win his immediate approval. He believes in being practical. When he makes a decision, it is generally one with a lot of thought behind it.

Health

People born under this second sign of the Zodiac generally are quite fit physically. They are often gifted with healthy constitutions and can endure more than others in some circumstances. Taurus is often vigorous and strong. At times his strength may astonish others. He can put up with more pressure than most. Pain or the threat of it generally does not frighten him.

He can be proud of his good health. Even when ill, he would rather not give in to it or admit it. But when a disability becomes such that it cannot be ignored, Taurus becomes sad and depressed. For him it is a kind of insult to be ill. When he is laid up with an illness, it generally takes awhile to recover. Although his constitution is strong, when struck down by a disease, his powers for recuperation are not very great. Getting better is a slow and gradual process for the average Taurus.

Males born under this sign are often broad and stocky. They may be wide-shouldered and powerfully built. They are seldom short on muscle. As they age, they sometimes become fat.

Females born under the sign of Taurus are often attractive and charming. They are fond of pretty things and like to see to it that they look fashionable. Although they are often beautiful when young, as they grow older some of them tend to put on a little extra weight. They often have unusually attractive eyes, and their complexions are clear and healthy.

The weakest part of the Taurus body is the throat. If ever he is sick, this part of his body is often affected. Sore throats and the like are often common Taurus complaints.

Occupation

The Taurus man or woman can do a good job—no matter what the work is. They have the ability to be thorough and accurate. They never shirk their duties. They may be looked upon as being slow, especially when they begin a task; but after they are thoroughly familiar with what they are doing, they work at an even and reasonable pace. They are methodical, which counts a good deal. They are good at detail. They seldom overlook anything.

Not all Taurus are slow. Some are quick and brilliant. In many cases, it depends on the circumstances they have to deal with. In any event, they never forget anything once they have learned it. They can be quite shrewd in business matters and are often highly valued in their place of business.

The average Taurus has plenty of get-up-and-go. He is never lazy or neglectful in his work. He enjoys working and does what he can to bring about favorable results.

In business, he will generally shy away from anything that involves what seems to be an unnecessary risk. He likes the path he trods to be a sure one, one that has been well laid out. When he has to make his own way, he sees to it that he is certain of every step of the route. This may often exasperate colleagues. His plodding ways generally pay off in the end, however. In spite of this, and because of his distrust of change, he often misses out on a good business deal. His work may become humdrum and dull due to his dislike of change in routine or schedule.

The Taurus man or woman does well in a position of authority. He is a good manager and knows how to keep everything in order. Discipline is no problem. He knows what scheme to follow and sticks to it. Because his own powers of self-control are so well developed, he has no problem in managing others. Taurus is not frightened by opposition. He knows how to forge ahead with his plans and will not stop until everything comes out according to plan.

Taurus is a stickler for detail. Every little point has to be thoroughly covered before he is satisfied. Because he is a patient person, he knows how to bide his time; he is the kind of person who will wait for the right opportunity to come along, if need be. This sort of person excels in a position where he can take his time in doing things. Any job that requires thoroughness and painstaking effort is one in which a Taurus is likely to do well. They make good managers and can handle certain technical and industrial jobs. Some Taurus are gifted with the ability to draw or design and do well in the world of architecture. Many of them are quite artistic, and it depends on the proper circumstances to bring this out. In most cases, however, Taurus is content with doing work that is sure and calculated. His creative ability may not have the proper chance to surface, and it is only through cultivation that he is able to make a broad use of it.

Although many people born under this sign work in the city, they prefer the peace and quiet of remote places to the hustle and bustle of the busy metropolis. Many of them do well in the area of agriculture. They have a way with growing things. A Taurus man or woman could easily become a successful dairy or poultry farmer. They find it easy to relate to things rural or rustic. Many of them are gifted with green thumbs.

When working with others, Taurus can be relied upon. His partner if possible should be similar in nature. The Bull may become annoyed if he works with someone who is always changing his mind or schedule. He doesn't care much for surprises or sudden changes. New ideas may not appeal to him at first; he has to have time to get used to them. Generally, he likes to think of something new as being a creation of his own. And by taking his time in approaching it, he comes to see it in that light. Taurus should be gently coaxed when working with others. He will give his consent to new ideas if his colleagues are subtle enough in their presentation.

Although the Taurus man or woman may not hold an important position in the place where he works, this does not disturb him. He doesn't mind working under others—especially if they are good and able leaders or managers. Taurus is a loyal worker. He can always be depended on to complete his tasks.

The Taurus man or woman understands the value of money and appreciates the things it can do. He may not be a millionaire, but he does know how to earn and save well enough so that he can acquire those material items he feels are important. Some people born under this sign can easily acquire a greedy streak if they don't watch out. So obsessed with material gain are some Taurus that they do not take time to relax and enjoy other things that life has to offer. Money-oriented, the ambitious Taurus sometimes turns into someone who is all work and no play. It is not surprising, then, that a great many bankers and financiers are born under this sign of the Zodiac.

The Taurus person is generally straightforward and well-meaning. If someone is in need, he will not hesitate to assist them financially. Taurus as children are sometimes stingy, but as they grow up and have enough money, they become reasonably free in their use of it. Still and all, the average Taurus will never invest all the money he has in anything. He always likes to keep a good portion of it aside for that inevitable rainy day. Although he may not be interested in taking many risks, the person born under this sign is often lucky. When he does take a chance and gambles, he quite often turns out the winner.

When a Taurus puts his best foot forward, he can achieve almost anything—even though it may take a little longer than it does with most. He has many hidden strengths and positive characteristics that help him to get ahead.

Home and Family

The Taurus person is a lover of home life. He likes to be surrounded by familiar and comfortable things. He is the kind of person who calls his home his castle. Generally, the home of a Taurus radiates comfort and hospitality. The Taurus woman knows how to decorate and arrange a house so that visitors feel immediately at home upon entering. The Taurus man is more often than not a good breadwinner. He sees to it that the members of his immediate family have everything they need.

The Taurus person usually likes the peace, quiet, and beauty of the country. If possible, he will see to it that he lives there—for part of the year if not for the whole year. The Taurus housewife has her work down to an efficient routine. She is interested in keeping everything neat and orderly. She is a very good hostess and knows how to make people feel at ease.

Being well-liked is important. Taurus likes to be surrounded by good friends. He admires important people and likes to include them in his social activities if possible. When entertaining, the Taurus woman usually outdoes herself in preparing all sorts of delicious items. She is skilled in the culinary arts. If ever she is poorly entertained or fed by others, she feels upset about it.

The Taurus man or woman usually has a tastefully furnished home. But what is more important to Taurus than beauty is comfort. His house must be a place where he can feel at home.

Taurus can be strict with their children and stand for no nonsense. They are interested in seeing that their children are brought up correctly. It is important for them that the youngsters reflect the good home they come from. Compliments from others about the behavior of their children make Taurus parents happy and proud. As the children grow older, however, and reach the teenage stage, some difficulties may occur in the beginning. The Taurus mother or father may resent the sudden change in the relationship as the child tries to assert his own individuality.

Social Relationships

Taurus generally does what he can to be popular among his friends. He is loyal and caring with people who are close to him. Because he is sincere and forthright, people generally seek him out as a friend. He makes a good talker as well as a listener. People in difficulties often turn to him for advice.

The Taurus person is genuinely interested in success, and there is nothing he admires more than someone who has achieved his goal. In making friends, it seems as though a person born under this sign gravitates toward people who have made a success of themselves or people on their way up. Influential people are admired by Taurus. Being surrounded by people who have met with some success in life makes the person born under this sign feel somewhat successful too.

The Taurus person is one who generally likes to keep his family matters to himself. He resents the meddling of friends—even close friends.

He is a person who sticks to his principles, and as a result he may make an enemy or two as he goes along.

Love and Marriage

In love matters, Taurus may go through a series of flings—many of them lighthearted—before settling down with the "right" person. By nature, Taurus is serious. In love matters, his feelings run deep; but he will take steps to guard himself against disappointment if he feels the affair won't be lasting. Taurus can be romantic. As with everything, once he has made up his mind about someone, nothing will stand in his way; he'll win the object of his affection if it's the last thing he does. Other suitors don't frighten him in the least.

Younger Taurus have nothing against light romances, but as they grow older they look for stability and deep affection in a love affair. Faithful in love as they are in most things, they look for partners who are apt to feel the way they do.

The Taurus in love does not generally attempt a coy approach. More likely than not he'll be direct in expressing his feelings. Once he has won the person he loves, the average Taurus is often possessive as well as protective.

Persons born under this sign generally do well in a marriage relationship. Matters at home go well as long as he is treated fairly by his mate. If conditions at home are not to his liking, he can be biting and mean.

There is no halfway in marriage as far as Taurus is concerned; it's a matter of two people giving themselves completely. As husbands and wives, they make ideal mates in many respects. They are usually quite considerate and generous. They like looking after the other members of their families. They are very family-oriented types, and nothing pleases them more than to be able to spend time at home with their loved ones.

Romance and the Taurus Woman

The Taurus woman has a charm and beauty that are hard to define. There is something elusive about her that attracts the opposite sex—something mysterious. Needless to say, she is much sought after. Men find her a delight. She is generally easygoing, relaxed, and good-natured. Men find her a joy to be with because they can be themselves. They don't have to try to impress her by being something they are not.

Although she may have a series of romances before actually settling down, every time she falls in love it is the real thing. She is not superficial or flighty in romance. When she gives her heart, she hopes it will be forever. When she does finally find the right person, she has no trouble in being true to him for the rest of her life.

In spite of her romantic nature, the female Taurus is quite practical, too, when it comes to love. She wants a man who can take care of her. Someone on whom she can depend. Someone who can provide her with the comforts she feels she needs. Some Taurus look for men who are well-to-do or who have already achieved success. To them, the practical side of marriage is just as important as the romantic. But most Taurus women are attracted to sincere, hardworking men who are good company and faithful in the relationship. A Taurus wife sticks by the man of her choice. She will do everything in her power to give her man the spiritual support he needs in order to advance in his career.

The Taurus woman likes pretty, gentle things. They enjoy making their home a comfortable and attractive one. They are quite artistic, and their taste in furnishings is often flawless. They know how to make a house comfortable and inviting. The Taurus woman is interested in material things. They make her feel secure and loved. Her house is apt to be filled with various objects that have an important meaning for her alone.

She is even-tempered and does what she can to get along with her mate or loved one, but once she is rubbed the wrong way she can become very angry and outspoken. The considerate mate or lover, however, has no problem with his Taurus woman. When treated well, she maintains her pleasant disposition, and is a delight to be with. She is a woman who is kind and warm when she is with the man of her choice. A man who is strong, protective, and financially sound is the sort of man who can help bring out the best in a woman born under this sign. She enjoys being flattered and being paid small attentions. It is not that she is excessively demanding, but just that she likes to have evidence from time to time that she is dearly loved.

The Taurus woman is very dependable and faithful. The man who wins her is indeed lucky. She wants a complete, comfortable, and correct home life. She seldom complains. She is quite flexible and can enjoy the good times or suffer the bad times with equal grace. Although she does enjoy luxury, if difficult times come about, she will not bicker but stick beside the man she loves. For her marriage is serious business. It is very unlikely that a Taurus woman would seek a divorce unless it was absolutely necessary.

A good homemaker, the Taurus woman knows how to keep the

love of her man alive once she has won him. To her, love is a way of life. She will live entirely for the purpose of making her man happy. Men seldom have reason to be dissatisfied with a Taurus mate. Their affections never stray. Taurus women are determined people. When they put their minds to making a marriage or love relationship work, it seldom fails. They'll work as hard at romance as they will at anything else they want.

As a mother, the Taurus woman does what she can to see that her children are brought up correctly. She likes her children to be polite and obedient. She can be strict when she puts her mind to it. It is important to her that the youngsters learn the right things in life—even if they don't seem to want to. She is not at all permissive as a parent. Her children must respect her and do as she says. She won't stand for insolence or disobedience. She is well-meaning in her treatment of her children. Although the children may resent her strictness as they are growing up, in later life they see that she was justified in the way she handled them.

Romance and the Taurus Man

The Taurus man is as determined in love as he is in everything else. Once he sets his mind on winning a woman, he keeps at it until he has achieved his goal.

Women find him attractive. The Taurus man has a protective way about him. He knows how to make a woman feel wanted and taken care of. Taurus men are often fatherly, so women looking for protection and unwavering affection are attracted to them. Because of their he-man physiques, and sure ways, they have no trouble in romance. The opposite sex find their particular brand of charm difficult to resist.

He can be a very romantic person. The number of romances he is likely to have before actually settling down may be many. But he is faithful. He is true to the person he loves for as long as that relationship lasts. When he finds someone suited to him, he devotes the rest of his life to making her happy.

Married life agrees with the man born under the Taurus sign. They make good, dependable husbands and excellent, concerned fathers. The Taurus man is, of course, attracted to a woman who is good-looking and charming. But the qualities that most appeal to him often lie deeper than the skin. He is not interested in glamour alone. The girl of his choice must be a good homemaker, resourceful, and loving. Someone kind and considerate is apt to touch his heartstrings more than a pretty, one-dimensional face. He is looking for a woman to settle down with for a lifetime.

Marriage is important to him because it means stability and security, two things that are most important to Taurus. He is serious about marriage. He will do his best to provide for his family in a way he feels is correct and responsible. He is not one to shirk his family responsibilities. He likes to know that the woman he has married will stand beside him in all that he does.

The Taurus man believes that only he should be boss of the family. He may listen and even accept the advice of his spouse, but he is the one who runs things. He likes to feel that he is the king in his castle.

He likes his home to be comfortable and inviting. He has a liking for soft things; he likes to be babied a little by the woman he loves. He may be a strict parent, but he feels it is for the children's own good.

Woman—Man

TAURUS WOMAN
ARIES MAN

If you are attracted to a man born under the sign of the Ram, it is not certain as to how far the relationship would go. An Aries who has made his mark in the world and is somewhat steadfast in his outlook and attitudes could be quite a catch for you. On the other hand, Aries are swift-footed and quick-minded; their industrious manner may often fail to impress you, particularly when you become aware that their get-up-and-go sometimes leads nowhere. When it comes to a fine romance, you want a nice broad shoulder to lean on; you might find a relationship with someone who doesn't like to stay put for too long a time somewhat upsetting. Then, too, the Aries man is likely to misunderstand your interest in a slow-but-sure approach to most matters. He may see you as a stick-in-the-mud. What's more, he'll tell you so if you make him aware of it too often. Aries speak their minds, sometimes at the drop of a hat.

You may find a man born under this sign too demanding. He may give you the feeling that he wants you to be at all places at the same time. Even though he realizes that this is impossible, he may grumble at you for not at least having tried. You have a barrelful of patience at your disposal, and he may try every bit of it. Whereas you're a thorough person, he may overshoot something essential to a project or a relationship due to his eagerness to quickly achieve his end.

Being married to a Ram does not mean that you'll necessarily have a secure and safe life as far as finances are concerned. Aries are not rash with cash, but they lack the sound head that you have for putting something away for that inevitable rainy day. He'll do his best to see that you're well provided for though his efforts may leave something to be desired.

Although there will be a family squabble occasionally, you, with your steady nature and love of permanence, will learn to take it in your stride and make your marriage a success.

He'll love the children. Aries make wonderful fathers. Kids take to them like ducks to water, probably because of their quick minds and zestful behavior. Sometimes Aries fathers spoil their children, and here is where you'll have to step in. But don't be too strict with youngsters, or you'll drive most of their affection over to their father. When they reach the adolescent stage and become increasingly difficult to manage, it would perhaps be better for you to take a backseat and rely on your Aries husband's sympathy and understanding of this stage of life.

TAURUS WOMAN
TAURUS MAN

Although a man born under the same sign as you may seem like a "natural," better look twice before you leap. It can also be that he resembles you too closely to be compatible. You can be pretty set in your ways. When you encounter someone with just as much willpower or stubbornness, a royal fireworks display can be the result. When two Taurus lock horns it can be a very exhausting and totally frustrating get-together. But if the man of your dreams is one born under your sign and you're sure that no other will do, then proceed with extreme caution. Even though you know yourself well—or think you do—it does not necessarily mean that you will have an easy time understanding him. Since you both are practical, you should try a rational approach to your relationship. Put all the cards on the table, discuss the matter, and decide whether to cooperate, compromise, or call it quits.

If you both have your sights set on the same goals, a life together could be just what the doctor ordered. You both are affectionate and have a deep need for affection. Being loved, understood, and appreciated is vital for your mutual well-being.

Essentially, you are both looking for peace, security, and harmony in your lives. Working toward these goals together may be a good way of eventually attaining them, especially if you are honest and tolerant of each other.

If you should marry a Taurus man, you can be sure that the wolf will stay far away from the door. They are notoriously good providers and do everything to make their families comfortable and happy. He'll appreciate the way you make a home warm and inviting. Good food, all the comforts, and a few luxuries are essential ingredients. Although he may be a big lug of a guy, he'll be fond of gentle treatment and soft things. If you puff up his pillow and tuck him in at night, he won't complain. He'll eat it up and ask for more.

In friendships, you'll both be on even footing. You both tend to seek out friends who are successful or prominent. You admire people who work hard and achieve what they set out for. It helps to reassure your way of looking at things.

Taurus parents love their children very much and never sacrifice a show of affection even when scolding them. Since you both are excellent disciplinarians bringing up children, you should try to balance your tendency to be strict with a healthy amount of pampering and spoiling.

TAURUS WOMAN
GEMINI MAN

Gemini men, in spite of their charm and dash, may make even placid Taurus nervous. Some Twins do seem to lack the common sense you set so much store in. Their tendencies to start a half-dozen projects, then toss them up in the air out of boredom, may only exasperate you. You may be inclined to interpret their jumping around from here to there as childish if not downright psychotic. Gemini will never stay put. If you should take it into your head to try and make him sit still, he will resent it strongly.

On the other hand, he's likely to think you're a slowpoke and far too interested in security and material things. He's attracted to things that sparkle and bubble—not necessarily for a long time. You are likely to seem quite dull and uninteresting—with your practical head and feet firm on the ground—to the Gemini gadabout. If you're looking for a life of security and steadiness, then Mr. Right he ain't.

Chances are you'll be taken in by his charming ways and facile wit. Few women can resist Gemini charm. But after you've seen through his live-for-today, gossamer facade, you'll be most happy to turn your attention to someone more stable, even if he is not as interesting. You want a man who's there when you need him, someone on whom you can fully rely. Keeping track of Gemini's movements will make your head spin. Still, being a Taurus, you're a patient woman who can put up with almost anything if you think it will be worth the effort.

A successful and serious-minded Gemini could make you a very happy woman, perhaps, if you gave him half the chance. Although Gemini may impress you as being scatterbrained, he generally has a good head on his shoulders and can make efficient use of it when he wants. Some of them, who have learned the art of being steadfast, have risen to great professional heights.

Once you convince yourself that not all people born under the sign of the Twins are witless grasshoppers, you won't mind dating a few to support your newborn conviction. If you do walk down the aisle with one, accept the fact that married life with him will mean taking the bitter with the sweet.

Life with a Gemini man can be more fun than a barrel of clowns. You'll never experience a dull moment. You'd better see to it, though, that you get his paycheck every payday. If you leave the budgeting and bookkeeping to him you'll wind up behind the eight ball.

The Gemini father is apt to let children walk all over him, so you'd better take charge of them most of the time.

TAURUS WOMAN
CANCER MAN

The man born under the sign of Cancer may very well be the man after your own heart. Generally, Cancers are steady people. They share the Taurus interest in security and practicality. Despite their sometimes seemingly grouchy exterior, men born under the sign of the Crab are sensitive and kind. They are almost always hard workers and are very interested in making successes of themselves in business as well as socially. Their conservative outlook on many things often agrees with yours. He'll be a man on whom you can depend come rain or come shine. He'll never shirk his responsibilities as a provider and will always see to it that his mate and family never want.

Your patience will come in handy if you decide it's a Moon Child you want for a mate. He doesn't rush headlong into romance. He wants to be sure about love as you do. After the first couple of months of dating, don't jump to the conclusion that he's about to make his "great play."

Don't let his coolness fool you, though. Underneath his starched reserve is a very warm heart. He's just not interested in showing off as far as affection is concerned. For him, affection should only be displayed for two sets of eyes—yours and his. If you really want to see him warm up to you, you'd better send your roommate off, then bolt the doors and windows—to insure him that you won't be disturbed or embarrassed. He will never step out of line—he's too much of a gentleman for that, but it is likely that in such a sealed off atmosphere, he'll pull out an engagement ring (that belonged to his grandmother) and slip it on your finger.

Speaking of relatives, you'll have to get used to the fact that Cancers are overly fond of their mothers. When he says his mother's the most wonderful woman in the world, you'd better agree with him—

that is, if you want to become his wife. It's a very touchy area for him. Say one wrong word about his mother or let him suspect that your interest in her is not real, and you'd better look for husband material elsewhere.

He'll always be a faithful husband; Cancers seldom tomcat around after they've taken that vow. They take their marriage responsibilities seriously. They see to it that everything in their homes runs smoothly. Bills will always be paid promptly. He'll take out all kinds of insurance policies on his family and property. He'll see to it that when retirement time rolls around, you'll both be very well off.

The Cancer father is patient, sensitive, and understanding, always protective of his children.

TAURUS WOMAN
LEO MAN

To know a man born under the sign of the Lion is not necessarily to love him—even though the temptation may be great. When he fixes most girls with his leonine double-whammy, it causes their hearts to throb and their minds to cloud over. But with you, the sensible Bull, it takes more than a regal strut and a roar to win you. There's no denying that Leo has a way with women, even practical Taurus women. Once he's swept you off your feet it may be hard to scramble upright again. Still, you're no pushover for romantic charm if you feel there may be no security behind it. He'll wine you and dine you in the fanciest places and shower you with diamonds if he can. Still, it would be wise to find out just how long the shower's going to last before consenting to be his wife.

Lions in love are hard to ignore, let alone brush off. Your "no" will have a way of nudging him on until he feels he has you completely under his spell. Once mesmerized by this romantic powerhouse, you will most likely find yourself doing things you never dreamed of. Leos can be like vain pussycats when involved in romance; they like to be cuddled and pampered and told how wonderful they are. This may not be your cup of tea, exactly. Still when you're romancing a Leo, you'll find yourself doing all kinds of things to make him purr. Although he may be sweet and gentle when trying to win you, he'll roar if he feels he's not getting the tender love and care he feels is his due. If you keep him well supplied with affection, you can be sure his eyes will never stray and his heart will never wander.

Leo men often turn out to be leaders. They're born to lord it over others in one way or another. If he is top banana in his firm, he'll most likely do everything he can to stay on top. And if he's not number one yet, then he's working on it, and will see to it that he's sitting on the throne before long.

You'll have more security than you can use if he's in a position to support you in the manner to which he feels you should be accustomed. He's apt to be too lavish, though. Although creditors may never darken your door, handle as much of the household bookkeeping as you can to put your mind at ease.

He's a natural-born friend-maker and entertainer. At a party, he will try to attract attention. Let him. If you allow him his occasional ego trips without quibbling, your married life will be one of warmth, wealth, and contentment.

When a little Lion or Lioness comes along, this Baby Leo will be brought up like one of the landed gentry if Papa Leo has anything to say about it.

TAURUS WOMAN
VIRGO MAN

Although the Virgo man may be a fussbudget at times, his seriousness and common sense may help you overlook his tendency to be too critical about minor things.

Virgo men are often quiet, respectable types who set great store in conservative behavior and levelheadedness. He'll admire you for your practicality and tenacity, perhaps even more than for your good looks. He's seldom bowled over by glamour. When he gets his courage up, he turns to a serious and reliable girl for romance. He'll be far from a Valentino while dating. In fact, you may wind up making all the passes. Once he does get his motor running, however, he can be a warm and wonderful fellow—to the right woman.

He's gradual about love. Chances are your romance with him will most likely start out looking like an ordinary friendship. Once he's sure you're no fly-by-night flirt and have no plans of taking him for a ride, he'll open up and rain sunshine over your heart.

Virgo men tend to marry late in life. He believes in holding out until he's met the right one. He may not have many names in his little black book; in fact, he may not even have a little black book. He's not interested in playing the field; leave that to men of the more flamboyant signs. The Virgo man is so particular that he may remain romantically inactive for a long period. His girl has to be perfect or it's no go. If you find yourself feeling weak-kneed for a Virgo, do your best to convince him that perfect is not so important when it comes to love. Help him to realize that he's missing out on a great deal by not considering the near-perfect or whatever you consider yourself to be. With your surefire perseverance, you'll make him listen to reason and he'll wind up reciprocating your romantic interests.

The Virgo man is no block of ice. He'll respond to what he feels to be the right feminine flame. Once your love life with a Virgo starts to bubble, don't give it a chance to fall flat. You may never have a second chance at romance with him.

If you should ever separate for a while, forget about patching up. He'd prefer to let the pieces lie scattered. Once married, though, he'll stay that way—even if it hurts. He's too conscientious to try to back out of a legal deal.

A Virgo man is as neat as a pin. He's thumbs down on sloppy housekeeping. An ashtray with even one used cigarette is apt to make him see red. Keep everything bright, neat, and shiny. Neatness goes for the children, too, at least by the time he gets home from work. But Daddy's little girl or boy will never lack for interesting playthings and learning tools.

TAURUS WOMAN
LIBRA MAN

Taurus may find Libra men too wrapped up in a dream world ever to come down to earth. Although he may be very careful about weighing both sides of an argument, that does not mean he will ever make a decision about anything. Decisions large and small are capable of giving Libra the willies. Don't ask him why. He probably doesn't know, himself. As a lover, you—who are interested in permanence and constancy in a relationship—may find him a puzzlement. One moment he comes on hard and strong with "I love you", the next moment he's left you like yesterday's mashed potatoes. It does no good to wonder "What did I do now?" You most likely haven't done anything. It's just one of Libra's ways.

On the other hand, you'll appreciate his admiration of harmony and beauty. If you're all decked out in your fanciest gown or have a tastefully arranged bouquet on the dining room table, you'll get a ready compliment—one that's really deserved. Libras don't pass out compliments to all and sundry. Generally, he's tactful enough to remain silent if he finds something disagreeable.

He may not be as ambitious as you would like your lover or husband to be. Where you do have drive and a great interest in getting ahead, Libra is often content to drift along. It is not that he is lazy or shiftless, it's just that he places greater value on aesthetic things than he does on the material. If he's in love with you, however, he'll do anything in his power to make you happy.

You may have to give him a good nudge now and again to get him to see the light. But he'll be happy wrapped up in his artistic dreams when you're not around to remind him that the rent is almost due.

If you love your Libra don't be too harsh or impatient with him.

Try to understand him. Don't let him see the stubborn side of your nature too often, or you'll scare him away. Libras are peace-loving people and hate any kind of confrontation that may lead to an argument. Some of them will do almost anything to keep the peace—even tell little white lies, if necessary.

Although you possess gobs of patience, you may find yourself losing a little of it when trying to come to grips with your Libra. He may think you're too materialistic or mercenary, but he'll have the good grace not to tell you, for fear you'll perhaps chew his head off.

If you are deeply involved with a Libra, you'd better see to it that you help him manage his money. It's for his own good. Money will never interest him as much as it should, and he does have a tendency to be too generous when he shouldn't be.

Although Libra is a gentle and understanding father, he'll see to it that he never spoils his children.

TAURUS WOMAN
SCORPIO MAN
In the astrological scheme of things Scorpio is your zodiacal mate, but also your zodiacal opposite. If your heart is set on a Scorpio, you must figure him out to stay on his good side.

Many people have a hard time understanding a Scorpio man. Few, however, are able to resist his fiery charm. When angered, he can act like a nestful of wasps, and his sting is capable of leaving an almost permanent mark. Scorpios are straight to the point. They can be as sharp as a razor blade and just as cutting.

The Scorpio man is capable of being very blunt, and he can act like a brute or a cad. His touchiness may get on your nerves after a while. If it does, you'd better tiptoe away from the scene rather than chance an explosive confrontation.

It's quite likely that he will find your slow, deliberate manner a little irritating. He may misinterpret your patience for indifference. On the other hand, you're the kind of woman who can adapt to almost any sort of situation or circumstance if you put your mind and heart to it. Scorpio men are perceptive and intelligent. In some respects, they know how to use their brains more effectively and quicker than most. They believe in winning in everything; in business, they usually achieve the position they desire through drive and intellect.

Your interest in your home is not likely to be shared by him. No matter how comfortable you've managed to make the house, it will have very little influence on him as far as making him aware of his family responsibilities. He doesn't like to be tied down, generally. He would rather be out on the battlefield of life, belting away at what he feels is a just and worthy cause, than using leisure time at home.

He is passionate in his business affairs and political interests. He is just as passionate—if not more so—in romance. Most women are easily attracted to him—and the Taurus woman is no exception, that is, at least before she knows what she might be getting into. Those who allow their hearts to be stolen by a Scorpio man soon find that they're dealing with a cauldron of seething excitement.

Scorpio likes fathering a large family. He gets along well with children and is proud of them, but often he fails to live up to his responsibilities as a parent. When he takes his fatherly duties seriously, he is adept with youngsters. Whenever you have trouble understanding the kids, Scorpio's ability to see beneath the surface of things will be invaluable.

TAURUS WOMAN
SAGITTARIUS MAN

The Taurus woman who has her cap set for a Sagittarius man may have to apply large amounts of strategy before being able to make him pop that question. When visions of the altar enter the romance, Sagittarius are apt to get cold feet. Although you may become attracted to the Archer, because of his positive, winning manner, you may find the relationship loses some of its luster when it assumes a serious hue. Sagittarius are full of bounce—perhaps too much bounce to suit you. They are often hard to pin down and dislike staying put. If ever there's a chance to be on the move, he'll latch on to it post haste. They're quick people, both in mind and spirit. And sometimes because of their zip, they make mistakes. If you have good advice to offer, he'll tell you to keep it.

Sagittarius like to rely on their own wit whenever possible. His up-and-at-'em manner about most things is likely to drive you up the wall occasionally. Your cautious, deliberate manner is likely to make him impatient. And he can be resentful if you don't accompany him on his travel or sports ventures. He can't abide a slowpoke. At times, you'll find him too breezy and kiddish. However, don't mistake his youthful demeanor for premature senility. Sagittarius are equipped with first-class brain power and know well how to put it to use. They're often full of good ideas and drive. Generally they're very broad-minded people and are very much concerned with fair play and equality.

In romance, he's quite capable of loving you wholeheartedly while treating you like a good pal. His hail-fellow well-met manner in the arena of love is likely to scare a dainty damsel off. However, a woman who knows that his heart is in the right place won't mind his bluff, rambunctious style.

He's not much of a homebody. He's got ants in his pants and enjoys being on the move. Humdrum routine, especially at home, bores him to distraction. At the drop of a hat he may ask you to whip off your apron and dine out for a change instead. He's fond of coming up with instant surprises. He'll love to keep you guessing. His friendly, candid nature gains him many friends.

When it comes to children, you may find that you've been left holding the bag. Sagittarius feel helpless around little shavers. When children become older, he will develop a genuine interest in them.

TAURUS WOMAN
CAPRICORN MAN

A Taurus woman is often capable of bringing out the best in a Capricorn man. While other women are puzzled by his silent and slow ways, Taurus, with her patience and understanding, can lend him the confidence he perhaps needs in order to come out from behind the rock.

Quite often, the Capricorn man is not the romantic kind of lover that attracts most women. Still, behind his reserve and calm, he's a pretty warm guy. He is capable of giving his heart completely once he has found the right girl. The Taurus woman who is deliberate by nature and who believes in taking time to be sure will find her kind of man in a Capricorn. He is slow and deliberate about almost everything—even romance. He doesn't believe in flirting and would never let his heart be led on a merry chase. If you win his trust, he'll give you his heart on a platter. Quite often, it is the woman who has to take the lead when romance is in the air. As long as he knows you're making the advances in earnest he won't mind. In fact, he'll probably be grateful.

Don't think that he's all cold fish; he isn't. Although some Goats have no difficulty in expressing passion, when it comes to displaying affection, they're at sea. But with an understanding and patient Bull, he should have no trouble in learning to express himself, especially if you let him know how important affection is to you, and for the good of your relationship.

The Capricorn man is very interested in getting ahead. He's ambitious and usually knows how to apply himself well to whatever task he undertakes. He's far from a spendthrift and tends to manage his money with extreme care. But a Taurus woman with a knack for putting away money for that rainy day should have no trouble in understanding this.

The Capricorn man thinks in terms of future security. He wants to make sure that he and his wife have something to fall back on when they reach retirement age.

He'll want you to handle the household efficiently, but that's no problem for most Taurus. If he should check up on you from time to time about the price of this and the cost of that, don't let it irritate you. Once he is sure you can handle this area to his liking, he'll leave it all up to you.

Although he may be a hard man to catch when it comes to marriage, once he's made that serious step, he's quite likely to become possessive. Capricorns need to know that they have the support of their women in whatever they do, every step of the way. Your Capricorn man, because he's waited so long for for the right mate, may be considerably older than you.

Capricorn fathers never neglect their children and instinctively know what is good for them.

TAURUS WOMAN
AQUARIUS MAN

The Aquarius man in your life is perhaps the most broad-minded you have ever met. Still, you may think he is the most impractical. He's more of a dreamer than a doer. If you don't mind putting up with a man whose heart and mind are as wide as the sky but his head is almost always up in the clouds, then start dating that Aquarius man who somehow has captured your fancy. Maybe you, with your Taurus good sense, can bring him down to earth before he gets too starry-eyed.

He's no dumbbell; make no mistake about that. He can be busy making complicated and idealistic plans when he's got that out-to-lunch look in his eyes. But more than likely, he'll never execute them. After he's shared one or two of his progressive ideas with you, you may think he's a nut. But don't go jumping to any wrong conclusions. There's a saying that the Water Bearer is a half-century ahead of everybody else. If you do decide to say yes to his will-you-marry-me, you'll find out how right some of his zany whims are on your golden anniversary. Maybe the waiting will be worth it. Could be that you have an Einstein on your hands—and heart.

Life with an Aquarius won't be one of total despair for you if you learn to balance his airiness with your down-to-brass-tacks practicality. He won't gripe if you do. Being the open-minded man he is, the Water Bearer will entertain all your ideas and opinions. He may not agree with them, but he'll give them a trial airing out, anyway.

Don't tear your hair out when you find that it's almost impossible to hold a normal conversation with your Aquarius friend. He's capable of answering your how-do-you-do with a running commentary on some erudite topic. Always keep in mind that he means well. His broad-mindedness extends to your freedom and individuality, a modern idea indeed.

He'll be kind and generous as a husband and will never lower himself by quibbling over petty things. You take care of the budgeting and bookkeeping; that goes without saying. He'll be thankful that you do such a good job of tracking all the nickels and dimes that would otherwise burn a hole in his pocket.

In your relationship with a man born under Aquarius you'll have plenty of opportunities to put your legendary patience to good use. At times, you may feel like tossing in the towel and calling it quits, but try counting to ten before deciding it's the last straw.

Aquarius is a good family man. He's understanding with children and will overlook a naughty deed now and then or at least try to see it in its proper perspective.

TAURUS WOMAN
PISCES MAN

The Pisces man could be the man you've looked for high and low and thought never existed. He's terribly sensitive and terribly romantic. Still, he has a very strong individual character and is well aware that the moon is not made of green cheese. He'll be very considerate of your every wish and will do his best to see to it that your relationship is a happy one.

The Pisces man is great for showering the object of his affection with all kinds of gifts and tokens of his love.

He's just the right mixture of dreamer and realist; he's capable of pleasing most women's hearts. When it comes to earning bread and butter, the strong Pisces will do all right in the world. Quite often they are capable of rising to very high positions. Some do extremely well as writers or psychiatrists. He'll be as patient and understanding with you as you will undoubtedly be with him. One thing a Pisces man dislikes is pettiness. Anyone who delights in running another into the ground is almost immediately crossed off his list of possible mates. If you have any small grievances, don't tell him about them. He couldn't care less and will think less of you if you do.

If you fall in love with a weak Pisces man, don't give up your job before you get married. Better hang on to it a long time after the honeymoon; you may still need it. A funny thing about the man born under this sign is that he can be content almost anywhere. This is perhaps because he is inner-directed and places little value on material things. In a shack or in a palace, the Pisces man is capable of making the best of all possible adjustments. He won't kick up a fuss if the roof leaks and if the fence is in sad need of repair. He's got more important things on his mind, he'll tell you. At this point, you're quite capable of telling him to go to blazes. Still and all, the Pisces man is not shiftless or aimless, but it is important to understand that material gain is never an urgent goal for him.

Pisces men have a way with the sick and troubled. It's often his nature to offer his shoulder to anyone in the mood for a good cry. He can listen to one hard-luck story after another without seeming to tire. He often knows what's bothering a person before the person knows it himself.

As a lover, he'll be attentive. You'll never have cause to doubt his intentions or sincerity. Everything will be aboveboard in his romantic dealings with you.

Children are often delighted with the Pisces man because he spoils and pampers them no end.

Man—Woman

TAURUS MAN
ARIES WOMAN

The Aries woman may be a little too bossy and busy for you. Generally, Aries are ambitious creatures and can become impatient with people who are more thorough and deliberate than they are—especially when they feel it's taking too much time. Unlike you, the Aries woman is a fast worker. In fact, sometimes she's so fast, she forgets to look where she's going. When she stumbles or falls, it's a nice thing if you're there to grab her. She'll be grateful. Don't ever tell her "I told you so" when she errs.

Aries are proud and don't like people to naysay them. That can turn them into blocks of ice. And don't think that an Aries woman will always get tripped up in her plans because she lacks patience. Quite often they are capable of taking aim and hitting the bull's-eye. You'll be flabbergasted at times by their accuracy as well as by their ambition. On the other hand, because of your interest in being sure and safe, you're apt to spot many a mistake or flaw in your Aries friend's plans before she does.

In some respects, the Aries-Taurus relationship is like that of the tortoise and the hare. Although it may seem like plodding to the Ram, you're capable of attaining exactly what she has her sights set on. It may take longer but you generally do not make any mistakes along the way.

Taurus men are renowned lovers. With some, it's almost a way of life. When you are serious, you want your partner to be as earnest and as giving as you are. An Aries woman can be giving when she feels her partner is deserving. She needs a man she can look up to and be proud of. If the shoe fits, slip into it. If not, put your sneakers back on and tiptoe out of her sight. She can cause you plenty of heartache if you've made up your mind about her but she hasn't made up hers about you. Aries women are very demanding, or at least they can be if they feel it's worth their while. They're high-strung at times and can be difficult if they feel their independence is being restricted.

If you manage to get to first base with the Ram of your dreams, keep a pair of kid gloves in your back pocket. You'll need them for handling her. Not that she's all that touchy; it's just that your relationship will have a better chance of progressing if you handle her with tender loving care. Let her know that you like her for her brains as well as for her good looks. Don't even begin to admire a woman sitting opposite you in the bus. When your Aries date sees green, you'd better forget about a rosy future together.

Aries mothers believe in teaching their children initiative at a very early age. Unstructured play might upset your Taurus notion of tradition, but such experimentation encouraged by your Aries mate may be a perfect balance for the kids.

TAURUS MAN
TAURUS WOMAN

Although two Taurus may be able to understand each other and even love each other, it does not necessarily hold true that theirs will be a stable and pleasant relationship. The Taurus woman you are dating may be too much like you in character to ever be compatible. You can be set in your ways. When you encounter someone with just as much willpower or stubbornness, the results can be anything but pleasant.

Whenever two Bulls lock horns it can be a very exhausting and unsatisfactory get-together. However, if you are convinced that no other will do, then proceed—but with caution. Even though you know yourself well—or, at least, think you do—it does not necessarily mean that you will have an easy time understanding your Taurus mate. However, since both of you are basically practical people, you should try a rational approach to your relationship: put your cards on the table, talk it over, then decide whether you should or could cooperate, compromise, or call it a day. If you both have your sights set on the same goal, life together could be just what the doctor ordered.

Both of you are very affectionate people and have a deep need for affection. Being loved, understood, and appreciated are very important for your well-being. You need a woman who is not stingy with her love because you're very generous with yours. In the Taurus woman you'll find someone who is attuned to your way of feeling when it comes to romance. Taurus people, although practical and somewhat deliberate in almost everything they do, are very passionate. They are capable of being very warm and loving when they feel that the relationship is an honest one and that their feelings will be reciprocated.

In home life, two Bulls should hit it off very well. Taurus wives are very good at keeping the household shipshape. They know how to market wisely, how to budget, and how to save. If you and your Taurus wife decide on a particular amount of money for housekeeping each month, you can bet your bottom dollar that she'll stick to it right up to the last penny.

You're an extremely ambitious person—all Bulls are—and your chances for a successful relationship with a Taurus woman will perhaps be better if she is a woman of some standing. It's not that you're a social climber or that you are cold and calculating when it comes to love, but you are well aware that it is just as easy to fall in love with a rich or socially prominent woman as it is with a poor one.

Both of you should be careful in bringing up your children. Taurus has a tendency to be strict. When your children grow up and become independent, they could turn against you as a result.

TAURUS MAN
GEMINI WOMAN

The Gemini woman may be too much of a flirt ever to take your honest heart too seriously. Then again, it depends on what kind of a mood she's in. Gemini women can change from hot to cold quicker than a cat can wink its eye. Chances are her fluctuations will tire you after a time, and you'll pick up your heart—if it's not already broken into small pieces—and go elsewhere.

Women born under the sign of the Twins have the talent of being able to change their moods and attitudes as frequently as they change their party dresses. They're good-time gals who like to whoop it up and burn the candle to the wick. You'll always see them at parties, surrounded by men of all types, laughing gaily or kicking up their heels at every opportunity. Wallflowers they're not. The next day you may bump into her at the library, and you'll hardly recognize her. She'll probably have five or six books under her arms—on five or six different subjects. In fact, she may even work there. Don't come on like an instant critic. She may know more about everything than you would believe possible. She is one smart lady.

You'll probably find her a dazzling and fascinating creature—for a time, at any rate—just as the majority of men do. But when it comes to being serious, sparkling Gemini may leave quite a bit to be desired. It's not that she has anything against being serious, it's just that she might find it difficult trying to be serious with you. At one moment she'll praise you for your steadfast and patient ways, the next moment she'll tell you in a cutting way that you're an impossible stick-in-the-mud.

Don't even try to fathom the depths of her mercurial soul—it's full of false bottoms. She'll resent close investigation, anyway, and will make you rue the day you ever took it into your head to try to learn more about her than she feels is necessary. Better keep the relationship fancy-free and full of fun until she gives you the go-ahead sign. Take as much of her as she's willing to give and don't ask for more. If she does take a serious interest in you and makes up her fickle mind about herself and you, then she'll come across with the goods.

There will come a time when the Gemini girl will realize that she can't spend her entire life at the ball and that the security and warmth you offer is just what she needs in order to be a happy, fulfilled woman.

Don't try to cramp her individuality; she'll never try to cramp yours.

A Gemini mother enjoys her children, which can be the truest form of love. Like them, she's often restless, adventurous, and easily bored. She will never complain about their fleeting interests because she understands the changes the youngsters will go through as they mature.

TAURUS MAN
CANCER WOMAN

The Cancer woman needs to be protected from the cold, cruel world. She'll love you for your masculine yet gentle manner; you make her feel safe and secure. You don't have to pull any he-man or heroic stunts to win her heart; that's not what interests her. She's will be impressed by your sure, steady ways—the way you have of putting your arm around her and making her feel that she's the only girl in the world. When she's feeling glum and tears begin to well up in her eyes, you have that knack of saying just the right thing. You know how to calm her fears, no matter how silly some of them may seem.

The Moon Child is inclined to have her ups and downs. You have the talent for smoothing out the ruffles in her sea of life. She'll most likely worship the ground you walk on or put you on a terribly high pedestal. Don't disappoint her if you can help it. She'll never disappoint you. She will take great pleasure in devoting the rest of her natural life to you. She'll darn your socks, mend your overalls, scrub floors, wash windows, shop, cook, and do just about anything short of murder in order to please you and to let you know that she loves you. Sounds like that legendary good old-fashioned girl, doesn't it? Contrary to popular belief, there are still a good number of them around—and many of them are Cancers.

Of all the signs in the Zodiac, the women under Cancer are the most maternal. In caring for and bringing up children, they know just how to combine the right amount of tenderness with the proper dash of discipline. A child couldn't ask for a better mother. Cancer women are sympathetic, affectionate, and patient with children.

While we're on the subject of motherhood, there's one thing you should be warned about: never be unkind to your mother-in-law. It will be the only golden rule your Cancer wife will probably expect you to live up to. No mother-in-law jokes in the presence of your mate, please. With her, they'll go over like a lead balloon. Mother is something special for her. She may be the crankiest, nosiest old bat, but if she's your wife's mother, you'd better treat her like royalty. Sometimes this may be difficult. But if you want to keep your home together and your wife happy, you'd better learn to grin and bear it.

Your Cancer wife will prove to be a whiz in the kitchen. She'll know just when you're in the mood for your favorite dish or snack, and she can whip it up in a jiffy.

Treat your Cancer wife fairly, and she'll treat you like a king.

TAURUS MAN
LEO WOMAN

The Leo woman can make most men roar like lions. If any woman in the Zodiac has that indefinable something that can make men lose their heads and find their hearts, it's the Leo woman. She's got more than her share of charm and glamour, and she knows how to put them to good use. Jealous men either lose their sanity or at least their cool when trying to woo a woman born under the sign of the Lion.

She likes to kick up her heels quite often and doesn't care who knows it. She often makes heads turn and tongues wag. You don't necessarily have to believe any of what you hear—it's most likely just jealous gossip or wishful thinking.

This vamp makes the blood rush to your head, and you momentarily forget all of the things that you thought were important and necessary in your life. When you come back down to earth and are out of her bewitching presence, you'll conclude that although this vivacious creature can make you feel pretty wonderful, she just isn't the kind of girl you'd planned to bring home to mother. Although Leo will certainly do her best to be a good wife for you, she may not live up to your idea of what your wife should be like.

If you're planning on not going as far as the altar with that Leo woman who has you flipping your lid, you'd better be financially equipped for some very expensive dating. Be prepared to shower her with expensive gifts, take her dining and dancing in the smartest nightspots in town. Promise her the moon, if you're in a position to go that far. Luxury and glamour are two things that are bound to lower a Leo's resistance. She's got expensive tastes, and you'd better cater to them if you expect to get to first base with this gal.

If you've got an important business deal to clinch and you have doubts as to whether it will go over well or not, bring your Leo partner along to that business luncheon. It will be a cinch that you'll have that contract—lock, stock, and barrel—in your pocket before the meeting is over. She won't have to say or do anything—just be there at your side. The grouchiest oil magnate can be transformed into a gushing, obedient schoolboy if there's a charm-studded Leo woman in the room.

Easygoing and friendly, the Leo mother loves to pal around with the children and proudly show them off. She can be so proud of her kids that she sometimes is blind to their faults. Yet when she wants the children to learn and to take their rightful place in society, the Leo mother is a strict but patient teacher.

TAURUS MAN
VIRGO WOMAN

The Virgo woman is particular about choosing her men friends. She's not interested in just going out with anybody. She has her own idea of what a boyfriend or prospective husband should be, and it's possible that image has something of you in it. Generally, Virgo is quiet and refined. She doesn't believe that nonsense has any place in a love affair. She's serious and will expect you to be. She's looking for a man who has both of his feet on the ground—someone who can take care of himself as well as take care of her. She knows the value of money and how to get the most out of a dollar. She's far from being a spendthrift. Throwing money around unnerves her, even if it isn't her money that's being tossed to the winds.

She'll most likely be very shy about romancing. Even the simple act of holding hands may make her blush—on the first couple of dates. You'll have to make all the advances, which is how you feel it should be. You'll have to be careful not to make any wrong moves. She's capable of showing anyone who oversteps the boundaries of common decency the door. It may even take a long time before she'll accept that goodnight kiss. Don't give up. You're exactly the kind of man who can bring out the woman in her. There is warmth and tenderness underneath Virgo's seemingly frigid facade. It will take a patient and understanding man to bring her enjoyment of sex to full bloom.

You'll find Virgo a very sensitive partner, perhaps more sensitive than is good for her. You can help her overcome this by treating her with gentleness and affection.

When a Virgo has accepted you as a lover or mate, she won't stint on giving her love in return. With her, it's all or nothing at all. You'll be surprised at the transformation your earnest attention can bring about in this quiet kind of woman. When in love, Virgos only listen to their hearts, not to what the neighbors say.

Virgo women are honest in love once they've come to grips with it. They don't appreciate hypocrisy, particularly in romance. They believe in being honest to their hearts, so much so that once they've learned the ropes and they find that their hearts have stumbled on another fancy, they will be true to the new heart-throb and leave you standing in the rain. But if you're earnest about your interest in her, she'll know and reciprocate your affection. Do her wrong once, however, and you can be sure she'll snip the soiled ribbon of your relationship.

The Virgo mother encourages her children to develop practical skills in order to stand on their own two feet. If she is sometimes short on displays of affection, here is where you come in to demonstrate warmth and cuddling.

TAURUS MAN
LIBRA WOMAN

It is a woman's prerogative to change her mind. This is a woman born under the sign of Libra. Her changeability, in spite of its undeniable charm, could actually drive even a man of your patience up the wall. She's capable of smothering you with love and kisses one day, and the next day she's apt to avoid you like the plague. If you think you're a man of steel nerves, perhaps you can tolerate her sometimeness without suffering too much. However, if you own up to the fact that you're only a mere mortal of flesh and blood, then you'd better try to fasten your attention on someone more constant.

But don't get the wrong idea: a love affair with a Libra is not all bad. In fact, it has an awful lot of positives. Libra women are soft, very feminine, and warm. She doesn't have to vamp in order to gain a man's attention. Her delicate presence is enough to warm the cockles of any man's heart. One smile and you're a piece of putty in the palm of her hand.

She can be fluffy and affectionate, things you like in a girl. On the other hand, her indecision about what dress to wear, what to cook for dinner, or whether or not to redo the house could make you tear your hair out. What will perhaps be more exasperating is her flat denial that she can't make a simple decision when you accuse her of this. The trouble is she wants to be fair and thinks the only way to do this is to weigh both sides of the situation before coming to a decision. A Libra can go on weighing things for days, months, or years if allowed the time.

The Libra woman likes to be surrounded with beautiful things. Money is no object when beauty is concerned. There'll always be plenty of flowers around her apartment. She'll know how to arrange them tastefully, too. Women under this sign are fond of beautiful clothes and furnishings. They'll run up bills without batting an eye, if given the chance, in order to surround themselves with luxury.

Once she's cottoned to you, the Libra woman will do everything in her power to make you happy. She'll wait on you hand and foot when you're sick, bring you breakfast in bed, and even read you the funny papers if you're too sleepy to open your eyes. She'll be very thoughtful about anything that concerns you. If anyone dares suggest you're not the grandest man in the world, your Libra wife will give him or her a good talking to.

The Libra woman, ruled by the lovely planet Venus as you are, will share with you the joys and burdens of parenthood. She works wonders in bringing up children, although you most always will come first in her affections. The Libra mother understands that youngsters need both guidance and encouragement. Her children will never lack anything that could make their lives easier and richer.

TAURUS MAN
SCORPIO WOMAN

Scorpio is the true zodiacal mate and partner for a Taurus, but is also your zodiacal opposite. The astrological link between Taurus and Scorpio draws you both together in the hopes of an ideal partnership, blessed by the stars. But the Taurus man with a placid disposition and a staid demeanor may find the woman born under the sign of Scorpio too intense and moody.

When a Scorpio woman gets upset, be prepared to run for cover. There is nothing else to do. When her temper flies, so does everything else that's not bolted down. On the other hand, when she chooses to be sweet, she can put you in a hypnotic spell of romance. She can be as hot as a tamale or as cool as a cucumber, but whatever mood she happens to be in, it's for real. She doesn't believe in poses or hypocrisy. The Scorpio woman is often seductive and sultry. Her femme fatale charm can pierce through the hardest of hearts like a laser ray. She doesn't have to look like Mata Hari—many resemble the tomboy next door—but once you've looked into those tantalizing eyes, you're a goner.

The Scorpio woman can be a whirlwind of passion, perhaps too much passion to suit even a hot-blooded Taurus. Life with a girl born under this sign will not be all smiles and smooth sailing. When prompted, she can unleash a gale of venom. If you think you can handle a woman who purrs like a pussycat when treated correctly but spits bullets once her fur is ruffled, then try your luck. Your stable and steady nature will have a calming effect on her. But never cross her, even on the smallest thing. If you do, you'll be in the doghouse.

Generally, the Scorpio woman will keep family battles within the walls of your home. When company visits, she's apt to give the impression that married life is one great big joyride. It's just her way of expressing loyalty to you, at least in front of others. She may fight you tooth and nail in the confines of your living room, but at the ball or during an evening out, she'll hang on your arm and have stars in her eyes. She doesn't consider this hypocrisy, she just believes that family quarrels are a private matter and should be kept so. She's pretty good at keeping secrets. She may even keep a few from you if she feels like it.

By nature, you're a calm and peace-loving man. You value dependability highly. A Scorpio may be too much of a pepperpot for your love diet; you might wind up a victim of chronic heartburn. She's an excitable and touchy woman. You're looking to settle down with someone whose emotions are more steady and reliable. You may find a relationship with a Scorpio too draining.

Never give your Scorpio partner reason to think you've betrayed her. She's an eye-for-an-eye woman. She's not keen on forgiveness when she feels she's been done wrong.

If you've got your sights set on a shapely Scorpio siren, you'd better be prepared to take the bitter with the sweet.

The Scorpio mother secretly idolizes her children, although she will never put them on a pedestal or set unrealistic expectations for them. She will teach her children to be courageous and steadfast. Astrologically linked, the Taurus-Scorpio couple make wonderful parents together. Both of you will share the challenges and responsibilities for bringing up gracious yet gifted youngsters.

TAURUS MAN
SAGITTARIUS WOMAN

The Sagittarius woman is hard to keep track of. First she's here, then she's there. She's a woman with a severe case of itchy feet. She'll win you over with her hale-fellow-well-met manner and breezy charm. She's constantly good-natured and almost never cross. She will strike up a palsy-walsy relationship with you, but you might not be interested in letting it go any further. She probably won't sulk if you leave it on a friendly basis. Treat her like a kid sister, and she'll love you all the more for it.

She'll probably be attracted to you because of your restful, self-assured manner. She'll need a friend like you to rely on and will most likely turn to you frequently for advice.

There's nothing malicious about the female Archer. She'll be full of bounce and good cheer. Her sunshiny disposition can be relied upon even on the rainiest of days. No matter what she'll ever say or do, you'll know that she means well. Sagittarius are often short on tact and say literally anything that comes into their heads, no matter what the occasion. Sometimes the words that tumble out of their mouths seem downright cutting and cruel. She never meant it that way, however. She is capable of losing her friends, and perhaps even yours, through a careless slip of the lip. On the other hand, you will appreciate her honesty and good intentions.

She's not a date you might be interested in marrying, but she'll certainly be a lot of fun to pal around with. Quite often, Sagittarius women are the outdoor type. They're crazy about hiking, fishing, white-water canoeing, and even mountain climbing. She's a busy little lady, and no one could ever accuse her of being a slouch. She's great company most of the time and can be more fun than a three-ring circus when treated fairly. You'll like her for her candid and direct manner. On the whole, Sagittarius are very kind and sympathetic women.

If you do wind up marrying this girl-next-door type, you'll perhaps never regret it. Still, there are certain areas of your home life that you'll have to put yourself in charge of just to keep matters on an even keel. One area is savings. Sagittarius often do not have heads for money and as a result can let it run through their fingers like sand before they realize what has happened to it.

Another area is children. She loves kids so much, she's apt to spoil them silly. If you don't step in, she'll give them all of the freedom they think they need. But the Sagittarius mother trusts her youngsters to learn from experience and know right from wrong.

TAURUS MAN
CAPRICORN WOMAN

You'll probably not have any difficulty in understanding the woman born under the sign of Capricorn. In some ways, she's just like you. She is faithful, dependable, and systematic in just about everything that she undertakes. She is concerned with security and sees to it that every penny she spends is spent wisely. She is very economical in using her time, too. She doesn't believe in whittling away her energy in a scheme that is bound not to pay off.

Ambitious themselves, they're often attracted to ambitious men—men who are interested in getting somewhere in life. If a man of this sort wins her heart, she'll stick by him and do all she can to see to it that he gets to the top. The Capricorn woman is almost always diplomatic and makes an excellent hostess. She can be very influential with your business acquaintances.

She's not the most romantic woman of the Zodiac, but she's far from being frigid when she meets the right man. She believes in true love and doesn't appreciate getting involved in flings. To her, they're just a waste of time. She's looking for a man who means business—in life as well as in love. Although she can be very affectionate with her boyfriend or mate, she tends to let her head govern her heart. That is not to say that she is a cool, calculating cucumber. On the contrary, she just feels she can be more honest about love if she consults her brains first. She'll want to size up the situation first before throwing her heart in the ring. She wants to make sure that it won't get crushed.

A Capricorn woman is concerned and proud about her family tree. Relatives are important to her, particularly if they've been able to make their mark in life. Never say a cross word about her family members. That can really go against her grain, and she won't talk to you for days on end.

She's generally thorough in whatever she undertakes: cooking, cleaning, entertaining. Capricorn women are well-mannered and gracious, no matter what their background. They seem to have it in their natures always to behave properly.

If you should marry a Capricorn, you need never worry about her going on a wild shopping spree. The Goat understands the value of money better than most women. If you turn over your paycheck to her at the end of the week, you can be sure that a good hunk of it will go into the bank and that all the bills will be paid on time.

With children, the Capricorn mother is both loving and correct. She will teach the youngsters to be polite and kind, and to honor tradition as much as you do. The Capricorn mother is very ambitious for the children. An earth sign like you, she wants the children to have every advantage and to benefit from things she perhaps lacked as a child.

TAURUS MAN
AQUARIUS WOMAN
The woman born under the sign of the Water Bearer can be odd and eccentric at times. Some say that this is the source of her mysterious charm. You may think she's nutty, and you may be fifty percent right. Aquarius women have their heads full of dreams, and stars in their eyes. By nature, they are often unconventional and have their own ideas about how the world should be run. Sometimes their ideas may seem pretty weird, but more likely than not they are just a little too progressive for their time. There's a saying that runs: the way Aquarius thinks, so will the world in fifty years.

If you find yourself falling in love with an Aquarius, you'd better fasten your safety belt. It may take some time before you really know what she's like and even then you may have nothing more to go on but a string of vague hunches. She can be like a rainbow, full of dazzling colors. She's like no other girl you've ever known. There's something about her that is definitely charming, yet elusive; you'll never be able to put your finger on it. She seems to radiate adventure and magic without even half trying. She'll most likely be the most tolerant and open-minded woman you've ever encountered.

If you find that she's too much mystery and charm for you to handle—and being a Taurus, chances are you might—just talk it out with her and say that you think it would be better if you called it quits. She'll most likely give you a peck on the cheek and say you're one hundred percent right but still there's no reason why you can't remain friends. Aquarius women are like that. And perhaps you'll both find it easier to get along in a friendship than in a romance.

It is not difficult for her to remain buddy-buddy with someone she has just broken off with. For many Aquarius, the line between friendship and romance is a fuzzy one.

She's not a jealous person and, while you're romancing her, she'll expect you not to be, either. You'll find her a free spirit most of the time. Just when you think you know her inside out, you'll discover that you don't really know her at all. She's a very sympathetic and warm person. She can be helpful to people in need of assistance and advice.

She's a chameleon and can fit in anywhere. She'll seldom be suspicious even when she has every right to be. If the man she loves slips and allows himself a little fling, chances are she'll just turn her head the other way and pretend not to notice that the gleam in his eye is not meant for her.

The Aquarius mother is generous and seldom refuses her children anything. You may feel the youngsters need a bit more discipline and practicality. But you will appreciate the Aquarius mother's wordly views, which prepare the youngsters to get along in life. Her open-minded attitude is easily transmitted to the children. They will grow up to be respectful and tolerant.

TAURUS MAN
PISCES WOMAN

The Pisces woman places great value on love and romance. She's gentle, kind, and romantic. Perhaps she's that girl you've been dreaming about all these years. Like you, she has very high ideals; she will only give her heart to a man who she feels can live up to her expectations.

Many a man dreams of an alluring Pisces woman. You are no exception. She's soft and cuddly and very domestic. She'll let you be the brains of the family; she's contented to play a behind-the-scenes role in order to help you achieve your goals. The illusion that you are the master of the household is the kind of magic that the Pisces woman is adept at creating.

She can be very ladylike and proper. Your business associates and friends will be dazzled by her warmth and femininity. Although she's a charmer, there is a lot more to her than just a pretty exterior. There is a brain ticking away behind that soft, womanly facade. You may never become aware of it—that is, until you're married to her. It's no cause for alarm, however, she'll most likely never use it against you, only to help you and possibly set you on a more sucessful path.

If she feels you're botching up your married life through careless behavior or if she feels you could be earning more money than you do, she'll tell you about it. But any wife would really. She will never try to usurp your position as head and breadwinner of the family.

No one had better dare say one uncomplimentary word about you in her presence. It's likely to cause her to break into tears. Pisces women are usually very sensitive beings. Their reaction to adversity, frustration, or anger is just a plain, good, old-fashioned cry. They can weep buckets when inclined.

She can do wonders with a house. She is very fond of dramatic and beautiful things. There will always be plenty of fresh-cut flowers around the house. She will choose charming artwork and antiques, if they are affordable. She'll see to it that the house is decorated in a dazzling yet welcoming style.

She'll have an extra special dinner prepared for you when you come home from an important business meeting. Don't dwell on the boring details of the meeting, though. But if you need that grand vision, the big idea, to seal a contract or make a conquest, your Pisces woman is sure to confide a secret that will guarantee your success. She is canny and shrewd with money, and once you are on her wavelength you can manage the intricacies on your own.

If you are patient and kind, you can keep a Pisces woman happy for a lifetime. She, however, is not without her faults. Her sensitivity may get on your nerves after a while. You may find her lacking in practicality and good old-fashioned stoicism. You may even feel that she uses her tears as a method of getting her own way.

Treat her with tenderness, and your relationship will be an enjoyable one. Pisces women are generally fond of sweets, so keep her in chocolates (and flowers, of course) and you'll have a very happy wife. Never forget birthdays, anniversaries, and the like. These are important occasions for her. If you ever let such a thing slip your mind, you can be sure of sending her off in a huff.

Your Taurus talent for patience and gentleness can pay off in your relationship with a Pisces woman. Chances are she'll never make you sorry that you placed that band of gold on her finger.

There is usually a strong bond between a Pisces mother and her children. She'll try to give them things she never had as a child and is apt to spoil them as a result. She can deny herself in order to fill their needs. But the Pisces mother will teach her youngsters the value of service to the community while not letting them lose their individuality.

TAURUS
LUCKY NUMBERS 2013

Lucky numbers and astrology can be linked through the movements of the Moon. Each phase of the thirteen Moon cycles vibrates with a sequence of numbers for your Sign of the Zodiac over the course of the year. Using your lucky numbers is a fun system that connects you with tradition.

New Moon	First Quarter	Full Moon	Last Quarter
Dec. 13 ('12) 7415	Dec. 20 8382	Dec. 28 1957	Jan. 4 7839
Jan. 11 9614	Jan. 18 8275	Jan. 27 1034	Feb. 3 4852
Feb. 10 2694	Feb. 17 7584	Feb. 25 6672	March 4 2859
March 11 9371	March 19 0816	March 27 8941	April 3 1725
April 10 5031	April 18 1685	April 25 9074	May 2 4826
May 9 0697	May 17 7355	May 25 4637	May 31 7058
June 8 8662	June 16 2459	June 23 6394	June 30 7253
July 8 3380	July 15 0263	July 22 1936	July 29 1422
August 6 2790	August 14 0528	August 20 7365	August 28 8662
Sept. 5 2459	Sept. 12 9637	Sept. 19 2059	Sept. 27 7735
Oct. 4 5607	Oct. 11 7482	Oct. 18 5697	Oct. 26 7168
Nov. 3 9417	Nov. 10 7256	Nov. 17 0311	Nov. 25 6923
Dec. 2 7405	Dec. 9 5836	Dec. 17 3449	Dec. 25 2783

TAURUS
YEARLY FORECAST 2013

*Forecast for 2013 Concerning Business
and Financial Affairs, Job Prospects,
Travel, Health, Romance and Marriage
for Persons Born with the Sun
in the Zodiacal Sign of Taurus.
April 21–May 20*

For those born under the influence of the Sun in the zodiacal sign of Taurus, ruled by Venus, planet of love, beauty, and money, 2013 promises to be a year of continual change and transformation. Expect to be bumped out of your comfort zone often this year, especially in April, June, July, September, October, and November. During these months major planetary aspects occur to shake up routines and habitual customs.

Venus, your planetary ruler, is steaming up fiery Sagittarius as the year begins. The sign of Sagittarius represents the sector of your solar horoscope that deals with shared resources, sex, and inheritance. Venus in Sagittarius gives you a chance to make improvements in these areas, improvements that might be a big part of your resolutions list as this new year starts. It is often said that the Bull is slower to fall in love than members of some other zodiac signs. But most of you are loyal and committed once you find the love of your life. This year you will have plenty of opportunity to test that possibility.

Mars, the planet of drive, is visiting Aquarius, your solar tenth house of reputation and destiny, as the year begins. If you sense that you are not in the right vocation, then the energy and enthusiasm to find a more satisfying career should be in plentiful supply. Expand your knowledge and expertise so that you can increase your value to an employer. Consider moving into self-employment. Find an academic or training course that can assist your growth and achievement. Expect to be busier than usual throughout 2013, particularly in January and February. During these months the harder you work, the greater are the chances of success. This is the period to invest resources in areas that can promote your cherished goals. Career and business interests can be changed in a positive manner if focus is applied to what needs to be done. Don't procrastinate. Hard work will pay dividends, and advancement can come both at home and at work.

Jupiter, the planet of abundance and wealth, is still visiting Gemini, your solar second house of personal money and possessions, as the year opens. Finances should be greatly improved, especially for the astute and grounded Bull. Jupiter conveys blessings and protection. And when placed in the second solar house, Jupiter often bestows great opportunities and gifts. Common sense, of course, must be applied. Taurus optimism and confidence around finances are buoyed from January to late June. More money should be flowing your way. Some wise investments made in the past should come to fruition. This is also a period when you could easily overextend and overindulge. So be diligent and monitor your spending. If you gamble, even modestly, on sports, games of chance, or lotteries, at least use your innate practicality and logic. When it comes to speculation, beware of risking your hard-earned cash. Financial concerns in committed partnerships could arise. Examine mutual spending habits to see if a shared understanding of economic aims exists. Remain alert and be ready. Someone close could convey good fortune, opportunity, or at least an advantage. This isn't the year to cut corners or to look for quick solutions. Instead, take a steady approach and things will get done.

Jupiter in late June enters Cancer, your solar third house of communication and the close environment, transportation and commerce, studies and information. Jupiter will visit Cancer for the rest of 2013 into mid-2014. Jupiter in Cancer is an opportune period to learn a new language, take creative writing classes, enroll in public speaking programs, and use short trips as a means of gaining knowledge. Any money spent on refresher courses as well as new studies would be beneficial. Lessons and workshops that provide employment training will be key. Taurus students putting in the effort are likely to excel during the second half of 2013. Some of you might tend toward laziness, relying on what you already know rather than hitting the books and broadening your knowledge. If you seek guidance counseling, choose someone with plenty of experience and wisdom in diverse fields.

Connecting and communicating with folk overseas either for business or personal reasons should be a positive experience. Some of you might travel for work or for study abroad. Buying a more expensive car, computer, home theater system, or other electronic equipment could be very tempting. You should be lucky with such purchases. Self-employed and entrepreneurial Taurus in import, export, and other foreign trade should find that commercial interests and profits on the rise. Jupiter in Cancer is also a good period to purchase real estate, but you must resist the temptation to take out a bigger mortgage than you can comfortably handle.

Young Taurus seeking a first home and coupled Taurus with

a growing family should actually enjoy the hunt for a house or apartment. September and October, when Mars moves through Leo and your solar sector of home and family, should be an especially fruitful period for this task. Your physical energy to go out and look for something that suits your needs will peak at that time. Know your lifestyle requirements, stick to a budget, and you should be pleased with the end results. A relocation, either planned or unexpected, might shake things up for some Bulls.

Creative talent is an innate quality of Taurus folk. Self-confidence is growing this year, helping you to deal more easily with obstacles, tricky people, and unforeseen circumstances. Your skill is also enhanced. Utilize it constructively in such various endeavors as broadening your knowledge, redecorating and renovating your home, generating more income, making noteworthy things, and enjoying a balanced lifestyle. Taurus with sporting prowess could receive a measure of fame this year. You may have a rise in your fan base, a better reputation with teammates, and requests to perform for local neighborhoods and communities. This is also a good year to seek a sponsorship or advertising deal that further develops your special gifts on the playing field.

Love and romance are under powerful vibes in 2013 while structured Saturn continues to visit the sign of Scorpio, your solar seventh house of relationship. Single Taurus has a good chance to find a permanent lover, if that is your choice. If not, you can look forward to romantic encounters that make you happy. If lack of time or a demanding work schedule has hindered your search for romance, don't discount matchmaking efforts through friends and various online websites.

With Saturn in Scorpio so strongly impacting all intimate as well as business partnerships, many Bulls will find that relationships are paramount this year. Your relations with coworkers, employers, creditors, members of the public, business partners, close family, some distant relatives, and especially lovers, spouses, mates, and best friends will be key. Lessons need to be learned about relating to the others in your life. Compromise and cooperation will be essential to lessen discord and to create harmony and agreement. If a marriage or relationship has been on the rocks for some time, then you can expect issues to arise that might bring you to the point of no return.

This transit of Saturn in Scorpio is all about commitment. You will be deciding if you are being supported by the others in your life as well as experiencing emotional fulfillment. If the answer is in the negative, you might have to come to an inexorable choice; whether to end a personal or professional relationship and move on or to apply more effort and resurrect the bond that once was. Even a happy and committed union will require constant work during the next couple of years to ensure that romance remains alive. It is important for Taurus individuals to choose wisely when it comes to a significant other. This can be a year when you fall deeply in love and take the plunge into committed couplehood.

Intense Pluto is transiting Capricorn, your solar ninth house of long journeys and higher education. Pluto here makes a powerful connection to Jupiter in Cancer, your solar third house of short journeys and studies. This planetary opposition in the second half of 2013 further emphasizes travel for business and learning. The Bull eager to expand your knowledge may become an exchange student abroad. Those of you leaving school or graduating may journey to various countries before moving into the work force. Research and in-depth explorations lead to discoveries. It is an excellent year to return to academic study on a part-time or full-time basis. Scholars and investigators should experience wonderful success, with the possibility of a grant for further study. Taurus novelists will find words flowing more freely, and you could be launching one or more books.

The Bull eager to immigrate will find it easier to get a visa. Take care when studying belief systems and religious doctrines, as there is a strong chance of becoming dogmatic. A second marriage or extramarital affair could be on the cards. Such triangles may be more about rivalry than love. There may be challenges and conflict coming from competitors in the business and sporting worlds. Dealings with patrons, clients, the press, and other media figures could be trickier because various complaints and problems are publicized rather than kept under wraps. Strive for patience with people who are not measuring up or following what you consider the right code of behavior. A flexible approach is recommended but if not achieved, you could be quite frustrated.

This is a year when you are willing to help friends and those you love but very unlikely to assist anyone who only wants to use your knowledge and generosity. Superficiality isn't your style. Relationships that are not working may be ended or at least mended so that equality and balance are maintained. Confusion might surround some friendships. From time to time you might not know where you stand. Both pals and associates might try to take advantage or even deceive you. Be on guard, as not everything you are told will be the truth. Welcome new friends with whom you can share common interests and values. Joining a group or a club may appeal, but be careful that you are not cajoled into taking on too many volunteer roles and tasks.

Uranus, planet of the unique and the unexpected, is traveling through your Aries solar twelfth house, so spending time on your own should be enjoyable and productive. Working alone might be your preference. Talented Taurus may find that your output of original and creative work increases considerably. Some of you will take a new direction, especially a creative or spiritual path that may develop into something wonderful. An art exhibition or a display of artistic creations could be a highlight. Confidential projects and ventures carried out behind the scenes should progress extremely well. The Bull who is helping the underprivileged might spend many hours in volunteer labor. The radical nature of the Uranus in Aries transit foresees interesting outcomes from losses, endings, and separations that lead to new beginnings. These are likely to set you on a fresh direction, one that will be very different from any experienced before, and may be a creative or spiritual path that will develop into something wonderful.

When it comes to health, Taurus folk often battle with problems relating to weight. The good things of life can at times be too tempting to resist. As a Taurus you consider yourself a connoisseur of food and wine. So it will be essential to watch how much you consume on a daily basis, and try to be moderate. Members of your sign must develop strict habits when it comes to fitness and health and well-being. Sons and daughters of Venus like all the comforts and indulgences, from fried vegetables to chocolate-coated fruits. The Venus-ruled temperament leans to the easy, sometimes the lazy. Although Taurus can be stubborn and persistent, that perseverance is not often observed around nutrition and exercise, the two areas that come into play as far as weight gain is concerned.

Cycling or walking can be a positive form of exercise for those of you who are not keen to partake of a more rigid workout. Such daily exercise is one method of keeping weight under control. Drinking plenty of water and reducing caffeine and alcohol can also be of major benefit in keeping your kidneys and liver in healthy condition. Take out a gym membership or purchase inexpensive home equipment. Using your money here is a wonderful motivation to use the facilities in order to be trim and taut.

Taurus rules the throat, voice, and neck. These are areas that need extra protection, especially through the winter months. Remember to dress appropriately. Protect your throat and larynx if singing or constant talking is part of your normal routine. If you are healthy, major problems should be minimal throughout 2013 as long as care is taken with areas that could be the cause of ongoing concerns. This year may be busier than usual, with lots of short trips, running errands, and driving around, so pace your activities and put plenty of rest and relaxation into your daily agenda.

The phases of the Moon and the retrograde phases of Mercury

are important for decision making and subsequent action, and these phases are noted and discussed in the daily forecasts that follow. The three Mercury retrograde phases this year all take place in water signs, which are compatible with and fertile for Taurus as an earth sign. Your ruler Venus also has a retrograde phase, which takes place from December 21 until the end of January next year.

Taurus individuals will be more able this year to embrace change. Modification and transformation are natural processes, and you will not be as resistant as usual. Being adaptable, on the other hand, will lessen the chance of becoming overwhelmed. Go with the flow of opportunities, and be especially flexible when the unexpected happens. Successful outcomes will lay strong foundations for the future.

TAURUS
DAILY FORECAST

January–December 2013

JANUARY

1. TUESDAY. Happy New Year! Taurus folk can have the best of two worlds today, the social as well as the domestic. Still, time spent around home and hearth may be your best bet. Your ruler Venus, the planet of love and beauty, is now visiting the party-loving sign of Sagittarius. So if you are looking for a peaceful day, you could be disappointed. Relatives or friends may drop in to take advantage of your innate ability to make everyone welcome. You are proud to show off your house, and people love to partake of your hospitality. Misunderstandings and mixed messages might complicate the simplest things, so choose easy pastimes that will not provoke controversy.

2. WEDNESDAY. Pleasant. Good things come to those who wait, and for many Bulls the wait may be over in some areas of your life. Change is in the air. Although embracing adjustments and being adaptable may not be a Taurus forte, there is no escaping a different landscape and horizon stretching out in front of you. Accept gracefully any transformations sent by the universe. Things should be looking much brighter as this new year gets under way. Abundant planet Jupiter is visiting your Gemini solar second house of personal money from now until late in June. So expect good fortune to flow and the bank balance to build as long as you keep savings up and spending down.

3. THURSDAY. Disruptive. Stand by and prepare for a roller-coaster ride over the next couple of days. Be flexible and watch for those things you weren't counting on to appear. Situations and events are likely to pop up out of nowhere, throwing a preset agenda into disarray. Loved ones might not seem to agree with you, so endeavoring to force your point of view could prove futile. Try to defer visits to relatives and in-laws if possible. Arguments and tension are bound to spoil the scene, and you will have no patience for discussing trivial or senseless issues. Concentration may be at low ebb, which can make it difficult for those of you studying or taking any kind of exam and test.

4. FRIDAY. Unpredictable. Expect the unexpected is the mantra again today. Decisions can be made because your judgment is sound, but it is advisable to maintain a realistic approach. Career and business interests are starred. Bulls keen to generate more income should find situations and events falling your way. Humility is something most Taurus folk practice. So make sure your ego is tucked safely away now, especially if you are representing a product or selling yourself. Special recognition, a promotion, or a pay raise could come to you. Those of you seeking favors should find these are quickly granted.

5. SATURDAY. Guarded. Take it easy shopping, or it won't be long before your hard-earned cash disappears. Although your ability to communicate clearly is strong, there is also a greater than usual propensity to exaggerate. Make sure all facts and figures are verified if you are presenting a lecture, selling anything, and even talking in general. You would be embarrassed if someone challenges your findings. It is not a wise move to approach relatives and in-laws for a loan or any favor that involves money. And you should not lend money to anyone right now. Don't be overconfident taking a driver's test, leading a debating team, or counting on a study report to satisfy a teacher.

6. SUNDAY. Diverse. A number of planetary trends prevail as the weekend comes to a close. Remaining focused and on track shouldn't be too arduous, although there may be a little confusion swirling around that throws you off track. Under current stars all projects requiring in-depth research should proceed successfully. With your persuasive powers and strategic thinking at a high, superficial conversations will not hold much appeal. Think over what you are told, it could be misleading. Dig around if finding out the truth of a matter is important. Taurus students preparing for an exam or writing an assignment should be pleased with the amount of work you accomplish.

7. MONDAY. Variable. Your social life could be on a high and your datebook is filling up nicely. However, this isn't the time to squeeze in too much activity. Current cosmic trends are likely to find your physical energies taking a dive but your emotions swelling considerably. Career achievements are highlighted. A new job could be on the agenda for some of you. Bulls experiencing issues with a superior or a parent should proceed carefully to keep the peace, as arguments could develop rapidly. Being bossed around or having to take orders is bound to increase your irritability and hinder productivity. The day is better for planning than for taking decisive action.

8. TUESDAY. Lively. Money matters are in the frame as the Moon travels through your Sagittarius house of joint finances and possessions. Go after an ambitious plan, negotiate an important contract, or rearrange your resources to get ahead. This is also a positive period to begin business activities and to initiate a career move. A moneymaking proposition should have potential, although you will need to do your homework to pin down realistic options. Taurus shoppers should keep a set figure in mind, especially for luxury items. The likelihood of spending more than the budget allows is strong. As a Taurus, though, you do opt for quality over quantity.

9. WEDNESDAY. Delightful. Your ruler, the lovely Venus, now enters the sign of Capricorn, your solar ninth house, and bestows a serious and stable tone on relationships. While Venus visits Capricorn over the next three weeks, Bulls have an opportunity to let love affairs develop and grow more solid and secure. Social and romantic pastimes that have a religious or cultural theme should be especially enjoyable and fun during this period. This is also a good time to consider likely destinations for summer vacations. You may find good sites that suit your needs, whether single and looking or committed and content. Your preference for beautifully tailored apparel can cost you a bundle, but it's worth it.

10. THURSDAY. Inspired. Let creativity flow rather than attempt tasks that are routine or repetitive or try to do work that requires precision. Develop your imaginative schemes, then iron out the bugs later on. A flirtation with someone from another country or culture could add an emotional zing to your mood, and you might be left wondering what the next step will be. A compliment will also do your heart good. If you are not fancy-free, don't read too much into a romantic overture; your admirer may just be having a little lighthearted fun. To avoid misunderstandings, write down the exact address of a social venue, or you could miss out on a good time.

11. FRIDAY. Pondering. Many Taurus folk could feel there is more to life than what is currently on offer. Keep smiling, as this mood of dissatisfaction may not last long. If you take the time to consider where you are in life right now and if the pathway you are on is the right one, then you should experience more happiness and less restlessness. Under today's Capricorn New Moon include a few special treats when planning an upcoming travel itinerary or special adventure. Do be mindful not to waste money on activities and pursuits that you can do anytime on home turf. Embrace the unknown, the unfamiliar. Opt for new experiences and encounters.

12. SATURDAY. Foggy. Even if this is a day off work, current employment conditions could be a focus for you as the changeable Moon visits Aquarius, your solar sector of career and reputation. Ambitions will be clouded if confusion regarding your direction in life is creating angst. Take time out for serious thought about what means the most to you. Strive for clarity as to what makes you happy so that important life decisions can be made. Whether going solo or with a partner, you can expect ups and downs in the love department over the next few days. Taurus folk on vacation should be especially prudent with your spending money; it could disappear in a flash.

13. SUNDAY. Productive. If work duties are still preying on your mind, get an early start and catch up on a number of tasks that are begging to be done. Bulls who are free from such obligations will enjoy a chance of scenery; it could be a learning experience as well as a chance to rest and relax. Research on the computer might bring positive results for students and for those of you seeking to upgrade skills and expertise. People are likely to be paying attention and interested in what you have to say. But approach tricky topics diplomatically, or someone might end up with wounded feelings. Group activities with an artistic outcome could nicely occupy part of your leisure time.

14. MONDAY. Active. With the Moon sailing through your Pisces solar eleventh house of friendships and cherished desires, this should be a lovely day to begin the new working week. Despite this fine lunar influence for Taurus folk, there are a couple of adverse planetary contacts that may throw a monkey wrench in the works if you are not on guard. Exaggeration should be avoided and moderation observed. Someone from your past could drop in unexpectedly, which might make you a little nervous or distracted. Those of you traveling away from home may encounter odd situations or incur unusual expenses. Try not to waste money on souvenirs.

15. TUESDAY. Bountiful. Pleasant vibes continue. You could find your star shining brightly among friends and associates now. This is an excellent day to reconnect, strengthen, or initiate new links in order to expand your social circle and network. Favorable news may be received concerning an employment application, a partnership offer, or a business opportunity. Don't let anyone convince you to change your mind when it comes to a special goal. Channel that renowned Taurus practical energy into feasible projects and aims. Love and affection will spark over the next few days, so be prepared for an extra dose of romance to brighten your life.

16. WEDNESDAY. Nurturing. Even if you are extremely busy, it is important to make sure you are getting enough sleep, good food, and relaxation over the next couple of days. Intensity and passion are on the rise. Love is in the air right now. A delightful turn of romantic events could set your pulse racing. Solo Taurus is in luck going out on a date this evening. Even those of you in a committed relationship should be pleased with the pleasant ambience prevailing and the loving affection bestowed. A holiday romance could be heating up, with the possibility of the affair enduring for a long time.

17. THURSDAY. Reassuring. Extra sleep might be in order for Taurus folk who are your own boss. With the Moon now slipping through your Aries twelfth house of secrets and solitude, it is very likely that dreams and imagination are making an indelible impression. The need for quiet and privacy becomes a priority as you take time out to recharge spiritual and physical batteries. Endeavor to retire earlier than usual tonight. Allow time for your body to recover, especially if you have been keeping a hectic pace lately. Although love and romance are under stable stars, jealousy may be a problem if you are feeling insecure or if your partner cannot reassure you enough.

18. FRIDAY. Constructive. Although energy could remain on the low side, your ability to think clearly and quickly is good. The Aries Moon continues to urge Bulls to slow down and let a feeling of oneness envelop you, but your mind is bound to be busier than usual. Students could be really fired up. Progress can be made with any form of writing, delivering a lecture, or researching a special assignment. Take time to organize your office files, clear away paperwork, pay outstanding accounts, and answer correspondence. Your hunches should be accurate, so pay attention. Focusing on more efficient methods to increase output and productivity should prove successful.

19. SATURDAY. Bright. The Moon now moves through your sign of Taurus, your solar first house of personality and self. You are in the bright spotlight. Your personal image is to the fore. This is the perfect time to make an appointment for a beauty treatment. Messenger planet Mercury is also on the move, entering your Aquarius solar tenth house of career and reputation. Aquarius here facilitates original and creative thought and enhances all your speaking and writing projects. Now is an excellent period to push forward with special plans, ask for favors, and help people who need assistance. If you are a romantic Bull, keep an eye out for a potential new love.

20. SUNDAY. Accomplished. Yesterday afternoon the glowing moved into Aquarius, reinforcing your focus on business and career prospects. With both Mercury and the Sun in Aquarius, Taurus individuals should continue to feel emotionally strong and ready to take on whatever the universe sends. Expect activity to increase. Restlessness can be a motivator, urging you to move out of your comfort zone even if it is only for the next four weeks. If your place of employment isn't providing the level of emotional gratification needed to keep you happily occupied, now is the time to seek new options and opportunities. Look for the niche that will inspire your enthusiasm.

21. MONDAY. Assertive. Determination and drive are enhanced as the new week gets under way. The cosmic trends continue to encourage you, boosting your confidence to move forward with personal goals and pursuits. This morning the Moon slips into your solar second house of Gemini, which puts the focus on your personal income and possessions. If going into business for yourself is under consideration, begin making plans now and ease into self-employment. Once all bases have been covered, it should be a smooth transition, with the chances of success high. If you are in line for a promotion or a special contract, you appear to have the edge on competitors.

22. TUESDAY. Advantageous. The day ahead is all about communicating and using your mind to the best advantage. Your ability to converse articulately is at a high, although you will need to watch the tendency to exaggerate. Thinking on your feet and outside of the box comes easier even for the most conservative Bull. People are bound to listen to your every word now. A financial concern could add pressure. Finding a way through the problem shouldn't be too difficult for the astute and money-conscious Taurus. If you are after a special gift, consider auction sites and estate sales where there is a good chance of your finding something original and tasteful.

23. WEDNESDAY. Good. Lucky trends continue to spread positive vibes your way. Take advantage. Participate in activities and functions that increase your chances of unexpected gains. Avoid restlessness by introducing a lot of variety into a dull routine, or your enthusiasm could quickly drain away. Those of you in financial discussions or negotiations should remember to look at the whole picture to ensure that all variables are taken into account. If you and a partner are shopping for home appliances, agree on what you both can afford. This can prevent tension from arising between you, and also will present a united front to salespeople who may try to talk you into spending more.

24. THURSDAY. Satisfactory. Flexibility may not come naturally to Taurus folk. But you can adapt, even quickly, when you have to. Make the effort today, or you could become overwhelmed by constant disruptions. If you can abide by the motto of expect the unexpected, then you should be able to handle whatever changes await you. People around you, especially on the job scene, are likely to be more chatty than usual. This is fine as long as productivity is maintained. If not, it might be wise to refrain from the discussions. Taurus members of a group dedicated to protecting the environment will enthusiastically champion a cause close to your own home or neighborhood.

25. FRIDAY. Complex. Contradictory trends are in play today. Any matters involving business, career, and financial transactions should proceed without a hitch. Excellence on the job may be rewarded by a pat on the back from an influential associate or the boss. But matters involving the law and public interests, especially where such interests touch partnership or client concerns, may experience delays and obstacles. Some projects might require another look or revision before you sign off the job as completed. Squeezing in time to have fun during the day will be challenging, so wait until the evening rolls around before you let your hair down.

26. SATURDAY. Fair. Home repairs and renovations will get a promising start as long as you and your helpers have a good idea of what the job entails. With self-confidence at a high, be careful that you don't take on more than you can comfortably handle. It would be very costly for a professional to repair the mistakes that you, as an amateur, might make. If you missed out on a party invitation, consider inviting friends over for dinner or throw your own party. But take care later on. The approaching Full Moon culminating at midnight tonight in the sign of Leo will increase everyone's emotions, making some angry and bombastic. There is also a potential for accidents, so drive sensibly.

27. SUNDAY. Unsettled. Full Moon influences color the day with fiery emotion, and a bevy of other cosmic trends will convey a sharp tone. If you are feeling less than inspired, just catch up on routine tasks at home. Taurus individuals who live with parents should quickly exit the scene, as trouble appears to be looming with a father or elderly relative. A social outing may be marred by disagreements and arguments, especially if siblings or other relatives are included in the gathering. Parents should teach youngsters how to perform household chores. Ensure that everyone pitches in and helps to keep a modicum of order so that you prevent minor mishaps and losses of treasured possessions.

28. MONDAY. Tricky. It is another day when the celestial trends are mainly adverse. However, by the time you leave work for home, improvements are likely to occur. Students should double-check that you have everything required for the day ahead, as you might leave something important at home. Travel plans may be disrupted. Bulls vacationing overseas should take care with personal treasures, wallet, and passport. Ensure that important items remain in your hands, not in the possession of an unsavory character. Home and career issues might clash, making decisions difficult to make. Relax and participate in a pleasant pastime this evening, but head to bed early.

29. TUESDAY. Smooth. Today's trends improve as the hours pass. By the time evening rolls around, you will be sharing a fun experience with your mate or a special friend, which will be a delightful way to end the day. The urge to produce could find many of you giving free rein to creative juices and artistic expression. Regardless of whatever form that takes, spend time constructing your masterpiece. Chemistry could spark a special attraction for single Taurus. Make sure you get to know a potential partner pretty well before giving your heart away. For those of you with children at home, making loved ones feel extra important will be rewarded by demonstrable appreciation and affection.

30. WEDNESDAY. Mixed. Although there might be an urge to party and have fun, this impulse may be fleeting. With a somber tone prevailing, any delays, obstacles, or problems could quickly deplete your enthusiasm and physical resources. A self-imposed target or deadline could push you to the limit. Believing in your goal can be the motivation you need to move forward. Jupiter, the planet of expansion, is about to go direct in the sign of Gemini, your solar house of personal money. Jupiter moving forward will free up money matters that have been stalemated, delayed, or placed on hold. Focusing on financial affairs and your ability to generate more money can serve you well in the coming weeks.

31. THURSDAY. Helpful. Your working day begins with the graceful Moon slipping through Libra, the sign of compromise and cooperation, and the sign that shares with you planet Venus as a ruler. Moon in Libra impacts your solar sixth house of work and service. Using compromise, fairness, and tact on the job or at home will ensure that harmonious vibes prevail. A health problem could improve rapidly, with your vim and vigor increasing considerably. If minor health problems have been causing concern, contacting a medical practitioner for a checkup can put your mind at ease. A major project will prove challenging. If anyone can persevere and stick with it, you can, Taurus.

FEBRUARY

1. FRIDAY. Quiet. The universe is sending very few planetary aspects today, at least through the working hours, so depend on yourself to get things going. It would appear that an employment matter will bring a feeling of been there done that, and now you have to revisit the matter yet again. Make the effort and go with a fresh approach; an important adjustment should make a significant difference very soon. Updating a resume to accompany a job application will be to your benefit. A fresh diet or exercise plan will be an eye-opening experience. The more effort you expend on your own health, the more you will learn about your own body, what makes you feel energetic, and what doesn't.

2. SATURDAY. Encouraging. Energetic planet Mars and affectionate planet Venus are both on the move today. Mars enters Pisces, your solar eleventh house of friends and cherished goals. Venus, your ruler, swings into Aquarius, your solar tenth house of career concerns. Expect the unpredictable when it comes to business and employment matters. Hopefully, you will be on the receiving end of some unexpected offers and messages. An admired associate may provide guidance with a special project. Although there could be a few challenges ahead, successfully mastering this project will raise both your profile and self-confidence. Include a short break from routine today.

3. SUNDAY. Harmonious. A loving partnership is a two-way street, and today's Scorpio Moon is ideal for Taurus lovers to make this happen. Reveal your own feelings. Give equal time to your partner's feelings and concerns. The more you and your mate understand each other's life experiences, the closer the bond of affection becomes and the stronger the relating is. Reconnecting with old friends and forming closer connections with newfound pals should be easier now. These ties will eventually help business matters, sales, and networking. A scintillating flirtation looks promising for singles. Couples should relax together and plan a candlelit evening just for two.

4. MONDAY. Variable. Morning sees the Scorpio Moon brightly impacting your solar seventh house of relationship and urging a more intimate connection with your personal partner. But your physical resources may be lower, making you susceptible to infections, so the early hours would be good for staying in and nurturing yourself and those close to you. Your moods begin to fluctuate as the Moon later visits Sagittarius, your solar eighth house of sex, shared finances, and power. Find positive and productive methods of releasing frustration if intense situations create angst over the next two days. Be wary of charlatans peddling get-rich schemes; you are not likely to benefit here.

5. TUESDAY. Good. Keep heavy and labor-intensive chores to a minimum. This is one time when running out of steam will triumph over your usual innate ability to persevere. The urge to become closer to your partner remains high, increasing delightful intimacy and passion for those of you in a hot couple. Mercury, the planet of talk, hops into Pisces, your solar eleventh house of goals, earnings from commerce, and social connections. Mercury moving forward in Pisces over the next three weeks will encourage the astute and business-savvy Bull to conduct further networking to improve the financial bottom line. Connect with old and new friends. Rewards will come by cultivating folk who have your interests at heart.

6. WEDNESDAY. Easygoing. Cosmic influences suggest a lively day. If boredom has been an issue lately, now is a good time to attempt something different. An unconventional person or relationship could test your boundaries, bringing a need to explore all angles to find understanding. Many Bulls should experience a wonderful day of love and romance. A flirtation is bound to give singles a buzz. But keep it light, and you should enjoy the fun vibes. Refrain from becoming too involved in studies and mental challenges. Your concentration is likely to lapse, possibly resulting in errors. Fortunately, imagination is enhanced, which will be a boon to creative pursuits.

7. THURSDAY. Restrained. Moderation is the key on this day when temptation is bound to be strong and willpower weak. As a Taurus you savor the good things of life. But be a little self-sacrificing now, especially if you are trying to lose weight or to regain a good fitness level. Even though there might be bargains displayed in every store window and sales signs on every corner, before you spend money consider whether you really do need all the products that grab your attention. Fortunate features of the day include flowing creative juices and a surge of popularity. Good luck may pay a brief visit as well. It might be a smart idea to buy a lottery ticket, then hope for a windfall.

8. FRIDAY. Adept. Give creative free rein to mental projects over the next few days. With Mercury and Mars merging in the sign of Pisces, original thoughts could increase productivity on the job and at home base. Let your musings take wing and see where they lead. This is a great period to stride forward on a positive note. You can advance a project that has been on hold for some time and finally bring it to a close. Making quick decisions isn't something that many Taurus advocate. However, right now you should excel at thinking on your feet, coming to swift conclusions, and choosing wisely. Socializing with colleagues helps to foster loyalty and friendship.

9. SATURDAY. Busy. There may be plenty on the agenda today, but there is the chance that you will try to do too much. Moving at a steady rate will be preferable to rushing through tasks. That way there will also be less chance of errors occurring. Steer clear of discussions that reveal philosophical and religious beliefs. Differences of opinion will most likely lead to strong emotional reactions and heated words. Avoid situations where you need to listen attentively, which might be a challenge you cannot meet right now. Pay your own way when you are out socializing with friends and associates. And refrain from lending cash to pals; it might take a long time before the money is repaid.

10. SUNDAY. Vibrant. Taurus energy and enthusiasm should be higher, but recklessness might be a problem. So this is a day to move ahead cautiously. Keep in mind that although you may meet with success, good luck is not always guaranteed. A friend or a member of a social group you belong to could introduce you to a new way of viewing things or to unusual interests that you will be tempted to explore further. A fresh perspective will be enlightening. But with anything you act upon, ensure that the bigger picture is taken into consideration as well as the minor points. A financial concern could throw a goal into disarray; all won't be lost, it just means the wait will be longer.

11. MONDAY. Challenging. The Moon is visiting the sign of Pisces, activating your solar eleventh house of friendships and cherished desires. Even though your star is shining brightly with pals and associates, responsibilities could be all consuming. Don't expect today's events to be easy. Venus, your life ruler, is challenging serious Saturn, so remaining happy and upbeat may prove difficult. If you can keep smiling throughout the day, any gloom, doom, or loneliness should be fleeting. Try very hard to cultivate influential people. Compromise is needed to keep a complaining client from going to the competition. Taurus singles seeking a new romance might be out of luck for now.

12. TUESDAY. Fine. Good planetary vibes promise a positive day ahead for Taurus folk. It should be easy to make decisions, seek special guidance, research a project, and dig for information. A resourceful approach will ensure that whatever requires action will be done to a very high standard for a good outcome. A realistic attitude will be most productive. Think through each step from a practical standpoint. Those of you looking for company this evening should plan an outing with special friends or catch up over dinner with extended family members. If being alone is your choice, pick up that mystery novel you've been meaning to read. Or watch a thriller that keeps you in suspense.

13. WEDNESDAY. Revealing. It is a day for quiet pursuits and pleasures. Defer activity that demands strenuous effort and rapt concentration. The Moon is moving through the sign of Aries, your solar twelfth house of secrets and the subconscious. You can remain productive by performing plenty of small tasks that require little time, effort, or energy. A secret wish could be fulfilled. Work behind the scenes may bring positive rewards. Someone from your past could return, arousing suspense, excitement, and even a bit of trepidation. The coupled Bull should let loved ones know if you desire peace and solitude. They are not mind readers and cannot guess how you feel.

14. THURSDAY. Mixed. Keep your wits about you today, Taurus. Power struggles could occur on the job. Stand your ground and stick to your principles, but don't set out to make waves or you could become unstuck. The Aries Moon impacting your twelfth house may sap your energy, but the thought of what may be in store this Valentine's Day should be a great pick-me-up. With romance in the air and a confirmed date for the evening, set the scene for two. Surprise your partner with a special gift that will delight the senses; use your imagination. Also buy a little treat for yourself, just to confirm that you are treating yourself well; remember, you're worth it.

15. FRIDAY. Renewing. The day begins slowly but picks up as the hours pass. The Moon enters your own sign of Taurus by mid-morning, Vim and vitality should return, so this is a good day to act on personal plans and strategies. It is also an excellent period to focus on a special goal or to begin something that increases self-assurance and self-confidence. Be thorough with any research you undertake, and you'll be led to the right choice. A special reunion might bring an important person back into your social circle, making you and others realize how lucky you really are. A visit to a salon or spa will revitalize your energy, just in time for a fun weekend ahead.

16. SATURDAY. Gratifying. The Moon traveling through your own sign of sensual Taurus and impacting your solar first house of personality makes it easy for you to impress and to influence. With extra charm and charisma at your disposal, ask and you should receive. Be confident that you have a lot to offer and that people are more than willing to listen to your many practical suggestions. A team sports event, a special committee meeting, or a volunteer community project might be on your agenda this weekend. Any activity that involves you with like-minded others pursuing a goal is highlighted. You can expect achievements to be permanent. Enjoy a bit of leisure time in between serious doings.

17. SUNDAY. Bright. The Moon traveling through your sign of Taurus and your first house of personality keeps the spotlight on you for much of the day. There may be some obstacles along the way, but you are in a strong position right now. Take advantage of the opportunities and chances presented. You may need to look outside of the square or move away from your comfort zone, but it should be worthwhile in the end. A new interest will be inspiring once you are prepared to discard preconceived ideas. Visitors could drop by, ready to have fun and share the costs of a good time. A display of affection from a romantic partner sets the scene for happiness tonight.

18. MONDAY. Active. This morning the golden Sun moves into peaceful Pisces, accenting your solar eleventh house of long-range aims, income from business and career, and network of friends and professional associates. The Moon rising in Gemini accentuates your solar second house of personal finances, personal possessions, and self-worth. Many Bulls could get the urge to splurge in a big way. A desire to keep up with the neighbors could be your downfall. Saturn, the taskmaster planet of the zodiac, turns retrograde in Scorpio at midday. Saturn retrograde here gives you a chance to reassess and redress frustrations and concerns in a personal or professional partnership.

19. TUESDAY. Meaningful. The Moon continues to roll through your Gemini house of personal finances. Be astute with your money. If you cannot afford high-end products now, wait until you can. The Gemini Moon also impacts your personal value system, encouraging you to give what you can. And the Sun in Pisces may lead you to use some of your leisure time to do volunteer work for a humanitarian group. Expect your social calendar to overflow with requests for your attendance at group gatherings. An invitation to an unusual event will bring delight but also trepidation. Don't stress, Taurus, as your innate creative ability will come to the fore and you will rise to the occasion.

20. WEDNESDAY. Resourceful. Many Bulls are likely to be very busy today making connections, confirming dates, and getting where you want to go. Listen carefully in discussions and meetings; there will be much to learn and follow through. You should also be careful what you tell to whom, especially in casual conversation. An offhand remark may betray some private information, and could come back to haunt you. If someone doesn't agree with your ideas or suggestions, take a deep breath and remember that all opinions expressed are as important and as valid as your own views. A pedicure, reflexology session, or foot massage will be a lovely treat at the end of the day.

21. THURSDAY. Spirited. A tendency to spread your energy too thinly should be avoided. Deadlines, employment pressures, or concerns relating to home affairs could send your stress level rocketing, so take steps to remain cool and calm. With the Sun and Neptune merging in the sign of Pisces, some complex celestial influences will mark the day with a bit of confusion and angst. You are being encouraged to connect or reconnect with your spiritual values. You are also in tune with close contacts. They are bound to appreciate your support. Having lunch with a relative or neighbor should be uplifting. Spread compassion and warmth to the people who would benefit the most from your kindness.

22. FRIDAY. Lively. The Moon still activates your Cancer solar third house of communication, which would account for a high frequency of phone calls, e-mails, and visitors. If a deadline is approaching, get to it as early as possible without wasting a lot of time chatting. On your way to an appointment you may meet a long-lost acquaintance. The conversation will be most worthwhile, especially if it means you can make interesting new contacts. This afternoon the Moon enters Leo, your solar fourth house of home and family. A prickly situation with loved ones may develop at the drop of a hat, and will require immediate mediation. Gentle words can set things straight

23. SATURDAY. Interesting. Home comforts may appeal the most. Taurus folk who also have a loving family and happy domestic environment should show appreciation by sincere caring gestures. Perhaps taking parents or siblings out to dinner would be a proper demonstration of your love and affection. Home entertaining should progress smoothly if you are eager to show off your hospitality and culinary skills. Mercury, the planet associated with messages, communication, commerce, and transportation, goes retrograde now in the sign of Pisces. Mercury retrograde here for the next three weeks can cause mix-ups with a special goal, misunderstandings with friends, and delays in transport.

24. SUNDAY. Fair. Most of the action appears to take place around home base today. Be observant, watching people's body language and listening to their comments. Arguments could erupt without warning. Even minor and petty remarks might be taken out of context now and over the next few days. It might feel as if you are surrounded by confused souls and strange situations. If something needs to be done right, see to it and be sure the facts are correct. Verify meeting times and places for professional meetings as well as social dates. Messages are likely to be passed on or heard incorrectly. Wind down with your favorite music, letting it wash away the pressures of the day.

25. MONDAY. Tricky. A Full Moon culminating in Virgo impacts both your solar fifth house of romance and pleasure and your Pisces solar eleventh house of friends and associates. Sensitivity rises, warning Taurus to take extra care when dealing with people's feelings; emotional scenes could quickly develop. Moderation is advised, as unrealistic expectations are to the fore. Be discriminating about forming casual friendships. Some who claim to be your pals do not have your best interests at heart. Venus, your ruler, enters impressionable Pisces tonight. Romance, illusion, and fantasy may become an everyday part of your life while Venus visits Pisces over the next few weeks.

26. TUESDAY. Opportune. Luck comes in various forms, and you might be on the receiving end of some good fortune. Taurus folk who earn a living through sports and are part of a winning team will appreciate hearty applause for your performance on the playing field. With your ruler Venus visiting imaginative Pisces, those of you with artistic talent are sure to excel. Recognition for your creative expertise may lead to a scholarship or sponsorship. Do not let an annoying friend or associate poach on your turf. Keep your cool while you protect what you value, or you might say something better left unsaid. Yearning for a perfect love will not lead to finding that soul mate; get out and circulate.

27. WEDNESDAY. Diverse. Current planetary trends encourage cooperation and compromise rather than conflict and complaint, despite any difficulty you might have achieving these worthy goals. Lazy colleagues can add to your workload, which will also add to the stress you are feeling. Just remain detached and be graceful under pressure; then most things should flow smoothly. Make time for casual conversation with coworkers, especially those who are generally unhelpful. It is amazing how a sincere effort to be friendly can turn contentious vibes into harmonious ones. Some Taurus individuals will have luck finding a cure for a long-standing health problem.

28. THURSDAY. Lovely. Despite an adverse lunar trend, you can expect a romantic day ahead. Your ruler, sexy Venus, merges with inspirational Neptune and bestows a dreamy quality to the events that transpire. This can be a magical period if you are in love, but it could bring a few clouds of confusion if you are unsure about your lover's commitment. However, this isn't the time to test his or her loyalty or even to ask sensitive questions; you probably won't get satisfactory answers. A glamorous function will add a touch of pizzazz to your social life, so take full advantage of the chance to dress up and be seen. Don't be surprised by sincere compliments. You deserve them.

MARCH

1. FRIDAY. Satisfying. As the new month begins, the Sun in Pisces makes positive aspects to disciplined Saturn in Scorpio and powerful Pluto in Capricorn. These planetary connections convey a practical, realistic tone. You are urged to keep a level head and to take things one step at a time as you navigate. While the Sun visits

Pisces until March 20, you might be pulled in different directions by friends and professional associates. You still should organize your priorities so that you share private thoughts and important activities with loved ones. Don't waste precious energy on household tasks and other routine responsibilities. Save some for creative action.

2. SATURDAY. Sociable. A concentration of planets populates your Pisces solar eleventh house of friends and associates, hopes and aims. Strong social influences surround Bulls, encouraging you to make the most of what is on offer. The sensual Moon is now glowing in Scorpio, your solar seventh house of marriage and partnerships, making it easy to connect with your mate in a pleasurable manner. If stress and pressure are plaguing you, create a mini environment at home that can relax and calm. It might be fun to build a small aquarium and take care of fish as pets. Make a wish for the things that you want in your life; some of your dreams will come true.

3. SUNDAY. Varied. Take advantage of every leisure day to relax and rest up. Attending to little chores at home probably will not appeal on your day off. Besides, with the Moon continuing to track through your opposite sign of Scorpio, progress in a number of areas is unlikely to be as smooth or as quick as you would want it to be. Get set for a fun day socializing with family members or your special pals. Even if you are single, you can still revel in the company of close companions. Enjoyment will come from going to a live concert, from viewing a new museum exhibit, and certainly from listening to your favorite music in your own home theater.

4. MONDAY. Limiting. Moderation is the key to success today. With your life ruler Venus challenging expansive Jupiter, enjoying the good things of life becomes extremely tempting. Combine these energies with a restless Sagittarius Moon, and this could propel many Taurus folk to look for entertainment, property, or goods and services that are out of the scope of your current budget. Because the Sagittarius Moon represents your solar eighth house, the mysteries of life, death, taxes, legacies, and all forms of other people's money may be on your mind. If there are problems in any of these eighth-house matters, you will want to act as promptly as possible once you decide on the path to be taken.

5. TUESDAY. Astute. Management of joint finances and resources, another eighth-house matter activated by the Sagittarius Moon, becomes an important focus for Taurus now. Gains can come to those of you who keep your eyes wide open for viable opportunities. Buying a gift for a loved one would be a great delight. But you probably should give the purchase serious thought, as it might put a huge dent in your savings plan. If sensitive emotions come to the surface, there will be no escape. Denying your feelings will only give them greater strength. A mentor might come into your life, offering significant support. Let intuition combined with clear thought be your guide, and the right choices will be made.

6. WEDNESDAY. Happy. This day has the potential to be very rewarding. Love and excitement are in the air and will more than likely be the underlying theme for the next few days. New ideas should be enticing. Right now your solar ninth house of travel, education, and adventure is being activated by the Capricorn Moon. If your feet are getting itchy, it is only going to get worse, so begin researching vacation packages. Keep an open mind about the places you might land. Don't reject out of hand a destination that is totally unfamiliar to you. Visiting somewhere different could be just what you need. Even if you can outdo the competition, wisely opt for cooperation rather than confrontation.

7. THURSDAY. Empowering. The day ahead is likely to begin with serious business to take care of, so set the alarm half an hour earlier and you should find that you can complete more work than usual. Your mental and practical capabilities are enhanced. Constructively use these gifts from the universe. Long-term plans and ambitions should be within easier reach, making it essential to fix any flaws in projects that are coming up for review. A journey to visit relatives who live somewhat far away may be on the cards. Conversation may reveal some fascinating tidbits of family history. Be alert for a secret admirer about to come out from the wings and send a come-hither signal.

8. FRIDAY. Penetrating. Insight and understanding on a deep level remain strong attributes of the Taurus persona right now. Hard work won't faze even the most laid-back or lazy among you. With your typical persevering approach, you can sustain difficult research and come up with excellent results. Right now you can learn just about anything you put your mind to. Focus on what really interests you, and you will make a breakthrough. People close are likely to seek your opinion on a personal or professional problem. They realize you have a knack for finding a solution and can get things done quickly. Choose stimulating and informative evening entertainment, but avoid noisy environments.

9. SATURDAY. Mixed. Keep a promise to spend time with loved ones. If the weather permits, this is the kind of day to take the children to the park and watch kites fly. In a moment of honesty an intimate may talk about an awkward emotional problem. Unless you can let go of old wounds and grievances, a resolution could be nearly impossible to find. For those of you still living at home, parents could be more difficult to deal with. Taurus folk on the job this weekend are likely to experience issues because of an inflated ego of a boss or other authority figure. If people are demanding, best observe the motto that silence is golden. Then you might escape further upsets.

10. SUNDAY. Imaginative. Plan a relaxing day surrounded by upbeat companions. Get into the great outdoors and do something exhilarating. Taurus who is part of a couple will prefer catering to a mate and being catered to in return. With the Moon floating through your Pisces solar eleventh house, don't be afraid to dream about ways to make a better future for yourself and loved ones. Consider realistic methods that can assist your efforts to forge ahead. Don't be too proud to ask for guidance from friends and associates. A casual acquaintanceship could fall away due to changing interests or values. But friendships of long standing will endure and be steadfast.

11. MONDAY. Promising. A variety of issues should work in your favor today, with the possibility of greater personal and professional incentives on offer. A New Moon culminates in the sign of Pisces, your solar eleventh house of hopes and aim as well as earnings from business and career. Progress on a project close to your heart should be swift. Bulls with fresh plans ready to be implemented can rest assured that the stars are beaming positive vibes on these undertakings over the next two weeks. Seize the opportunity to join a prestigious club or association. There you can meet people who have live-wire interests and connections. An alluring attraction could be developing into a full-blown affair.

12. TUESDAY. Diverse. Before dawn dynamo planet Mars enters Aries, your solar twelfth house of things unseen. And at dawn the Moon moves into Aries. Vim and vigor may seem to slip away. Listen to the signals from your body. If necessary, give yourself a chance to rest and recharge your physical, emotional, and spiritual batteries over the next two and a half days. It is a time for introspection. Wily thinking can turn a vague plan into quiet yet determined action. A secret wish might be fulfilled. A special request is likely to involve you in hard work. Postpone it for now and choose a soothing pastime instead.

13. WEDNESDAY. Challenging. With both Moon and Mars in your Aries solar twelfth house, your energy level is likely to dip. But with Mars in Aries, the sign that Mars rules, a more rosy hue is cast. You can take action and make things happen if the desire to change your life is strong enough. Passive aggression could be evident now, which would be a waste of this positive planetary influence. Consider what you want, commit to a plan, then begin to implement a short-term goal or longer-range lifestyle change. Solitude may be a strong yearning whenever your twelfth house is activated, as it is now through Mars and the Moon. Work alone if you can. That doesn't mean you are hiding anything or hiding from anybody.

14. THURSDAY. Good. Dragging yourself out from under a heavy sleep could be difficult for you this morning. Once you are up and on the go, there shouldn't be any problems becoming motivated. Don't expect or demand too much from yourself. Plod along as only a Taurus knows how. Then you should be pleased with your productivity at the end of the day. When the Moon swings into your own sign later this afternoon, things should certainly begin to look brighter. If assistance is required from any source or direction, there isn't a better time than now and the next two days to request favors, help, and advice.

15. FRIDAY. Heartening. An astrological principle states that the Moon is exalted when placed in the sign of Taurus. So while the Moon visits your sign through tomorrow night, prepare to be in the spotlight. This is a great time to put your best foot forward, dress to impress, and enjoy the good things of life. Don't be shy when it comes to taking the lead with a group activity or money matter. Current influences are terrific for showing people exactly what you are capable of. If a new outfit is required for a special function, finding just what you need should be quick and easy. With plenty of energy at your disposal and a lively mood prevailing, make sure that plans to socialize are more upbeat than usual.

16. SATURDAY. Eventful. It is another day when you should be ready to take advantage of your increased charm and charisma. But don't try to do any strenuous chores; your vim and vigor might be a little under par as the Sun creates friction with restrictive Saturn. Dealing effectively with underlying issues relating to a personal matter may be necessary before you venture out this morning. Social or community plans, perhaps your attendance at a game or at a public meeting, may be thrown into disarray because you partner objects to one of your friends or associates. If you are unable to talk your partner out of this attitude, it might be politic to give in. Have fun up until midnight, when the Moon leaves your sign of Taurus.

17. SUNDAY. Encouraging. Daydreaming about what could be done if you had access to unlimited cash resources can be enjoyable and perhaps even enlightening. Don't get too carried away, though. Silly mistakes may be made with money matters unless a realistic stance is taken. Spend time doing whatever takes your fancy. Try not to watch upsetting newscasts, unless you are willing to have a really good cry as a constructive form of release. Shopping for new shoes will be a bit frustrating but satisfying when you find a perfect pair. Messenger Mercury finishes its retrograde today, bringing an end to transportation delays, problems with electronic equipment, and misunderstandings with friends.

18. MONDAY. Subdued. Lunar trends are practically nonexistent today, and you can almost feel the quiet. There is bound to be a certain amount of detachment in the air as your ruler Venus challenges somber Saturn. This planetary aspect poses potential disappointment in a love affair or a social undertaking. If coworkers are not as warm and forthcoming as usual, just let it be. Do not look for assurance, because you may not receive a positive response. How you value your worth to others is often expressed through your actions, so be aware of what you do and make adjustments if needed. Defer any new financial undertakings at this time. Delayed gains or even a loss on investments could occur.

19. TUESDAY. Lively. Squeezing in leisure time to have fun could prove very challenging. Even if close companions are not in a light-hearted mood, you can rise above their pettiness and try at least to perk them up. A thoughtful message of encouragement could also provide the lift to spirits that someone, perhaps even you, might be seeking now. Steer clear of discussions about major financial issues, especially through the first half of the day. Be extra prudent shopping, or money could disappear at a fast clip. Taurus presenting a lecture, speech, or sales report should feel confident. Your delivery is likely to be slick, to the point, and of vital interest to your audience.

20. WEDNESDAY. Variable. At dawn today the Sun enters the sign of Aries, your solar twelfth house. A burdensome situation could come out of left field. If you aren't sure what action to take, consult someone whose opinion you value. With the Moon in Cancer accentuating your solar third house of communication, many Bulls may feel caught up in a whirlwind of meetings, appointments, phone calls, and messages. If your datebook is crammed full and your in-basket top-heavy, schedule a quiet walk at lunchtime to catch your breath, clear your head, and relax even for a brief spell. Skip caffeinated beverages this evening; trying to sleep could be difficult enough without added stimulation.

21. THURSDAY. Uncertain. Ups and downs may be experienced now. Of special significance for Taurus folk is that Venus, your ruler, is changing signs tonight, leaving Pisces and entering the action-oriented sign of Aries. For the next few weeks both the Sun and Venus will be transiting Aries, your solar twelfth house. As the twelfth house is your house of secrets, most activity could be conducted in confidence or behind closed doors. Although you might sense you can achieve anything and everything and experience the urge to rush in, a slow and steady pace will bring the best results. Don't be rushed, even by a loved one; expectations may create an environment where mistakes and errors creep in.

22. FRIDAY. Manageable. Diverse and active celestial influences characterize the day. You can expect to be busy and on the go from dawn to dark. There should be plenty of energy at your disposal as dynamo Mars merges with erratic Uranus. The challenge will be to use this increased vim and vigor in a constructive and practical way. If you can curb restless behavior and deal with surprising events that throw a money wrench into the works, you can accomplish a lot. A special treasure or sentimental object that has been mislaid for some time could be unearthed while you are looking for something else. Drivers, slow down and obey the rules of the road.

23. SATURDAY. Soothing. Taurus folk really appreciate the comforts of home and hearth, probably more so than usual now with today's Leo Moon impacting your solar fourth house of property, the domestic abode, and family. These areas are to the fore. A home-related project could require a major rethink, especially if you and your partner are at loggerheads over how much money to spend on it. A family get-together might be emotional, but it will offer a chance to clear up unfinished business. Whatever it takes to strengthen the ties that bind will be worth the effort. Whether or not you are getting along with in-laws, at least show respect out of consideration and respect for your mate.

24. SUNDAY. Enriching. Complete the household chores as early as possible so that the rest of this leisure day is free for pleasurable pursuits. During mid-morning the Moon glides into Virgo, your solar fifth house of leisure pursuits, so the emphasis switches from serious to playful. If the budget is stretched to the limit, it might be time to carry out severe cost-cutting measures. Involve your partner in the process so that you both are aware of current income and outgo. Then if you both sacrifice and adjust equally, resentment is avoided on both sides. Taurus parents engaged in sports activities with the children may learn more about a game than you ever wanted to know.

25. MONDAY. Fair. Mixed trends prevail throughout the day. Popping out for a spot of fresh air whenever stress becomes overwhelming should help repair frayed nerves. Financial matters could create friction, and there may be problems with someone in authority or with a business partner. Refrain from asking for a promotion or salary increase, and don't expect any favors to come your way right now. A physical activity, either a team or individual sport, could prove to be very taxing. But the more energy you exert, the more you will benefit from the challenge. Taurus singles can make a good impression on a first date; such an outing will not be your last with this particular partner.

26. TUESDAY. Interesting. Mars rules the day ahead and makes a number of planetary connections that will introduce contradictory influences. Luck and opportunity come your way, so you can afford to be more optimistic. You do need to be mindful of your personal safety, as this can be an accident-prone period for the unwary. Even if everything on your current to-do list isn't completed by the end of the day, you should successfully finish the important tasks that require immediate attention. Money from an unusual and unexpected source is a feature of today's good fortune, perhaps just when it is needed the most. Buy a lottery ticket and double your chances of boosting the bank balance.

27. WEDNESDAY. Effective. Over the next two days the more efficient you are, the more you can accomplish. This is because the Moon will be visiting Libra, your solar sixth house of health, daily working conditions, and service to others. You are encouraged to tidy up the home and business office, empty old files, and implement up-to-date employment processes. Evaluate your state of health, lifestyle habits, and current regimens. Some of you have strayed off the path and are now in danger of undoing past good work. The Libra Full Moon is apt to increase stress on the job, as emotions and sensitivities will rise. Keep your cool and take care in discussions with colleagues. Aim to get a good night's sleep.

28. THURSDAY. Restless. Complex trends exist today as a number of planetary links light up the cosmos. Restlessness may be extra strong. Even the most stable and fixed Taurus individual may feel impelled to do something different or to take part in an adventure. Introduce plenty of variety into your day to reduce the chances of tedium taking over. This is a very good period to begin a new project, find a new lover, or open a special savings account. A partner could unexpectedly pop the question, creating delight, anticipation, and excitement. Artistic juices flow freely and your output could be great. Draw on your heightened level of ingenuity to create something entirely new.

29. FRIDAY. Buoyant. Life continues to be busy, although some Bulls might be wishing for the pace to slow down a little. There still is a lot of activity happening in the cosmos, notably the Moon sailing through your opposite sign of Scorpio in your solar seventh house of relationship. You probably will not get a lot of peace and quiet today. Regardless of how much work needs attention, do not ignore a loved one's needs just to make points with a boss or colleague. Any matter requiring in-depth research can be carried out to a high standard. Students and investigators digging for facts and figures should beware of information overkill; sometimes less is more. Keep social expenses within your budget.

30. SATURDAY. Uneasy. Serious Saturn rules the airwaves, creating problems for those of you prone to taking on obligations belonging to other people. Being a martyr or at the beck and call of others is a real but unpleasant possibility today. Do the minimal amount of household chores if you can get away with it. If you are on the job, let colleagues do the work assigned to them. Social events might seem more like a duty than a pleasure. Or you may be so busy organizing the entertainment that you don't have a moment to spare for your own enjoyment. Love and romance might be hard to come by for the currently unattached. The coupled Taurus will have to work hard to rouse a partner to passion.

31. SUNDAY. Uneven. A complex planetary pattern forms today, with intense situations possibly putting a strain on relationships. People in authority may be inflexible and demanding. Postpone a visit to in-laws or parents if some tension already exists or if there is a contentious issue that is bound to be discussed. Still, there is the possibility of some good news and luck being bestowed on Taurus folk today. You might be able to share in someone else's good fortune. Those of you single might find a new love partner appearing on the horizon. The coupled Bull should aim to be alone with your mate. While socializing, try to avoid situations that could trigger jealousy or power issues.

APRIL

1. MONDAY. Reassuring. Good vibes fall in most areas of your life as the new month gets under way. With four planets transiting your Aries twelfth house of solitude, the tempo should ease off a little. Here is your chance to regroup, relax, and recharge spiritual, emotional, and physical batteries. There are also plenty of opportunities coming along for you to turn around negative situations and circumstances. The Sun and Jupiter are happily linked, expanding your vision and luck, so begin making plans. If you have always had an interest in meditation, yoga, or other metaphysical activity, now is the time to attend classes. Outdoor pursuits seem tailor-made to increase your enjoyment.

2. TUESDAY. Expansive. A happy atmosphere continues around you. Taurus folk are on a roll, and good fortune remains a constant for now. You can move successfully ahead with a number of special projects, large or small, that have been on the back burner for some time. If you yearn for more excitement and adventure in your life, don't be content to just daydream. Instead, take a peek at ways you can experience more of what life has to offer. Whether it is snorkeling at a coral reef, gazing at the wonders of a theme park, or surfing at a tropical beach, get away from familiar turf. Research lively destinations, then implement a savings plan so you can soon be on your way.

3. WEDNESDAY. Low-key. Relatively easy energies prevail. It might be a bit of a reach to stay awake. Rather than daydreaming, give serious consideration to what you hope to achieve this year. Take inventory every now and then to ensure that you are heading in the right direction. Dealing with a difficult financial decision could provide some challenges. If the homework is done thoroughly, it shouldn't take long for things to be put into perspective. Someone may be working against you behind the scenes, but you are in a position to foil any unscrupulous plot. Feel free to spread knowledge and wisdom among the people close to you who need a helping hand.

4. THURSDAY. Variable. Vexing trends exist throughout a good part of the day, and you might be a little out of sorts. Your capacity to remain alert and focused may be challenged. Today's Aquarius Moon impacting your solar tenth house of career suggests that a new colleague or associate could become a great friend. Don't worry too much, but do return any aid or assistance you get from another. If business and employment matters intrude heavily on personal pursuits, you will have to make the domestic environment a work-free zone. A revision of plans might be required this evening, and your romantic partner or steady date will not be happy if you favor the job over personal life.

5. FRIDAY. Encouraging. Focus sharply on your business and community interests, and you should see good progress. The chances of your hopes coming to fruition will increase in proportion to the effort you put forth. Career-minded Taurus should be mindful that keeping emotional and vocational concerns in balance offers the best way for you to be happy and also for things to function smoothly. Give equal time to the personal and to the professional, and no one will feel neglected or left out. Turning work into a pleasurable activity can keep your motivation and enthusiasm alive. Volunteer work for a local organization will fulfill a need, and you can make new friends there.

6. SATURDAY. Uneasy. A few tiffs with friends could mark the day, so be on guard and be aware of people's sensitivities. Perhaps unrealistic expectations are adding extra pressure and tension. If you are in charge of organizing a party or of providing transport to a particular venue, enlist the help of others. That way you are not left to assume all the guilt if things go wrong. Friendly Taurus will grab the opportunity to join a group, club, or class and meet new people. But move slowly. Don't jump in and volunteer your services for every task or project on the agenda. See first where you would best fit in. Be clear about what you hope to receive and also what you are prepared to give.

7. SUNDAY. Guarded. Be careful over the next few days, Taurus. Sexual desire quickens, romantic sensitivity rises as dynamo Mars merges with saucy Venus, your ruler, in your Aries twelfth house of behind-the-scenes activity. Mars and Venus here often indicate a secret love affair. Such a liaison could develop swiftly, especially if you are going through a rough patch with a partner. Better not stray. The affair will eventually come out into the open, possibly wounding those you love. Keep your sights firmly fixed on cherished aims. This is a good time to launch a special project. With heightened imagination, you have the best of creative energy at your disposal. Let inspired thoughts flow without restraint.

8. MONDAY. Uplifting. Today's lovely scenario is set for romantic and emotional ties to come into focus. Love is in the air. Plan an evening of togetherness for you and your steady date or long-time mate. Expressing strong emotions as well as delicate feelings should be easier for all Bulls now. A magnetic and passionate attraction to a beguiling newcomer could be reciprocated, soon becoming a full-fledged affair of the heart. Taurus workers will be forging ahead on a special aim, and the outcome appears promising. But don't push too hard. Your social life seems set to receive a delightful boost, with a flurry of invitations to a variety of events coming your way.

9. TUESDAY. Opportune. An unusual activity or event could get your adrenaline pumping. Moving forward with your own plans is under auspicious stars. This is also a positive period to lend a helping hand to someone who might require assistance in some form. The Aries Moon lasting until midnight tomorrow night represents your lunar low period. So for the next two days you have chances to factor in a spot of quiet reflection, contemplate where you are, and tune in to all forms of beauty in the environment. Kicking a bad habit might be under consideration. Tactics can be designed to do something positive along this line on Thursday when the Moon enters your sign of Taurus.

10. WEDNESDAY. Challenging. This morning's New Moon in assertive Aries carries the energy of fresh beginnings and provides a sense of freedom. Formulate plans, then initiate appropriate action. Deliberate carefully, though, as decisions made now could have a long-lasting influence. Because Aries does represents your twelfth house, a bit of gloomy thinking may linger. If current tactics are not working as successfully as envisioned, don't despair. Fresh opportunity to achieve success will present itself soon. The trick is to draw on your ingenuity while you make good use of the positive celestial influences. That way, facing a challenging professional undertaking will be far easier.

11. THURSDAY. Empowering. Influencing your own life positively should be a priority as the Moon flits through your own sign of Taurus. With your solar first house of self and personality in the spotlight, it won't take much for you to get into high gear and attract favorable attention. Even if there are a couple of obstacles to overcome, your renowned persistence and perseverance ensure that goals can be reached and favors will be granted. Some of you aspire to be a leader and an initiator. So be alert for opportunities, however small, to organize, to take charge, or to provide guidance.

Gently let people know how you feel. Romance is starred under current cosmic trends.

12. FRIDAY. Burdensome. Indecision, angst, and frustration could be the overall tone of the day. Taurus at work might see extra responsibilities being added to your agenda. Getting an early start and scheduling a long lunch might be helpful in keeping you grounded and on track, but don't count on it. Establishing priorities will be problematic on this last day of the workweek. Everyone has an opinion about the when, where, how, and who of various jobs. Avoidance, resistance to change, and an inflexible approach will hinder progress. Powerful planet Pluto goes retrograde today, giving you a chance to review and revise. Don't fight the inevitable. Once you take the first positive step, things will slowly improve.

13. SATURDAY. Trying. With structured Saturn and unpredictable Uranus bringing tension to your solar horoscope, this is another day when things are unlikely to run smoothly. Stress and tension within a partnership might need attention, and the only way to resolve issues may be through cooperation and compromise. Responsibilities may be many, even if it is a supposed leisure day for you. It seems like a case of two steps forward and one step back. Reorganizing letters, photos, and music could be a pleasant pastime for those of you without set social plans, and you should experience a sense of accomplishment once everything is in order.

14. SUNDAY. Attentive. A moderate approach is needed today. Taurus folk appreciate the art of good dining and fine wine. At times, though, you are prone to overindulgence, which can lead to a growing waistline and a declining bank balance. An upcoming visit to a naturopath or dietician could get to the bottom of the problem and put you back on track. A modified diet and an individually tailored fitness regimen would also be worthy of further consideration. Checking financial records and credit card statements should be beneficial, as you may discover an error or two made by your financial institution.

15. MONDAY. Promising. The limelight is certainly shining your way now, Taurus. Venus, your lifetime ruler, enters into your sign and carries the promise of lots of fun and excitement over the next few weeks. If you haven't had a beauty makeover or arranged a new wardrobe for the upcoming summer holidays, take advantage of positive trends and do it now. Healthwise, you should be glowing. Your finances look set to remain stable. Romance is on the horizon; and your charm and charisma are on the rise. Don't be discouraged if you feel a little weighed down at times, because this trend will quickly pass and things should greatly improve as the day wears on.

16. TUESDAY. Assertive. Taurus persuasive skills and negotiation expertise are advanced, and you can take pride in successful outcomes achieved. If you need financial backing or a special favor, ask now because your requests should be looked upon favorably. The romantic nature of Bulls is primed with Venus in your sign now. You might be inclined to take a more assertive approach toward a potential lover or a significant other. Choose your tactics carefully, basing them on a good knowledge of your partner. If you are currently single and seeking a permanent relationship, make the first move gently and adapt as you begin to understand what a mate or date expects from you.

17. WEDNESDAY. Bright. Energy levels rise dramatically now as the Sun and fiery Mars merge together in Aries, your twelfth house of personal limitations and solitary action. A few words from a brother or sister could trigger a long-delayed decision, so it might be advisable to have a frank chat. Many Taurus individuals could feel inspired to write either for pleasure or practice. Some of you are gearing up to write your first novel or memoir. Attending a creative writing or language class would be a wonderful hobby pursuit and might also help your chances of gaining satisfying employment and climbing up the career ladder. As you seek opportunity, remember to always be tactful.

18. THURSDAY. Satisfying. Mixed trends are in force today. Getting a head start on all projects means you should see a lot more output with less time and energy exerted. Finances are to the fore, especially if home improvements currently in the pipeline are eating into the household budget. Taurus imagination and inspiration are greatly enhanced. Your ability to see beauty in many different forms graces your artistic and creative expression. Under current stars those of you playing the dating game may be on a winning streak now. The coupled Bull can rekindle loving feelings if a romantic scene is set for two. A school concert would be a good choice for family entertainment.

19. FRIDAY. Fair. Progress will appear to be slower if people drag their feet and situations unfold at a snail's pace. Just do your best to make what you can of the day. Put a smile on your face, exhibit a friendly attitude, enjoy the good, ignore the bad. Refrain from gossip. If you are told something in confidence, make sure you keep it to yourself. If relocation, repairs, or renovations are on the agenda, make sure everything is in place to avoid holdups. Don't fret if loved ones cannot keep up your pace. After all, you are getting a boost from the universe today. The Sun, the bright star of the solar system, enters your sign of Taurus this afternoon, throwing the spotlight your way for the next four weeks.

20. SATURDAY. Surprising. Chatty Mercury meets up with erratic Uranus, sparking an element of unpredictability and excitement today. Another planetary event adds to the exhilaration you may feel. Energetic planet Mars is now entering your sign, so Sun and Mars both in Taurus will encourage you to take the initiative and enjoy new experiences. Exposure to fresh ideas and a greater involvement in a group project should bring pleasure to your weekend. Choose leisure activities wisely. Remaining focused on one project at any given time may become difficult, so try not to spread yourself too thinly.

21. SUNDAY. Dynamic. With Mars in your sign of Taurus now firing up your energy level, your vim and vitality receive a huge boost. As a Bull raring to go, you should be ready to take on the world. Most of you will feel more robust, with high adrenaline surges that enable you to get plans and activities under way. Believing that you can get somewhere is the first step, taking the relevant action is the second step. Asserting yourself is easier now, but just watch that you don't push yourself or other people too hard. Socializing will give you pleasure as well as opportunity. Cooperative vibes predominate, and everyone will benefit from one another's input and feedback.

22. MONDAY. Sticky. Relationships will probably be at the forefront of attention for many Taurus individuals today, and certainly so if a disappointment is experienced on the romantic front. If you are single and content to remain that way, then it might be finances that are the cause of angst for some of you. The agitated Bull will hope that this first day of the workweek ends as quickly as possible. A superior could offer encouragement one moment, then fly off the handle the next. Refrain from answering back or even defending what you believe. Making a difference is not on the cards. Even trying to get through to people probably will not be worth the effort.

23. TUESDAY. Hopeful. With the Moon moving through Libra, your solar sixth house of health and service to others, it is time to evaluate employment conditions and daily lifestyle habits. Check how long it has been since your last dental appointment, medical checkup, or visit to the gym. If your eating patterns have become unbalanced, you need to return to healthful home cooking; select fare that provides a full range of the nutrients your body requires. The current stellar pattern is excellent if you have important decisions to make and business concerns to take care of. Financial dealings conducted behind closed doors should be profitable.

24. WEDNESDAY. Interesting. The test results from a recent medical appointment could prove illuminating, giving you blessed peace of mind. If you are worried about your fitness and vitality, ask your doctor if a stress test might be a worthwhile procedure. Niggling ailments, usually relatively easy to cure, nevertheless cause anxiety. So get a diagnosis and follow the prescribed regimen. Creativity is welling up in the artistic Taurus. Further cultivate your imagination and forge ahead. Persuading others of the value of your ideas won't be difficult. Your passion and power to inspire are very strong now. A promising romantic encounter while traveling far from home lies ahead for some Bulls.

25. THURSDAY. Sensitive. Continue to believe in your dreams and allow creative juices to foster inspiration and fantasy. Avoid taking irritability out on your mate, clients, or the general public. Today's Full Moon in your opposing sign of Scorpio will more than likely increase emotions and sensitivities in everyone. If harmony and equality are not constants in your significant relationship, then it is time to take the necessary steps and make the relevant adjustments that will restore balance. Both you and your partner should discuss as openly and honestly as possible any areas that are creating dissatisfaction. Doing so will lessen the chances of resentment building up and may lead to a good resolution.

26. FRIDAY. Bumpy. Mixed planetary trends form in the cosmic, and confusion may cloud the day. Defer doing any kind of task or activity that requires mental concentration. You may find that your mind wanders and your focus is limited if you attempt such things. It is probably best not to fight it. Instead, make plans to catch a fantasy film, attend a live concert, or just hang out with close friends. The community-minded Bull will gain satisfaction from helping the needy. A quiet dinner for two could be a healing experience in a rocky relationship. When you and your mate let each other know what is happening in your daily lives, you reconnect on a truly honest plane.

27. SATURDAY. Beneficial. Intensity and passion mark the day ahead. These vibes encourage romantic togetherness and creative inspiration. Joint money matters could benefit from critical attention. Some of you angling for home insurance or car insurance might be able to get a better deal if you do some research and let the agent know that you know what you're talking about. Catching up with overdue business and tax accounting can be a constructive move. Staying on top of your finances is an essential ingredient of successful business management. Taurus singles looking for love could be spoiled for choice. It seems there are a few admirers out there vying for your attention.

28. SUNDAY. Demanding. The time-honored adage that patience is a virtue will hold true today. But only if you insist on fulfilling a duty. Frustration on the one hand and lethargy on the other may discourage even the most enthusiastic, energetic Bull. The people around you are not likely to be up to any task they promised to perform. Even a pleasurable social activity may be too much for your relatives or friends. Their physical resources seem to be on the verge of decline just when you need a helping hand. There are apt to be a number of hurdles to jump over when it comes to relationships. You may decide to ignore the signs and carry on regardless, but that will only prolong the inevitable.

29. MONDAY. Harmonious. A healthy bank balance and a supportive partner can take away stress, which will contribute to a strong sense of overall well-being. Bulls lucky enough to have both should thank the universe for your good fortune. In return, show loved ones due appreciation. A progressive approach can inspire, so remain focused on what you want to happen in your life. Taurus students should enjoy a productive day. Careful research carried out under ideal condition is apt to unearth some startling information. Those of you interested in purchasing a new piece of artwork should consider commissioning a local artist to produce something unique that suits your taste and home decor.

30. TUESDAY. Uneven. Although it may be a topsy-turvy day for many Bulls, having confidence in your ability should help you cope with whatever challenge comes along. Containing a restless urge will take a bit of willpower. But if you don't, the resulting edgy behavior will distract the people around you and hinder productivity. For Taurus individuals with a demanding lifestyle, a new laborsaving gadget is just what you need to reduce your workload and free up some leisure time. A reunion of college pals may bring special joy as well as lots of surprises. A long-held secret may be revealed, but you may have known it anyway. Do not let on that you knew.

MAY

1. WEDNESDAY. Mixed. With the Sun shining from your sign of Taurus, you are basking in the spotlight and feel that you are the center of the universe. So the more demanding loved ones become, the less you will like it. But if you want harmony and happiness in your life, you have to work hard to achieve equality and balance. Only small changes might be needed to reach the desired balance in an intimate relationship. Move slowly, and improvements will occur over time. Your energy resources could fluctuate today, and it won't take much for you to overreact and vent. Let people know that your patience and tolerance are limited. Start investigating travel and vacation options for later this year.

2. THURSDAY. Bright. Intellectual planet Mercury has stepped into your sign of Taurus and joints the Sun, Venus, and Mars there in your first solar house to place more focus on personal attributes and ambitions. Expect the pace of life to continue to rise as your calendar fills up with short trips, meetings, social functions, errands, and daily excursions. The next few weeks will be a great period to network and to talk to influential people. Tension could develop in a family or professional relationship, which may signal that the time is right to talk about a problem so an adjustment can be made. Strive to meet deadlines, or stress will build if projects are left uncompleted.

3. FRIDAY. Promising. With Venus, the planet of love and money, in your own sign of Taurus, the next week is all about love. If you have been waiting for romance to come knocking on your door, be ready. This is a period when it just might happen. Business owners and independent operators should implement a time management system, which will help to establish the balanced lifestyle you are seeking. As far as your daily routine is concerned, consider all options before discarding or introducing various projects and procedures. Confidence is essential when trying something new or different. You can expect assistance from members of a group.

4. SATURDAY. Happy. Taking pleasure in the small joys that life serves up is a wonderful way to retain a positive outlook. As the Moon glides through your Pisces solar eleventh house of friends, hopes, and wishes, you'll want to take every chance for enjoyment and happiness that comes along. Artistic projects should hold spe-

cial appeal, as imagination can be used to give form to the form-
less. You may start such an activity now, perhaps expressing ideas
and feelings through poetry, building an extension on a property,
designing a home theater system, creating a landscape that mirrors
the mind's eye. If you are keen to seek entertainment outside the
home, join a community group. Some Bulls will officiate at the wedding of a best friend.

5. SUNDAY. Unsettling. With talkative Mercury and restrictive
Saturn linked adversely, remaining upbeat and happy could be
a very difficult task. However, your energy is at high level. If
you keep busy and on the go, you should make steady progress.
With a critical eye and enhanced imagination, many Taurus folk
should be brimming with creative ideas that can be utilized productively. Students should find that any blocks and obstacles you are
currently experiencing around an assignment, a teacher, or a study
project are likely to disappear. Unexpected issues could crop up in
a romantic relationship.

6. MONDAY. Focused. A quiet mood could dominate throughout
the day even though there is plenty of powerful energy around you.
You should have a great deal of vim and vitality available to propel
you into any adventure that you wish to embark upon. As a Taurus you
know more than most other people that no one should underestimate
the power of persistence and determination. Have a clear direction
or outcome in mind so that you can set the course you wish to sail.
Passion and intensity are on the increase, which augurs a word of
caution for those of you prone to flirting. Tone it down to avert jealous and potentially ugly scenes.

7. TUESDAY. Stabilizing. Mellow vibes continue with the Moon
slipping through your Aries twelfth house of secrets, sorrows, and
private interests. Nevertheless, there is a difference today. Because
of other planetary influences, you are a force to be reckoned with.
Sharp, alert, and articulate are just some of the attributes you possess in abundance now, and they should ensure that whatever you
start will be completed to a high degree. Your ability to research
and collect plenty of useful information through the use of modern technology is also a plus, which will assist those of you who
are students and researchers digging deeply for facts, figures, and
promising leads.

8. WEDNESDAY. Energetic. If you have been burning the candle
at both ends, you might feel a little lethargic as the day begins. How-

ever, as the hours pass and the Moon enters your sign, your energy peaks and your charisma becomes evident. Taurus willpower and determination are a powerful combination. Your decisions could have a long-lasting effect, but make sure the views and circumstances of loved ones are taken into consideration. Updating your personal image, if this is a little tired and outdated, could up new doors of opportunity. For singles, a shining new image will attract the attention of that person you are aiming to impress.

9. THURSDAY. Insightful. Your future is looking bright right now. Self-confidence and self-assurance in your ability continue to spiral upward. Those of you who have worked hard can look forward to realizing a number of personal aims and ambitions. Putting the groundwork in now has the potential to increase the chances of success later on. With a New Moon culminating in your sign of Taurus tonight, you are impelled to seed new ideas, shape a fresh course, and implement change. The New Moon phase marks the beginning of fresh endeavors and projects. This is also a perfect period to see an astrology counselor for information on upcoming trends of the year ahead.

10. FRIDAY. Purposeful. Another red-letter dawns for lucky Bulls. Venus, planet of love and money and your lifetime ruler, is now visiting Gemini, emphasizing your solar second house of personal money, possessions, and values. Now to early June while Venus transits Gemini is an excellent period to focus on daily economies and finances. By doing so, you become more creative generating extra income, cutting down expenses, and saving money. Is your money working for you? Consult a professional, perhaps someone connected to your business or workplace, and get some answers about useful ways to invest. Don't neglect your nearest and dearest, including your pet animals and even the neighbors.

11. SATURDAY. Active. Paying attention to your surroundings and to what is happening close by. A busy day ahead is likely, so getting an early start would be a great way to ensure that progress occurs on many different levels. Taurus individuals are by nature drawn to luxury products and luxury pursuits, even if there isn't a lot of money in your wallet. You are not averse to spending what you have. But right now you are advised to refrain from splurging. Do not to buy things just because they appeal to your senses. Later on, when the bills roll in, finding spare cash might prove difficult. If possible, wait until this afternoon before signing important financial paperwork.

12. SUNDAY. Alert. A brighter image and sharper mind seem to create a new you, at least a new persona, in the minds of your nearest and dearest now. Take advantage of this period of the Sun's transit through your sign of Taurus, which lasts another eight days. Let people know what you want. It shouldn't be hard to get your message across. Courage, energy, and fortitude are readily available to you. You will surprise yourself and others by a more easygoing and confident approach. Some Bulls are keen to begin a collection of stone, ceramic, or metal artwork. Whatever takes your fancy, start slowly and build wisely. Purchase pieces that should grow in value, expand your portfolio, and pay dividends in the future.

13. MONDAY. Chancy. Imagination may be working overtime, so inspirational thoughts should be reviewed carefully. Your ruler Venus is adversely linked to foggy Neptune now. Things could seem out of whack, which will limit a realistic and practical outlook. Although creative projects might benefit, deceptive thinking and self-delusion may be present. Pursuing a fantasy is sure to send you off in the wrong direction. When it comes to romantic attachments and money concerns, remain alert, as you could be easy prey to the dishonest dealings of others. Defer any major involvement in financial negotiations and transactions. Remember, if something looks too good to be true, it probably is.

14. TUESDAY. Tricky. It is another day when you need to be alert and on the ball. However, the best method of managing difficult situations is to go with the flow and remain as flexible as possible. Obsessing over minor matters or fixating on issues that are out of your control will only increase the pressure and result in a buildup of stress and anxiety. Be warned, Taurus, there are strong indications that you are prone to arguments and disagreements, particularly with a lecturer, an in-law, or a grandchild. Verify information presented to you. Don't take people at face value, as once again there may be folk who are not looking out for your best interests.

15. WEDNESDAY. Pressured. Your priorities might be evolving, and you are urged to accept change as natural and inevitable. Stubborn resistance will not help. Planet Mercury now enters Gemini, a sign Mercury rules and your solar second house of personal money and values. So it is essential that you keep on top of financial concerns; don't overlook details or seemingly minor matters. You may feel obliged to take on more responsibilities for the people who mean so much to you. Someone you care about may be struggling with a tough problem or suffering from anxiety. Consider if your intervention will be worthwhile in the long term. Open up to a close friend when things become overwhelming.

16. THURSDAY. Demanding. Personal or domestic problems could interfere with your employment duties today. The answer might be to take a day off work and to stay at home to straighten everything out. If the pressures of business or career are causing neglect to family and emotional ties, then perhaps it is time to take a hard look at what can be done to reverse the situation. Remember, though, it isn't possible to control everything in your immediate environment. Know that, and you will weave a smoother path through the day's events, which are bound to include a confrontation that you will have to resolve. A blast from the past could be disconcerting.

17. FRIDAY. Fruitful. Discovering resources that you might not have realized existed is the gift of today's cosmic trends. Family matters take center stage as the Moon slips through the sign of proud Leo and your solar fourth house. Energy channeled into property matters, from major renovations to minor repairs, can bring emotional gratification to home-loving Taurus folk. Improving the appearance and ambience of the place where you live will have great appeal. Entertainment close to home will prove relaxing. Hosting a dinner party will provide an opportunity to display your culinary skills. The unattached Bull should accept a blind date arranged by a family member.

18. SATURDAY. Complex. A few contradictory cosmic trends prevail today. This certainly isn't the most auspicious period to take part in a debating team, to star in a quiz show, or try to unravel a complex mystery. Confusion and lack of concentration will more than likely hinder your attempts at clear and concise thinking. It would be wise to defer projects that require an astute brain and a nimble response to a challenge. Do not volunteer for any heavy mental lifting. Singles might fare better in the love department if you are only seeking a casual affair or a one-night stand. Keep an eye out for promising romantic encounters, but be discerning and don't blindly accept everything you are told.

19. SUNDAY. Variable. Although a lighthearted vibe should rule the day, you might have to work hard to keep gloomy thoughts from casting dark shadows over your mood. Taurus parents might have unexpected expenses, resulting in a need to trim the household budget or cut an activity from a child's schedule. Contending with an unplanned event could test your resilience and patience. But most Bulls have plenty of both qualities, so take a deep breath and you should sail through the situation relatively unscathed. When it comes to relaxing, it should be easy to choose pleasurable pastimes over more serious pursuits.

20. MONDAY. Challenging. Today the Sun enters Gemini, impacting your solar second house of personal money, material possessions, and values for the next four weeks. With Mercury in Gemini, there should be a lot more talk about financial plans and planning. A challenging planetary aspect occurs later today when unpredictable Uranus squares off against intense Pluto. Be on guard, as you are prone to making impulsive changes without first considering the consequences. A bit of mental and physical housekeeping would be productive. New friends who stimulate your mind may enter your life, and pals with whom you no longer have anything in common might move on.

21. TUESDAY. Meaningful. There should be plenty to keep you occupied today. This will be great if you like to keep busy but not so good if you are trying to catch up on overdue tasks. The Sun, Mercury, Venus, and Jupiter all moving across your Gemini money house increases the focus on the generation of income, the acquisition of possessions, and your ethical and moral value system. Self-worth could become a big issue and might impel you to take specific actions to assert yourself in a positive sense over the next four weeks. Taurus workers will be emboldened to ask for a raise, a promotion, or more responsibility. You want every chance to prove your capabilities.

22. WEDNESDAY. Moderate. Venus, planet of the good things in life, is your life ruler. So you do need to watch your eating and drinking habits. If you are losing the battle of the bulge, do something about it. Home gym equipment might be help if you cannot get to a fitness center. Eating right, exercising daily based on a gentle program, drinking plenty of fresh water, and sticking to a sensible sleep pattern are all positive ways to maintain good health and general well-being. You may now be a major player in the workplace as you develop and inspire new ideas. If certain colleagues have difficulty keeping up with you, spend extra time bringing them up to speed.

23. THURSDAY. Attentive. Partnership matters could require attention today. The Scorpio Moon is activating your solar seventh house of relationships, so it may be difficult to meet the demands of an intimate or professional partner without resentment building. Don't take what others say too seriously; some folk could be dishonest and lack integrity. Your mind may be in a whirl dreaming up schemes and plans to increase income, but make sure everything started is finished or there could be a lot of tasks left undone. Finding methods to please your significant other will improve the chances of harmony being maintained and emotional satisfaction gained.

24. FRIDAY. Diverse. Taurus folk are not as disciplined as usual today. Mercury, the planet of walk and talk, is merging with saucy Venus, your planetary ruler. The urge to chat and socialize instead of performing essential chores could find you receiving the wrath of a boss or superior. Know your limits if you are heading out on a shopping trip; it would be easy to overindulge on luxury items and nonessential purchases. Today's good news is that it is an excellent period to negotiate a profitable business deal, because your ability to network and interact charmingly with other people is at a peak. This goes for your romantic magnetism as well. Set the scene and enjoy.

25. SATURDAY. Tense. Before dawn a Full Moon culminates in Sagittarius, your solar eighth house of assets and liabilities shared with other people. Emotional tension can arise, with the possibility of power struggles developing. Becoming too agitated will get you nowhere fast, so it is better to remain calm and controlled. Issues relating to shared money, resources, and debts could be the source of arguments, especially for those of you going through a divorce or property settlement. Nevertheless, this can be a very romantic period for coupled Taurus. With passion and sensitivity magnified, you will need to ensure that an inflated ego and emotional manipulation are kept to a minimum.

26. SUNDAY. Uneasy. Another pressure-filled day arrives with a number of celestial influences carrying challenges and obstacles. Confused thinking is possible. You might not be sure where you stand on certain issues. Don't let your emotions control your choices. Find a way to defer coming to decisions that cannot be easily reversed. Gossip circulating around your social network might be malicious, and rumors will get quickly out of hand. Be sure you do not spread any. Quell the urge to shop; your usual good sense of style and quality may be lacking now. Refrain from lending or borrowing, especially when it comes to friends.

27. MONDAY. Varied. Mixed trends exist again, although there may be a serious undertone permeating the air. New insights and ideas increase the excitement as the Moon moves into your Capricorn solar ninth sector of travel and adventure. Religious and philosophical beliefs could also appeal now, especially systems that have a traditional foundation. Continue to do your homework when it comes to the purchase of expensive items. There are a number of factors that should be taken into account before laying out too much hard-earned cash. Business interests should proceed smoothly as long as minor points are given due consideration while you keep your eye on the larger picture.

28. TUESDAY. Opportune. Luck might arrive in unexpected ways today. Keep in mind that moderation is essential, and you will be able to refrain from overdoing or overindulging. A special gift or thoughtful favor should add gloss to the day. Even in-laws with whom you normally clash could be more affable and responsive. You are on a creative roll, but might still experience the sense that you are short on time. Pace your activities without rushing, and things will slip more easily into place. For the unattached Taurus an online dating pool should be producing a number of standout potentials. Be daring as well as discerning; take a chance, and you might find someone who is just right.

29. WEDNESDAY. Good. Abundant fortune continues to shower goodies your way. Shining in the spotlight seems to be your forte now. Today's Aquarius Moon is impacting your solar tenth house of career and status. An award, promotion, or rise in profile could spell a significant change for the lifestyle and destiny of many Taurus folk. Enjoy the accolades. Don't allow niggling annoyances or envy from others to intrude on your optimism and confidence. If your luck seems to be holding steady, take the plunge and buy a lottery ticket or enter a competition. You could become an instant winner even if it only a token prize is handed to you.

30. THURSDAY. Positive. Business activities conducted from dawn to dusk are likely to turn out as envisioned today. Whether you run your own small operation or work for a larger firm, remember that delegating tasks is the key to your productivity. This way you can free up your time to tackle more important tasks. Minor as well as major achievements are a hallmark of the day. Sign checks and financial documents in the morning. The day is good for buying, selling, negotiating, and connecting with people who can support and assist your efforts. Beautifying the working environment by adding a few plants or colorful posters will work wonders for staff morale.

31. FRIDAY. Cooperative. Getting along with many different types of people should be easier today. You might be impelled to hurry things along because Mercury, planet of movement, is now visiting Cancer, your solar third house of communication and short trips. Being very busy is one thing, but rushing can lead to errors and thereby create more work for everyone. Slow down, especially while driving, and act methodically. Trying to straighten out other people's problems will leave little time for yourself. Before you jump in, remember that it is your choice to do so, not theirs. The more you trust that things will work out in your favor, the better is the chance this will happen.

JUNE

1. SATURDAY. Motivating. Things are lively today, and can get hectic and unpredictable. Accomplishments can be many if you stay sharp and keep your eye and mind constantly on the way ahead. As the new month begins, there are six planets moving through Gemini, your solar second house of personal finances and possessions. This provides a welcome boost of energy, enthusiasm, and motivation for Taurus individuals to earn more money and to focus on building personal wealth. Change is a constant. If something isn't working out, look ahead and make the adjustments to develop a brighter future. In matters of romance, you'll be reassured and made happy by your mate.

2. SUNDAY. Tranquil. A yearning for the simple and sweet things of life arrives now for many Bulls. Before dawn this morning the Moon entered Aries, your solar twelfth house, so arranging for a peaceful and quiet Sunday would be perfect. Heading off to a lake, a pool, or the beach might appeal. A picnic in a shady, relatively secluded spot with a loved one or beloved family member could provide the needed relaxation. The Aries Moon represents your lunar low period, and strange dreams might wake you out of a deep sleep during this two-day period. Record your dreams for further analyzing. Perhaps a problem that has been worrisome could be answered by these nightly visions.

3. MONDAY. Serene. Expect a fairly calm and relaxing day, even if the work environment is busy and noisy. This is a great period to tie up loose ends. Venus, your life ruler, is now visiting the sign of home-loving Cancer. Venus in Cancer stimulates your solar third house of neighborhood activities, communication on all levels, matters relating to siblings and other relatives as well as commerce and trade in general. Over the next few weeks while Venus visits

Cancer, make it your business to meet new people, converse more with those who live close by, and take an interest in whatever is happening in your local community.

4. TUESDAY. Harmonious. The stars are on your side again today. With the Moon now gracing your sign of Taurus, you should feel your vim and vitality rising. You should also feel at home regardless of whatever appears on the horizon. Activities that require attention to detail and focus will move smoothly ahead. Profitable, tangible results will be the likely outcome. Your calm and steady presence should be soothing to the people in your immediate environment. You could wind up working two jobs instead of one. Any problem that arises can be quickly dealt with as long as you know which steps to take and which teammates you choose to help you.

5. WEDNESDAY. Favorable. A thoughtful and meaningful mood may be the result of the spotlight shining on your sign of Taurus. Today is perfect for self-examination to ensure that you are happy with events of the past and the pathway along which you are heading. The most important thing for Bulls now is to stay true to your own aims and ambitions and to remain on track. Your charm and charisma should be higher than usual. By virtue of your ability to perceive things from a larger perspective, you can make an impact on other people. Singles, someone special might stand out from the crowd. Be responsive, as this interesting individual might have an eye on you as well.

6. THURSDAY. Eventful. Today's trends offer diverse activities and situations. Once you start making your way through, you should pass any tests with flying colors. Inattention or carelessness, most likely because of other people, could be costly. Watch your step and take extra precautions when traveling. Students conducting research should double-check facts and figures from a variety of sources to ensure that the information gathered is not flawed. If anyone has trouble keeping up with your pace, be alert and offer assistance. Try not to let a loved one or associate fall behind. It will be hard not to give in to the irresistible urge to flit and flirt like a social butterfly.

7. FRIDAY. Active. A very busy day with lots of planetary activity presents itself in the cosmic realm. You can expect an equal measure of excellent and not so great events to occur as the hours pass. The main thing is to keep smiling. One noteworthy event is Neptune, planet of image and illusion, starting a retrograde in Pisces.

Your creativity is on the rise. Personal interests, especially relating to love and romance, look to be highly rewarding. Enchanting moments with loved ones should be uplifting. Refrain from beginning new enterprises, as a number of confusing matters could see you discarding a project from sheer frustration and before giving the whole enterprise a chance to evolve.

8. SATURDAY. Troublesome. A bumpy day is foreseen, even though a New Moon culminates in Gemini, the sector of your solar horoscope that impacts your personal finances and possessions. You may lack the physical resources to tackle anything worthwhile, so this isn't the best time to go out into the world without the support of others; protection and patience may be thin on the ground. Take care of tasks that require only short bursts of concentration. Restlessness could be a problem. Seek a variety of activities, or boredom will creep in. Refrain from confiding in others, even siblings or best friend, as your secrets are bound to be public knowledge before the weekend ends.

9. SUNDAY. Renewing. New Moon influences continue to place importance on your personal cash flow and matters concerning self-worth. During the next week this lunar phase can be utilized constructively to improve your financial prospects and to implement plans that can positively alter your lifestyle. Take action now and watch the bank balance grow. It may be necessary to juggle income and expenditure. But make sure you are not too critical if money is being spent on the needs of others which whom you share a life. Do not be stingy if your partner or a beloved family member requires a few more essentials now. Remain close to home tonight.

10. MONDAY. Subdued. It might be very easy to succumb to disillusionment under current planetary transits. Keep a low profile. Getting along with superiors may be fraught with difficulties, and people in authority are bound to be harder to please than usual. Resolve to straighten out financial matters before they get beyond your control. Neptune, the planet of inspiration and imagination but also of illusion and unreality, is retrograding through Pisces, your solar eleventh house of friends, income from business interests, and cherished desires. So some situations touching on these areas may be unclear and disappointing over the next few months.

11. TUESDAY. Purposeful. Today's events are bound to mirror yesterday's, although you are better able to cope. Even if assistance, support, and guidance from other people are not forthcoming, you probably won't be too concerned. Self-reliance is a Taurus trait, and it comes in handy now. Sexual drive is heightened. Emotions are intense, which can give you the passion and fervor to devote yourself to a creative undertaking. Those of you who are writers and artists will benefit from such zeal, but be careful that you don't become obsessive. Good companions and good conversation will add enjoyment to the day. Watch that you are not too outspoken, and show respect for differing opinions.

12. WEDNESDAY. Tricky. The universe is challenging and testing you today. It might seem as if every little thing you try to do takes twice the effort and delivers half the result. Domestic affairs could require a change in your schedule. An unexpected turn of events may involve a rethink and revision of plans. Family matters that should take center stage might be shifted to the background if a curveball comes flying in your direction. Clashes with a lover are likely if you are unable to compromise. Taurus singles seeking love could find more than you bargained for. If you can drop that innate stubbornness, simplify your approach, and go with the flow, harmony is within reach.

13. THURSDAY. Testing. Rash behavior, especially on the love front, and impulse shopping are the problems delivered by the universe today. Your challenge will be to avoid these traps. This isn't the best time to arrange a beauty treatment or try out a new hairstyle; unexpected results could cause displeasure at the very least. Although a senior member of the family might not be happy with your ideas for a special occasion, most other relatives will more than likely embrace your plan. If a helping hand is needed with household chores, try to get everyone involved doing their fair share putting in some time and energy. And ask everyone to contribute toward the expenses.

14. FRIDAY. Fine. Astrologically speaking, this is a relatively problem-free day. Go with the flow, Taurus. It will take more energy to go against the tide than with it. Right now the trend is more about smooth sailing than rocking the boat. Accept people's kindness and thoughtfulness, then spread your gentle goodwill to others. A major breakthrough on a family or domestic project will give you a big sigh of relief and a large dose of happiness. Now you can move on, feeling lighter and freer. Friends offer support and encouragement. Invite them over to your place to enjoy your special brand of hospitality and culinary expertise.

15. SATURDAY. Prickly. Today the Moon is sliding through Virgo, your solar fifth house of pleasure, leisure, and treasure. However, don't expect everyone to be content and happy. Situations are likely to occur that may be confronting. You will need to avoid a bull-headed attitude if you wish to keep the peace and retain the harmony. Staying cool and controlling your temper may be challenging for even the most placid among the Taurus-born, especially when someone's ego clashes with yours. If a child isn't responding to your coaxing, be firm and fair. If a youngster is behind the learning curve, hire a private tutor to supplement what is being taught at school.

16. SUNDAY. Varied. Fun is where you find it, and sometimes the simple pleasures of life are the most enjoyable. Don't make elaborate plans for amusement. Folks could cancel out of a social event, or your choice of a pleasure pursuit might fizzle out through their lack of interest. So if you sense resistance, it is advisable not to force the issue. Previous networking could pay dividends, and a short course of study may provide a chance to learn new skills. A short trip could have a positive romantic undertone, and there may be a pleasant surprise thrown into the mix. Taurus shoppers should really examine merchandise you want to buy; there is a high probability of hidden faults escaping notice.

17. MONDAY. Challenging. Diverse aspects prevail, with frustration, restlessness, and a willingness to take risks forming the pattern of the day's events. Employment matters could be unpredictable, although things aren't likely to be too stressful if you proceed in an organized and practical manner. You are very likely to reap the rewards of labor conducted behind the scenes or in confidence. What is told to you might not be what you wanted to hear, but will be to your advantage in the long term. Relationships with coworkers may be a little tricky, so keep a low profile. And refrain from signing lease agreements and other legal documents pertaining to trade and commerce.

18. TUESDAY. Restrained. Some very ordinary pitfalls can assail Bulls who are on the job today. It could seem as if you are going nowhere fast, with your concentration continually lapsing. Your mind might wander off to more pleasant situations. Or there may be constant interruptions from people calling and visiting, and all demanding attention. Even if it doesn't seem like it, you are up to the challenge. Learn to say no to requests from people who should be more self-reliant. Help them to be so by delegating to them more consistently. Sensible management of a diet and exercise plan is a key to good mental health as well as physical health, and it keeps your focus sharp. Take more responsibility here.

19. WEDNESDAY. Lucky. Planetary trends are encouraging. The Sun and Jupiter are merging in the sign of Gemini, your solar house of personal money and values, so this is a very lucky day for Bulls. Let your confidence and enthusiasm shine forth. You might be overly excited and ready to express yourself wholeheartedly in nearly everything you do now. Things are positive on the financial front just as long as you do not gloss over details or ignore potential problems or downplay hidden flaws. Overcome a tendency to see through rose-colored glasses and imagine a perfect scenario. If people ask you for favors, you might unthinkingly agree without considering the time and energy it will take.

20. THURSDAY. Bright. The popularity of Taurus folk continues to climb. Moving forward on the job due to recent efforts seems likely. Tact and diplomacy will be to the fore. You are all about cooperating, compromising, and effecting harmonious resolutions. Most of you will also feel free to speak your mind and let others know of your secret worries as well as your secret wishes. If there are problems causing concern and limiting progress, bringing such issues into the light of day can help clarify them. That is the way to lessen stress and strain. Feel-good energy is like a magnet, attracting people to you as it radiates outward. Spend quality time with someone you love.

21. FRIDAY. Accomplished. Before dawn the Sun enters Cancer, your solar third house, and will visit Cancer for the next four weeks. If you need to change direction, now would be a good starting point. Sun in Cancer will be an ideal period to visit relatives, to take a public speaking course, to study creative writing, to express yourself freely, and to interact with diverse types of people. Bulls in commerce should find that delivering a sales pitch increases the bottom line, and you might be swamped by offers too good to refuse. A legal matter should go your way as negotiations become easier to conduct. You can speak the words that impress influential people.

22. SATURDAY. Guarded. Conditions today might be slightly off-putting under planetary trends that are slow and quiet at best. Adopt a tactful approach to everyone who crosses your path, as they could be exceedingly sensitive. Differences of opinion concerning shared resources might create friction, and a showdown between you and your partner could arise. Try to avoid arguing over pointless matters; heated discussions will only disturb harmony and increase stress. Take a deep breath, then aim to work things out rationally and quietly. Bulls interested in writing should find this a rewarding period. If socializing isn't on the agenda, slip into something comfortable and cuddle up to your mate.

23. SUNDAY. Variable. Sensitive feelings and emotions might be on display. Expect a tricky day ahead as the Full Moon in Capricorn activates both your solar ninth house of extended travel and higher learning and your solar third house of short trips and quick study. Differing views and opinions could mar a visit to in-laws unless a very tactful and diplomatic stance is taken. Bite your tongue if keeping the peace is important. Gossip you hear is upsetting, especially if you know the facts are false. A longtime writing or communication project could finally conclude, conveying a sense of relief and liberation. Good company and stimulating conversation will be a nice close to a busy weekend.

24. MONDAY. Fair. Current influences encourage Bulls to avoid conflicts and to channel energy into constructive tasks. News from a distance could find you having to postpone a long trip or overseas journey. Although this may be upsetting for now, try to see beyond the immediate concern and look at the broader picture. Stretch yourself beyond the normal routine if possible. It would be helpful to get out into the great outdoors and breathe the fresh air. Communing with nature is something that can always revitalize and stabilize the earthy Taurus. Some of you experimenting with ethnic flavors in the kitchen will create a unique and delightful sauce.

25. TUESDAY. Promising. You are known for your persistence and patience, but both may be in short supply now. Be organized and clear when dealing with work-related issues and nervous colleagues. Any unexpected developments can be handled with ease if you believe in yourself and your abilities. When it comes to business interests, cast aside any tendencies to doubt yourself. You know that you have the knowledge and expertise to accomplish what is needed to be done. Your relationship with a significant other can be strengthened with a little extra affection and special attention. A surprise gift could pull at the heartstrings.

26. WEDNESDAY. Easygoing. Inspiration and practicality happily combine today, assisting the talented and artistic Taurus. Don't worry too much about a major task. Your ability to remain grounded and to follow through is enhanced. Most of you should excel when it comes to dealing with difficult associates, clients, and authority figures. Do not shy away from issues and problems no matter how complex or troublesome they appear. Mercury, the planet associated with the thought processes and communication, is retrograde in the sign of Cancer from now until July 20. Mercury retrograde gives you an opportunity to rethink various decisions and plans.

27. THURSDAY. Manageable. Getting an early start this morning promises increased productivity on the job. Financial negotiations and transactions should also progress very smoothly early in the day. Take extra care when signing important paperwork and legal documents while Mercury is retrograde for the next three weeks. It may be all too easy for mistakes to creep in to your work and for you to overlook small but significant details. Remember, whenever Mercury is retrograde, it is essential to read the fine print. Those of you who enjoy seeing your name in print or expressing your views to the public will be very active writing and speaking over the coming weeks.

28. FRIDAY. Vexing. It might appear that nothing flows easily today. Physical energy may be under par, and everything you attempt could take longer to do than usual. Be patient even if situations seemingly come from out of nowhere. If you can stay calm, then thinking on your feet and finding answers should be reasonably straightforward. Self-expression and creativity increase now that Venus, your life ruler, has entered showy Leo, your solar fourth house of home and family. Relationships with parents should improve. Young Bulls living far from loved ones are likely to make an extended journey to visit a parent, a sibling, or other close relative.

29. SATURDAY. Sparkling. Social groups have a lot to offer for the Bull keen to mix and mingle today. Get to know some members individually, and you could add a couple pals to your friendship circle. This is also a good time to make contact with someone you are unable to see on a regular basis. Jupiter, the planet of expansion and abundance, has left the sign of Gemini and is now settled in Cancer, your solar third house of communication, studies, and short travels. Jupiter in Cancer over the next year is a wonderful period for writers, students, and communicators in all forms of media. Confidently exchange ideas and share plans with close companions.

30. SUNDAY. Useful. Creative enterprises or spiritual activities might be a feature today. Many of you could be selflessly engaged in assisting a charitable event or supporting and counseling folk in need. Unfinished business may be a priority. Complete that study assignment. Neglected tasks and shirked duties will benefit by your desire to tidy up and to make amends. Someone's careless words can be revealing or confusing, depending on what is said. Listen closely to understand the hidden agenda. If writing a novel has always appealed, now is an excellent period for research to find a suitable creative writing course or an agent and editor who can help you realize your dream.

JULY

1. MONDAY. Turbulent. The first day of the month brings the potential for a number of scenarios to occur under forceful planetary patterns. Now isn't the most auspicious period to make a sales pitch or presentation, to ask for a favor, or to formalize agreements or contracts. Love and relationship issues could be either exciting or upsetting while free-spirited Venus, your ruler, conflicts with serious Saturn but happily connects with erratic Uranus. Bulls can be very stubborn, and today you might be more demanding of loved ones than usual. When they do not give in as you wish, a battle of wills is likely to ensue. Expect the unexpected at a diverse social function.

2. TUESDAY. Uneasy. The Moon in your sign of Taurus represents your lunar high period, which gives you the opportunity to start out on a positive note. But other planetary forces may be somewhat in opposition. Obtaining what you want right now might be fraught with difficulties, even if you are very persistent, because people are not cooperative. You will perceive some jealousy from a person who envies your position, power, or personal charisma. Mercury remains in retrograde motion, increasing the chances of mix-ups and delays. Remember to continually check messages, verify addresses, and back up computer data.

3. WEDNESDAY. Helpful. Tricky celestial transits are still sending challenges your way. But the lunar influence helps combat and smooth over testing trends. The Moon still in your sign of Taurus gives you motivation to set new goals and ambitions. And the support of close companions will help build your courage and confidence to go after those goals. You can be very persuasive. Even if others don't agree with your point of view, backing down might not be an option. Bulls looking to rent or buy a new abode could find a few promising places; just don't expect more for your money than is realistic. Treat yourself to a manicure or pedicure at day's end.

4. THURSDAY. Erratic. You can expect a number of disruptions and demanding situations to occur periodically on this busy day. If you have to deal with someone who appears cranky or in a bad mood, give him or her a wide berth. Restless energy prevails. If you are joining in the holiday celebrations, you will be spared from boredom. Otherwise, it would be advisable to alter your daily routines and add variety to your activities. Don't lose your cool or be too concerned if plans are changed, even canceled. That is to be expected when the Sun is in a testing link with erratic Uranus, as it is today. Be spontaneous, and you'll have fun.

5. FRIDAY. Guarded. Money and how you manage it could be on your mind. If you have been spending more than your current income allows, you could be caught short today. Perhaps someone demands payment of an overdue loan. Or a household emergency requires instant funds. Adjusting your spending habits and cutting costs might be necessary, even if family members are reluctant to go along with your plans. Bulls who are inclined to smother loved ones should try to refrain from acting this way now. They need the space and freedom to handle their own affairs. Romance improves if your partner is allowed to do the talking.

6. SATURDAY. Purposeful. Money matters continue to be of concern. If you decide to implement cost-cutting measures, be sure your concepts and strategies are explained to loved ones so that everyone is on the same page. An issue from the past could take on more meaning than it once did. The workaholic Taurus on the job this leisure day should endeavor to leave early and spend time with your nearest and dearest. Plans to change the decor indoors or to add a splash of color outdoors could find you frantically shopping for excellent materials that will suit your designs. Social functions could be beneficial in more than one way, so dress to impress.

7. SUNDAY. Opportune. Financially, this looks to be a lucky day. Sometimes, it is fine to take a small risk. Taurus shoppers could come across a number of unexpected finds, maybe some at bargain prices, that will look good at your place. However, know your limits to avoid going overboard and spending more than the budget can cope with. If plans are flexible, consider just taking off somewhere and seeing where you end up. The most enjoyable outings often are the ones that involve the least arranging. Conversations tend to be spontaneous and amusing. For some Taurus folk, the news you receive should end your suspense. Take care of your loved ones' needs, and be rewarded doing it.

8. MONDAY. Vital. Most Bulls should experience a resurgence of energy and feel happier and brighter than you have for some time under the New Moon that culminates before dawn in the sign of Cancer. Close relationships with relatives, next-door neighbors, and other locals should be enhanced. You could be recruited by a political leader to join an action group aiming to implement quality-of-life policies in your community. Short trips and errands are well worth the effort if people power wins the day. Serious planet Saturn now ends a retrograde and goes forward in the sign of Scorpio, impacting all your relationships. You will be pleased and empowered by successful romantic encounters.

9. TUESDAY. Fine. The energy mix today should see most things work out well for Taurus folk. An alert mind and the ability to think on your feet will aid most business and career matters. Students taking exams or presenting papers should also receive benefits. Originality of thought is always a plus, and today that capability will inform those of you who want to solve problems quickly, create a masterpiece, or win over an audience. Well-chosen words to the right people will do wonders for your reputation. Domestic changes are foreseen, and you may soon have a new home address. The social scene should be stimulating and offer up a surprise or two.

10. WEDNESDAY. Lovely. Your lifestyle in general and your living quarters in particular are likely to have a higher priority now that a new season is under way. Your home is your castle. Making it a showplace may be a project you start soon. Implementing a new budget might be the best way to save toward a major item that improves home comfort. Even flowers, scents, and knickknacks that have eye appeal will give you as well as visitors sensual and emotional stimulation and satisfaction. Memories of the good old days could arouse nostalgia until you remember what you didn't have back then. Find a quiet place to retreat, rest, and nurture mind, body, and spirit.

11. THURSDAY. Satisfactory. Sharing your thoughts and feelings is a positive method of releasing emotions. A sibling or a neighbor could be on hand to listen to your ideas. The chances of being pulled in two separate directions are stronger as the demands of employment and home duties clash. Displaying a sense of humor will be one way to ease the pressure and help you get through the day. Participating in social functions should be stimulating, with lots of interesting people encountered along the way. The unattached Bull could be attracted to someone very different from the type of person who usually takes your fancy.

12. FRIDAY. Rocky. The day gets off to a rather rough start and could remain that way though the passing hours. Stick with what you know best. It would be wise to leave practical pursuits for another time. Creative and spiritual activities, on the other hand, should progress well under current influences. Physical energy might be at a low level or work duties more physically strenuous than usual, making it difficult to keep on top of routine obligations. Try your best. Although your performance might not excel, it should at least be up to par. This isn't the best time to attend a job interview or to launch a new enterprise.

13. SATURDAY. Lively. Luck and opportunities abound today, being given a push by energetic planet Mars entering the sign of Cancer early this morning. If the home is in need of a new decor, begin planning an extension or renovation. As a Taurus you probably have expensive taste. Extra money spent on improving the living quarters should increase the comfort there but significantly decrease the bank account. So budget, budget, budget. The chances of biting off more than you can chew will be quite high. Before making promises and granting favors, see that you have taken care of major as well as routine responsibilities. Love life heats up, especially for the unattached looking for a good time.

14. SUNDAY. Balancing. You may be a bit fatigued, possibly self-inflicted through too much socializing. The Moon now in Libra, your solar sixth house of health and daily routine, signals that it is time to launch a get fit-program and prioritize your general well-being. Dynamo Mars now visiting the sign of Cancer for the next six weeks will be emphasizing your solar third house of communication and travel. You will need good health to cope with this busy period. Running errands, taking short trips, and generally being on the move may be dominant themes this month and next. Siblings or neighbors may be touchier, making it difficult to broach sensitive subjects.

15. MONDAY. Challenging. A new workweek poses a bit of confusion and conflict at the start of the workday. Authority figures could be on the warpath, and tense situations may need to be confronted. You are up to the challenge. Solving problems with coworkers or clients can bring you all closer together. Your effort and expertise won't go unnoticed, so take the lead and show others how capable you are. An after-hours session at the gym should provide relief from the stress and strain of the job. Regular workouts will help make your figure trim, taut, and terrific. Deep breathing is a good practice to keep your blood pressure down and to keep you centered.

16. TUESDAY. Constructive. You should be productive and efficient on the job. You can advance fairly smoothly, making up for lost time but avoiding haste and impatience. This morning the Moon slides into Scorpio, your solar seventh house of relationship. Excellent aspects exist today between the Moon in Scorpio and Saturn in Scorpio. You can get your ideas across in a straightforward manner. Finding a balance between your home life, your emotional life, and your work life is essential. Otherwise, you might begin to resent the area that is demanding too much. Social and romantic incentives promise excitement for tonight.

17. WEDNESDAY. Important. A trio of major planets in water signs rules the cosmic airwaves now. Jupiter in Cancer happily connects to Saturn in Scorpio and to Neptune in Pisces. This is a very favorable planetary conjunction: Jupiter, planet of luck, combining with both Saturn, planet of structure, and Neptune, planet of inspiration. A change of direction seems very likely. If something you have always dreamed of appears now and it looks realistic or plausible, then it is time to take action. This is an excellent period to travel overseas in order to improve your skills and talents, whether in a creative or commercial field. Find time for two this evening and enjoy the togetherness.

18. THURSDAY. Demanding. This is a rather uncertain day. Uranus, planet of surprise and of radical change, has just gone retrograde in Aries, your solar twelfth house. Despite how unsettled things might appear, they should ultimately work out favorably. Your judgment appears to be sound in most areas of your life, except perhaps for romance. Passion and intensity are on the rise. Taurus experiencing tension within a close relationship could hit more bumps in the road. Jealous and obsessive behavior can stir things up. To retain harmony, sacrifice a social outing in order to stay home and cater to your significant other.

19. FRIDAY. Meaningful. Another noteworthy day in the cosmos features structured Saturn and inspirational Neptune in step with each other, encouraging Bulls to take action toward making dreams a reality. By getting involved in something that you totally believe in, accomplishments are likely. The sky can be the limit. Work and career matters should have turned a corner and become positive. If you are searching for the right career path, you should receive insight to steer you toward the main goal. Someone special living at a distance will surprise you, perhaps by announcing an upcoming visit. A romantic declaration is cause for great joy.

20. SATURDAY. Complex. Being practical and sticking with the tried and true will serve you well as you are confronted by contradictory trends. High excitement as well as a chaotic episode or two might make this a day to remember. Getting along with your in-laws should be easier, especially if you usually experience difficulties with your partner's relatives. Right now Taurus individuals are being encouraged to expand your horizons. Looking farther afield will have untold benefits. If there is a topic or a belief system that intrigues you, this is an excellent period to extend your knowledge. Make the most of romantic and social vibes as you interact with various types of people.

21. SUNDAY. Stable. Study plans can resume now that planet Mercury has ended a retrograde and is moving forward again in the sign of Cancer, your solar third house. Travel delays and communication malfunctions are likely to be less frequent. Contracts and other important documents can be signed. Major purchases can go ahead. People who require an honest assessment of a situation will be drawn to your sound reasoning power and trustworthy advice. You will not let them down. The talented Taurus should easily find inspiration and imagination to produce works of art that have a practical application and moneymaking potential. Romance is waiting in the wings for some.

22. MONDAY. Sensitive. A busy day in the cosmos! Early this morning Venus enters Virgo, your solar fifth house of creativity and self-expression. At mid-morning the Sun enters Leo, a sign that emphasizes creativity and self-expression as well as the sign that activates your solar fourth house of roots and close environment. Early this afternoon a Full Moon culminates in Aquarius, your solar tenth house of career and business. Emotional outbursts might be par for the course. Bite your tongue unless there is a matter of principle you are honor bound to defend. If the work you do isn't offering emotional satisfaction, it might be time to consider other employment options open to you.

23. TUESDAY. Motivating. Taurus physical vitality gets a boost from the Sun's transit of Leo, your solar fourth house of family and close environment, for the next month. You might put this renewed energy, enthusiasm, and drive into your home, perhaps renovating it or moving to a new one. Or you might focus on your employment and professional life, possibly relocating to a new company or fresh industry. Some of you may take a vacation and live a little, especially over the next few weeks while Venus visits Virgo, your solar fifth house of fun and play. Bask in the romantic attention of a lover and the social glow of friends with whom you are so popular.

24. WEDNESDAY. Moderate. There is some danger of going over the top, so slow the tempo a little. You will still get where you want to go. The influence of the Aquarius Full Moon lingers all morning, continuing to activate your solar tenth house of professional concerns and business interests. Small obstacles and curveballs will test your mettle and patience. Concentrate on getting as much work done as possible until early afternoon. At that time the Moon slides into Pisces, your solar eleventh house of friendships and alliances. Associates keen to socialize could defeat your good intentions. Loyal friends are worth cultivating, and right now one might guide you through a tricky issue.

25. THURSDAY. Inspiring. Taurus creativity, enhanced by inspirational thinking, flows freely today. Look for a monetary reward from something you produce. Those of you who pursue an artistic hobby should find that people are prepared to pay for unique wares. Keep at it, and you could build up a profitable side business. Preparing the family home either for sale or renovation is featured now. Your efforts to improve your living quarters and home comforts are under good stars. It shouldn't be difficult to obtain quotes from contractors willing to tackle the necessary repairs and refurbishing. Unexpected changes in your friendship circle provide new initiatives and fresh opportunities.

26. FRIDAY. Mixed. Complex trends are in force as your ruler Venus challenges foggy Neptune and harmonizes with disciplined Saturn. The Moon slips into Aries, your solar twelfth house of things hidden and subconscious wisdom. Unconscious and subconscious desires come to the surface, making this a good day to really think about what makes you happy. An inclination to look deep within can be a bonus for the talented Taurus, as you are bound to find a source of inspiration that can be utilized constructively. Don't try to convince yourself or others that cleaning the house from top to bottom will be enjoyable. Give that a miss and explore your creative flair instead.

27. SATURDAY. Tricky. Another bundle of cosmic trends arrives to test your patience and resolve. With the Moon residing in your twelfth house of solitude, today should be about resting, relaxing, and recharging spent batteries. But peace and quiet may be hard to find. Although a subdued mood could prevail, your competitive nature is tapped. The challenge will be for you to discern when it is the right time to be assertive and when to allow things to flow. Pressure to make a judgment call could be intense, but resist for now. Do whatever makes you happy, whether this is shopping, going to the movies, or having a beauty treatment. Joy comes from doing your own thing.

28. SUNDAY. Fortunate. Yesterday's problems should begin to disappear as your life ruler, the lovely Venus, happily links with expansive Jupiter. A ton of luck and good fortune are sure to come your way, so look for promising opportunities. Even a bit of modest gambling could pay off, but keep it small. Allow the artist's soul within to come out into the open. Bask in your creative inspiration; turn a product of the imagination into a moneymaking venture. Send old habits and dependency patterns packing; implement plans for a new you to emerge. Hanging out with young siblings or your own children should be delightful on this day meant for leisure.

29. MONDAY. Spirited. With the Moon in your own sign of Taurus, there is a chance to shine in many ways. This is a good time to reinvent yourself with a new look, to change your image for the better. Making your home, family, and personal life more stable and secure could also be of concern. Taurus parents may be focused on keeping youngsters safe, perhaps on teaching teenagers how to drive as well as cautioning them where not to drive; steering clear of dangerous areas and nasty people is important. This is also a good time to be sociable and spontaneous, so get out and mix and mingle with like-minded folk you can trust. Enter a competition with a friend, and play to win.

30. TUESDAY. Promising. It might not be a totally smooth passage throughout the day, but after any stormy patch along comes some calm. The cosmos is sending positive vibes that should uplift your spirits and keep your momentum going. The Moon still in your sign of Taurus is accenting all your traits, and there is more than one reason to celebrate now. With enhanced charm and charisma, you are bound to be popular and flying high on the social scene. Romance beckons. Some of you will fall in love under the current intense and passionate vibes. A strong spark of creativity could find some Bulls embarking on a promising artistic venture.

31. WEDNESDAY. Uneven. The urge to be free from restraints could be the main challenge for Taurus folk today. Try to curb your impatience when on the job. Arrange for a break from boring routines, or settling down to perform a specific task might be problematic. A tendency to be overly opinionated might alienate people around you, so proceed carefully. Physical energy will fluctuate. Restlessness may hinder your ability to focus, also to know which tasks to tackle and which to leave for another day. Avoid rash behavior and risk taking. This can be an accident-prone marked by a careless attitude and wishful thinking.

AUGUST

1. THURSDAY. Chancy. The inclination for you to take risks is tapped by the Gemini Moon accenting your solar second house of personal money. You are a caring and trusting individual, but now isn't the day to blindly accept the word of others as reality. Confirm statements made and verify facts in order to protect your best interests. With the Leo Sun impacting your solar fourth house of property and home, the urge to tidy up your living quarters and add a touch of flair increases. And so does your urge to spend big to create your idea of how a home should be. Even if changes are desperately needed, be practical and prudent as only a Taurus can be. Try not to live beyond your means.

2. FRIDAY. Buoyant. Venus and Mars, the planets of romantic love and sexual desire respectively, are in tandem driving the love boat forward today. It is a time of improvement for couples, despite some undercurrents of tension. If you've been yearning to get away for an intimate retreat, take advantage of the loving influences prevailing. Creativity and inspiration spark your imagination, giving rise to a flow of ideas that may be successfully and profitably harnessed. Even if this passion is only used to participate in a hobby, pleasure can come from work produced. Finances are looking up, and a small win or a pay raise should help ease the strain on household expenses.

3. SATURDAY. Practical. The renowned Taurus common sense will probably be on display today. Even if it is your day off of work, expect to be busy. You might find a few urgent calls or text messages waiting, and you may be continuously involved with neighbors or other visitors. Because today's Cancer Moon is impacting your solar third house of communication, it should be easier for those of you working from home to get things done as well as to express your needs and concerns. If frustration mounts, discuss this with others and ask for help if chores seem overwhelming. Use your strong intuition wisely when planning social events and recreational pursuits.

4. SUNDAY. Lively. Excitement builds for the Taurus who is lucky enough to be taking a short trip to a scenic locale. Even the most staid Bull will want to experience the full extent of life's potential adventures now. This certainly isn't the day to remain around the house unless a fun celebration will be taking place there. Instead, get out and about; go sightseeing, swimming, sailing. Your urge to interact with people will be very strong. So if you have specific obligations to fulfill, you might find it hard to turn away from the many distractions encountered through the day. News received might be disconcerting, but don't become involved in needless and petty gossip sessions.

5. MONDAY. Slow. Add plenty of variety to your routine today, or the hours are likely to move by very slowly. Dealing with paperwork, signing documents, or attending meetings should proceed without too many obstacles. The sense that you are in a rut and need more autonomy could hinder productivity a little. But it might also encourage you to take a few calculated risks and to implement plans so that you can experience more of what life has to offer. Have confidence in your abilities. Undertake projects that you know you can handle even though the thought of carrying the mission through to completion may seem daunting right now.

6. TUESDAY. Manageable. Conflict among family members could put a damper on the morning events. Although you might not be the one involved in arguments, it would be wiser to steer clear of contentious people, especially in-laws. How best to create home sweet home will be on your mind. Taurus folk like to know that regardless of the pressures applied in the outside world, you do have a safe haven to come home to at day's end. Today's New Moon falls in Leo, your solar fourth house of family and real estate. So those of you looking for a new residence are sure to find what you want over the next week or so. This is also a great time to begin restoring furniture and renovating property.

7. WEDNESDAY. Stimulating. Powerful energies are in play today, although don't expect everything to fall your way. In terms of making decisions, weighing things in the balance first is recommended. Expansive Jupiter conflicts with passionate Pluto, advising that a cautious approach is essential throughout the next week. A desire to move ahead is admirable. Great strides can be made now, as it will be easier to focus on ambitions and aims. Problems could develop if you stubbornly cling to your views without even considering, let alone accepting, that the opinions of others hold merit. An editor could advise you that a manuscript has been accepted for publication.

8. THURSDAY. Uneasy. Confusion abounds as the working day gets under way. First thing this morning review all important decisions and legal documents. Then you will be ready to act by mid-morning when fast-moving planet Mercury crosses into Leo, your solar fourth house. Mercury in Leo starts a favorable period to sign a rental agreement or purchase an apartment. The Virgo Moon brings some lightheartedness today. But there are indications that a more somber mood will prevail, making it difficult to move away from a subdued and serious tone. A sense of isolation could also creep into your thoughts. Remember, you are not alone and people are very willing to help if asked.

9. FRIDAY. Playful. Leave home earlier than usual, as traffic delays could delay your arrival at wherever you are going. Then the cosmic trends improve, and enthusiasm for the good things of life returns. If focus is applied, moneymaking ideas could come to mind or a speculative investment with potential might appear on the horizon. During your leisure hours don't sit around the house watching television. If you are a parent, take the children out to play, teach them a new game, maybe show them how to use a simple tool or machine. A night out dining and dancing should appeal to Bulls in a committed union. For the currently solo Taurus, the romantic signals look quite promising.

10. SATURDAY. Confusing. Maintain a methodical approach regarding decision making today. Wishful thinking and negative thinking are likely, and neither of these states is positive when it comes to choosing the right avenue to take. The health of a family member might be cause for concern, so just be on hand in case your services are needed. Double-check that all messages left for you are fully understood. Taurus individuals who are venturing out to a new club or to an unfamiliar location should plan your route before leaving home; there is a chance of becoming lost. Write down or record in some way anything you think important; right now there is also a chance of a memory lapse.

11. SUNDAY. Variable. Sharp, realistic thinking might be lacking again today, so be especially careful. Clarity of thought will be hard to come by, and its absence will hinder your ability to articulate ideas effectively as well as to express your emotions honestly. Be on guard when conversing with others or when receiving instructions. Wastefulness might also be an issue now. However, money used for maintaining general fitness is money well spent. So commit whatever funds you can to help ensure a healthy future. Search various media for sales of secondhand gym equipment; you are bound to find plenty of bargains in the many ads displayed. A day spent outdoors can be revitalizing.

12. MONDAY. Stable. A strong work ethic is an innate quality of Taurus individuals. There are, however, times when you cannot do it all, so sharing the workload is essential. If that time is now, call on others to assist and tasks should be completed with hours to spare. No acts of kindness ever go unnoticed. If things have been tense on the job, perhaps an impromptu coffee gathering or a casual lunch together will lessen the stress and help restore harmony. Disagreements with a partner don't have to turn into arguments. Agree to disagree, and save yourself and your mate from unwanted pressure.

13. TUESDAY. Varied. Mixed trends prevail today. The Scorpio Moon is placing attention on Taurus personal and business partnerships, so you might find it a struggle to retain balance and a steadfast approach. While you might not want to be rushed into making decisions, someone close might be thinking very differently. Sticking to your guns isn't difficult for a stubborn Bull, and under current trends this is exactly what you should do. Others can voice opinions, but don't be swayed by their views. Make time for your mate or steady date. Working to maintain a harmonious relationship is always worthwhile, and rewards come from being one half of a happy union.

14. WEDNESDAY. Mixed. Restlessness mounts and the tempo rises, making this a day when you need to put your foot on the brake at regular intervals. Running around in different directions scattering your energy willy-nilly would be an extremely wasteful activity. So try to plan your day's agenda as wisely as possible. Tension could build as career, home, and the needs of a partner clash, sending your emotions all over the place. Plenty of business should be conducted at group or team meetings. Right now you have the ability to make quick decisions and get right to the point. Do something out of the ordinary this evening to add variety to recreational pursuits.

15. THURSDAY. Useful. As the morning gets under way, you will have the confidence to make the right decisions and to do the right thing. The Moon is gliding through Sagittarius, your solar eighth house of the other people in your life as well as other people's money. You may be optimistically looking to the future and deciding on the best approach to broaden your horizons. Joint finances might need attention. Some of you may be visiting various financial institutions in order to obtain a mortgage or car loan. If you are finding it difficult to pay monthly bills, it is time to begin eliminating debt; start paying off credit cards as well as loans from in-laws or family friends.

16. FRIDAY. Productive. Lovely planet Venus, your ruler, now enters harmonious Libra, a sign also ruled by Venus. Avoiding power struggles could be a test of your fortitude today. You might try to do too much in a short span of time, so it would be wise to tone it down and cut expectations by half. Focus on strengthening your personal assets and increasing your wealth. Prosperity can be achieved, especially if tried-and-true financial advice is followed. Curbing the urge to splurge and steering away from get-rich-quick schemes will help you build up a nice little nest egg. Sweet words spoken and intimacy with the one you love the most should be very rewarding.

17. SATURDAY. Promising. Your well-being becomes a focus for the next four weeks while your ruler Venus visits Libra, your solar sixth house of health, service, and daily work. The close environment of the workplace increases in importance. Peaceful and clean surroundings, as well as order and method, will suit your mood best over these next weeks. Resist slowing down the exercise regimen. Do not be tempted, as you often are, to sample tasty but fattening delights. Taurus students should ensure that your learning tools are up to date, especially because your ability to understand complex topics rises now. Nonacademic topics will be enjoyable as well as broaden your mind and give you food for thought.

18. SUNDAY. Venturesome. Adventure and variety should be on the agenda now. Plans for a long journey could be finalized. There are bound to be a number of minor but niggling issues that require attention to ensure that your vacation is a fun-filled experience. Students can make steady progress by locking yourself away from a noisy or distracting environment. Taurus home buyers may be visiting several neighborhoods in search of a location that appeals. You should find the selection process easier as you have a very good idea of what suits your needs, even if your desires do run a little over budget. Uninvited relatives dropping by your place are inconvenient arrivals, to say the least.

19. MONDAY. Trying. The new working week begins on a perplexing day. Issues involving career and business could have disappointing outcomes, and you are likely to spend plenty of time running around in circles. Taurus can usually attract the good things of life due to the rulership of Venus. Today, however, be prepared to meet up with a few obstacles and problems that might make you think you are not so lucky after all. Relatives, especially siblings, might be more irritating than usual, but it would be wiser to just grin and bear annoying antics for now. Socializing on the job front can be fun. The single Bull might find a new partner among coworkers.

20. TUESDAY. Challenging. Productivity is apt to be hampered by distracting elements again today. Running endless errands might be on the agenda, but pacing yourself will bring the best results. With the Full Moon culminating in Aquarius, your solar tenth house of career and business, prepare to be in the limelight. Emotions and pressures rise both at home and on the job when various challenges come from professional matters and the public arena. You will have to put your best foot forward in order to avoid criticism from an authority figure. Be discerning. Give plenty of latitude if advising when deadlines will be met, as you could be off the mark.

21. WEDNESDAY. Disruptive. Diversity is a feature of the various cosmic forces again today. Moving ahead could be extremely slow under the adverse planetary vibes sent by expansive Jupiter and erratic Uranus. Restlessness and an urge for freedom from restrictions could hold you back. Some Taurus folk may feel out of sorts and unable to focus on the issues at hand. There are likely to be problems with friends. The outcome of a meeting behind closed doors may be unsatisfactory. Travel arrangements might need to be altered. Be careful making any other changes in your life right now because impulsiveness could lead to more troubles down the road.

22. THURSDAY. Interesting. Plans for the day are unlikely to come together as well as expected. Most Bulls could be continually stymied with efforts to get your act together and move successfully ahead. Good ideas might come to the fore, but it is unlikely that others will be prepared to listen or to take your ideas on board. Before evening, the Sun moves into earthy Virgo and lifts your spirits. Gather good friends around for a meal, a drink, and meaningful conversation. You can all vent about the trials and tribulations of daily life. Once views are aired, everyone should realize that he or she isn't alone and that shared knowledge will lighten the load so that you all can enjoy what is to come.

23. FRIDAY. Bright. Trends look good for you now as the golden Sun transits Virgo, your solar fifth house, which is one of the happiest areas of your solar chart. Get ready to play more. Self-expression, creative pursuits, romance, and children come into the spotlight for Taurus individuals. The little things of life are likely to convey a lot of pleasure. This is a great period to plan a vacation, join a hobby group or drama club, and enroll in a class specializing in the development of your creative side. A boost of confidence aids all projects and enterprises. Single Bulls could find your thoughts turning to love and romance. The job site might be a good place to start the search for your perfect match.

24. SATURDAY. Volatile. With planet Mercury moving overnight into Virgo, the universe favors short-term tasks and projects. Today there are a number of edgy planetary patterns forming. The Moon slipping through Aries, your solar twelfth house of personal interests and solitary pursuits, indicates that you may run out of steam before completing all chores started. Intense emotions and issues within a close union are brewing beneath the surface, and could erupt in a volatile or manipulative manner. With your articulation sharp and to the point, this isn't the day to dredge up past failings or current foibles of your partner. Watch out for flirtatious behavior, which is likely to arouse jealousy and anger.

25. SUNDAY. Intense. Passions remain strong and powerful. This is another day when you should strive for harmony. Keep serious discussions to a minimum, as the likelihood of mix-ups and misunderstandings is high. When the Moon swings into your sign of sensual Taurus this morning, your energy and charisma rise and your creative juices flow. Mercury joining the Sun in Virgo will be accentuating your solar fifth house of pleasure, treasure, and leisure. Speculative projects on the drawing board could be examined to see if there is merit in moving ahead now. This is an excellent time to research health issues suffered by you or by a loved one. Seek to understand conditions, causes, and possible outcomes.

26. MONDAY. Bumpy. Confusion abounds, and it will be easy to become lost in daydreams, fantasy, and wild imaginings. In addition, any laziness will certainly impede progress. It would be in your best interests to keep a low profile. It is not a time to do any major decision making, sign important documents without legal advice, or lay out a lot of money. Be alert for people who seem to be offering something for nothing; you might unwittingly become a victim for the shrewd con artist. Romance could be bumpier over the next few days, with some Bulls being attracted to someone who is unavailable or so unusual that the possibility of real love is nonexistent.

27. TUESDAY. Uncomfortable. Avoid involving others in your personal affairs. The cosmic vibes offer a diverse range of influences, and you will need to work hard to remain grounded and focused. However, there does appear to be an underlying tone of practical common sense that can provide assistance. Laziness on the job won't be tolerated by a boss or coworkers. Although you might not feel inclined to give employment duties your all, be aware that teammates are watching your performance. Overindulgence could upset health and digestion unless a moderate approach is taken with diet. Taurus shoppers have to reckon with impulse spending, which is always costly and only gratifying at the moment.

28. WEDNESDAY. Good. Energetic planet Mars moved overnight into Leo. Improvement is on the way, although taking a steadier approach with your cash flow remains necessary. The impact of your personality should be much more forceful now. It won't be difficult to drive a hard bargain or to get to the bottom of an issue. Financial and business negotiations should bring gains. Many Bulls could be leading the way with the most innovative ideas for a family celebration or a college reunion. You may be moving closer to cherished goals. Good news could arrive concerning a school scholarship, a grant for foreign study, or funding for a special project.

29. THURSDAY. Vexing. Tricky trends descend today. Although your ability to think things through remains strong, ideas might be whirling through your mind. Periodically stop and focus to stay on track. Impulsiveness could encourage faulty decision making, which may cause regrets later on. Expect the unexpected is the mantra to follow now. If you can be flexible, take a deep breath, and deal with each situation as it arises, then things probably won't seem so bad. When close companions share a confidence, make sure you keep their secrets safe. Mars transiting Leo, your solar house of close environment and property, energizes your interests in residential and commercial real estate.

30. FRIDAY. Smooth. Expect most things to run like clockwork now. A responsible and practical attitude provides the best outcomes. Making headway at work or at home seems assured. Discussions around business and career will be inspiring, possibly leading to some fortunate mutual decisions that will guarantee your future advancement. Look also to Lady Luck, as she may be an unexpected visitor brightening your day with a number of goodies. Even if you don't usually buy a lottery ticket, doing so today could double your investment. Expect smooth sailing if you are setting off on a long journey.

31. SATURDAY. Fair. The ability to tackle several tasks at once serves you well now. Refuse to allow the views of others to hold you back, especially if they haven't any experience with the subject matter and don't really know what they are talking about. Over the next six weeks or so, Mars will be transiting Leo, your solar fourth house of close environment, property, and home life. Focus on protecting loved ones as well as material possessions; make sure all is safe and secure. Family conflicts could occur more often unless a gentler and diplomatic stance is taken. If you are meeting coworkers for a get-together, double-check the address; someone could accidentally give the wrong location.

SEPTEMBER

1. SUNDAY. Stimulating. Your leisure choices are highlighted as this new month begins. There will be plenty of scope for Taurus individuals to do something entertaining and uplifting. Cheerfulness is addictive right now, but don't gloss over practical facts or settle for unrealistic details. Venturing forth with a positive attitude, you should find that a number of opportunities are available to you. A delightful educational or travel proposition could come your way. It is a good time to socialize, to participate in artistic ventures, and to pursue romantic pleasure. But it isn't a good time to gamble or to shop for large-ticket items. There probably are no bargains or sure things right now.

2. MONDAY. Diverse. Mixed influences carry contradictory trends today. Your undying sense of optimism usually works to your advantage, but discontent could bring negative thinking now. Be considerate. The people around you will be easily offended by careless words or actions. A lazy attitude on the job will alienate some of your teammates. Unless you are alert and can spot the elements of deception, you might be so gullible that anyone can fool you. Some Taurus individuals may receive a promotion for past good work. Begin to set everything in motion so you are ready to accept the increased responsibility that comes with a move up the career ladder.

3. TUESDAY. Obstructive. Unexpected obstacles and distractions could hold back progress today. Responsibilities for your home or other property could mount and become so overwhelming you might feel that life is spiraling out of control. Becoming more organized, implementing a roster of chores, and delegating some chores to loved ones, even to young children, can lift some of the burden from your shoulders. What you have to say should be of interest to others. So don't shy away from discussions and debates, especially on the job. Allow plenty of time to breathe and to take stock of what it is you want from life. Be ready to prune whatever deadwood is strewn across your path.

4. WEDNESDAY. Reassuring. Social and love involvements are likely to bring a smile to your face. But try not to worry about situations with loved ones. Just leave things for a little while, as it shouldn't take long for issues to be resolved. Romance is a theme now. Regardless of how busy you are, ensure that quality time is spent with a beloved or a best friend. Someone could be crying out for attention, and you haven't stopped long enough to take notice. Demonstrate with words and outward displays of affection what you feel; no one can read your thoughts. Finances appear stable. But don't be fooled into taking on more debt; first repay what you owe.

5. THURSDAY. Supportive. Getting more pleasure and play may be a priority for many Bulls today. A New Moon in Virgo, your solar house of fun, places a delightful accent on creative pastimes and leisure pursuits. This is a great day to make plans for a special celebration, a child's birthday party, or a romantic getaway. A love affair may be in the process of blossoming. Taurus on the job should compartmentalize tasks, or you could become highly stressed thinking about so many things you have to do. It could be a little unnerving for youngsters to start the new school term or to be in a new school altogether. Try to reassure and encourage them through any rough patches.

6. FRIDAY. Uplifting. An upbeat day dawns. Self-determination and self-discipline are the keys to productivity, and Taurus folk have plenty of both now. So you can expect lots of achievements today. Don't allow petty issues to spoil harmony with family members or with friends. Your sporting prowess could be on display, and a winner's trophy might soon be taking pride of place in your home. Self-promotion brings rewards, and those of you seeking a special sponsorship might get lucky. You and a romantic tie are bound to be on the same wavelength. Make plans to be somewhere different and do something special so that the whole weekend can be enjoyed together.

7. SATURDAY. Promising. Luck is on your side now, so try out new ideas and plans. There should be plenty of reason to celebrate. A proposal or special proposition that gets approval may be the forerunner to future advancement and success. Taurus eager to move up the career ladder can make yourself indispensable by initiating, organizing, and shepherding projects along. This might mean a lot of overtime work, but it will serve its purpose. Choose a healthy outlet for relieving stress. A brisk walk is a much better option than taking a drink or lounging around doing nothing. Social life promotes romantic hopes.

8. SUNDAY. Pleasurable. On this leisure day pleasurable activities should appeal more than ever. Over the next few days a period begins that is excellent in terms of traveling abroad, for importing and exporting, and for various dealings with foreign companies. If tension exists in the domestic quarters, an exercise regimen or energetic pursuit that everyone could do together would be a constructive method of channeling energy. Some Taurus might enjoy working out at a gym while others of you might prefer a long walk along the beach or a stroll through public gardens. The talented and artistic Bull will feel truly inspired, so allow your imagination to soar.

9. MONDAY. Structured. Before dawn intellectual planet Mercury enters Libra, a sign also ruled by Venus and the sign that represents your solar sixth house of daily living. Be methodical and deliberate; do not charge ahead without thinking or looking. You might be at loggerheads with friends, family, and colleagues as frustration or anger brews beneath the surface. Refrain from attempting strenuous or long-enduring tasks. Your physical resources and patience could be limited. There is always another way to view things if you look hard enough. Rise above the pettiness of others as well as any self-pity. Being tactful, you can avoid senseless dispute. Maintain a sense of humor.

10. TUESDAY. Constructive. With Mercury transiting Libra for the next three weeks, activity increases around daily living, health, and employment. This is an excellent period to implement lifestyle changes, to gather information on chronic ailments, and to schedule appointments with a medical practitioner or a clinic. Pay particular attention to eyes and teeth. Address any fears regarding overall well-being. Professional advice given now should be acted upon. Try not to be pushy or demanding. If you feel that the people with whom you work are causing unnecessary problems, this is a good time to initiate discussions and aim for resolution. An office flirtation could be heating up.

11. WEDNESDAY. Mixed. It could be hard work to get up and get going. Dissatisfaction with your home life or place of residence might be behind the urge to make changes, perhaps even to move out and on. Mull over decisions before coming to conclusions; your thinking is apt to be faulty today. Avoiding family arguments could also be difficult because you are inclined to take a rigid approach rather than let things flow. Venus, your ruler, now moves into Scorpio, your solar seventh house of marriage, partnerships, and the other important people in your life. Under this Venus transit, Taurus lovers and mates can expect passion and intensity over the next few weeks.

12. THURSDAY. Favorable. Other people's money will figure in your fortunes today. A decision regarding a partnership or joint assets may be made. If you are not receiving adequate emotional satisfaction or financial returns from your current employment, then it might be time to look farther afield. Update your resume, arrange job appointments, sign up with an agency specializing in your field. If you wish to retain your reputation as a good customer who always pays bills on time, make sure your account records are correct. Intimacy is deep and rewarding now, giving lovers a wonderful opportunity to strengthen affectionate ties.

13. FRIDAY. Adventurous. The Moon gliding through Capricorn, your solar ninth house of travel, education, and belief systems, heralds an uplifting period for widening your horizons and broadening your knowledge. This can be done in a number of ways. Get out into the wider world beyond your doorway; make connections within the community as well as outside it; commit to a special adventure with other people, even if they are strangers, because you will make new friends besides learning a lot. Start clearing away the old so that you can embrace the new. News from loved ones abroad will be a highlight of the day. Whether single or partnered, romantic Taurus will not be disappointed tonight.

14. SATURDAY. Fruitful. Opportunity could knock when you least expect it. A bevy of planetary patterns will awaken your creativity, increase self-confidence, and boost your love life. The desire to branch out, to escape, or to change old patterns of behavior within relationships could find you taking the appropriate action to help you on your way. Enrolling in a course of study or booking a ticket to faraway places may be just the thing to open your mind to new adventures and experiences. Getting your message across should be easier, although not everyone will be straightforward with you. Some of you are apt to be swept off your feet by an intriguing admirer.

15. SUNDAY. Busy. A day of high energy should be used to advance important projects, even on this day of leisure. A secret need for control could emerge, posing a potential power struggle with a love partner and putting a damper on entertainment plans. Due to a need for excitement, maybe just to make things happen, you may commit to obligations you cannot possibly fulfill without scattering your energy and making what should be an easy day a hectic one. In-depth discussions can be carried out, but don't misread what people say and certainly do not put words in their mouth. Inspired creative work comes from the talented Bull now.

16. MONDAY. Demanding. Work and responsibility are under the spotlight today. Expect the pressure to increase in your professional and business life. This may occur because of missed deadlines or fewer staff members available to take up the slack. Or a promotion has plunged you into a whole new set of tasks, directives, and initiatives. A crucial discussion could be the catalyst needed to make a positive change of direction. Sudden developments on the job could also put you on a different pathway. Be particularly careful when driving through detours and construction areas. Home will be a welcome haven tonight from the stresses of daily life.

17. TUESDAY. Lively. Mental alertness and clarity will promote productivity. A new agreement could bring fresh energy to the work environment, so be ready to jump on the bandwagon and get things moving. Wherever you are today, everyone you encounter seems to want to chat and gossip. Of course, you cannot avoid places where you have to be just to evade talkative others. Open up to the people you trust. Sharing joys, sorrows, and problems with friends can be a wonderful release. There may be a special pal who needs your wise counsel now. A positive difference in health could be experienced, and you might be introduced to a revolutionary new diet or beauty aid.

18. WEDNESDAY. Ardent. Venus, planet of love and money, two things that are always of interest to Taurus folk, will rule the airways today by making interesting aspects to other planets. A special social invitation could have an air of mystery, increasing the likelihood that a good time will be enjoyed by all. A very nice collectible or antique may be discovered at a thrift shop or yard sale, so keep your eyes open. If assistance is needed, now is the time to ask friends and associates who owe you a favor. Romance is highlighted. You could receive a marriage proposal or an invitation to set up house with your lover. An amorous evening foresees couples reaching a new depth of understanding.

19. THURSDAY. Sensitive. Emotions are likely to run high today as a Full Moon culminates in Pisces, your solar eleventh house of social activity, alliances, and associations. Relationships with the opposite sex should be happy and positive. This is a creative and fertile period. Bulls endeavoring to become pregnant should take advantage of the upcoming two weeks in which the lunar influence will enhance romance, passion, and fertility. Don't make firm commitments to a group over the next week, as you might be asked to expend more time and energy than is realistic. If you do accept, realize that you will need to follow a project through to completion. This isn't the best day to set off on vacation.

20. FRIDAY. Variable. It could be hard to think clearly today. Defer formalizing agreements or signing important documents unless you totally understand the fine print. Care should also be taken when delivering a lecture, presenting a sales spiel, or passing on messages. Forgetfulness could prove embarrassing, so take notes and record important information. The social calendar looks exciting, but a lack of money could be the factor that limits you having a really good time. Look on today's bright side, though. Pluto ends a retrograde and goes direct in Capricorn, your solar ninth house of higher learning. Tapping into your intuition is a way to gain knowledge. Insights you receive could provide enormous help in shaping your future.

21. SATURDAY. Purposeful. Pluto now moving forward in Capricorn is a significant planetary transit. There may be changes that encourage you to become involved in projects you never dreamed would be possible. This Pluto transit gives you tremendous ability to organize, to remain focused, and to use willpower to implement plans and enterprises that propel you toward achieving major aims. Although security and stability are the underpinnings that help you maintain your happiness, right now you may also recognize that change is needed to ensure a bright future. If you have been lazing around most of the day, your energy will zoom by the time you are ready to hit the town and play.

22. SUNDAY. Spirited. Energy peaks and charisma rises as the Moon sails through sensual Taurus, your sign and your solar first house of self and persona. With your self-confidence high, this is a good time to undertake special projects and ventures. If you are suffering a bit of a letdown because of late-night entertainment, too much stimulation, and lack of sleep, this leisure day off work gives you a chance to recoup and recover. Important changes regarding religious or cultural beliefs are indicated. For some Bulls, an increase in spiritual awareness may be taking place. This afternoon the Sun moves into Venus-ruled Libra, your solar sixth house of daily living, and begins a fruitful new period for bringing into balance the various elements of your lifestyle.

23. MONDAY. Opportune. The next four weeks while the Sun transits Libra, your solar sixth house emphasizing work, service, and health, will be a significant period. A chance to change jobs could be presented. It is a promising time to sign a long-term employment contract. Comfort comes from making sure that everything is in order, a routine is followed, and the pace is kept even. You can profitably search for ways to make lifestyle improvements and to increase your income. Effort applied should pay off. Check out help-wanted positions, enroll in job fairs, sign up for volunteer work. A volunteer service role can often lead to being hired on as a paid worker.

24. TUESDAY. Rejuvenating. Personal finances and possessions become prominent now as the Moon slips into Gemini, your solar second house of money. A moneymaking opportunity could suddenly appear. Check the details thoroughly. Although there is a strong possibility of gains, you could be a little unrealistic about the expected outcomes. As always, if a proposition looks too good to be true, more than likely it will be exactly that. For Taurus individuals, anything you really value and believe in can become an area of growth and expansion. An unhealthy habit that is affecting your well-being could be kicked by putting your famed persistence and tenacity to the test.

25. WEDNESDAY. Challenging. Prepare for extra expenses and obstructions that can alter your financial plans. There may be more to a money situation than meets the eye. Someone might not be imparting the correct information about an important fiscal consideration. Self-confidence and self-assurance could be eroded, making it difficult to concentrate or to move ahead with a number of tasks. Stop and tell yourself you are efficient and capable. That belief should help you realize there isn't anything to fear. Put a few shopping treats on your agenda and surprise a loved one, a family member, or a friend. Going out to socialize would be wiser than entertaining at home tonight.

26. THURSDAY. Beneficial. This relatively quiet day in the cosmos is nevertheless quite benevolent. With your ruler Venus harmoniously linked to jolly Jupiter, there shouldn't be anything low-key about current activities. You could start a winning streak. But do differentiate between greed and real need. If you have an interest in the performance arts, music, and literature, chase your most cherished goals. Fortune abounds for those of you with creative pursuits on the drawing board. Whatever you do should turn out just the way you like it. Fields associated with travel, advertising, writing, and publishing are favored. A vacation begun now should surpass your expectations.

27. FRIDAY. Fortunate. Financial luck appears to be on the way. This could come through new negotiations, a prize, or the selling of an unwanted item for a profit. Good humor and optimism prevail, giving you a chance to interact with a variety of people and thereby gain a wider perspective. Be discerning, as you could be tempted to spend more money on the good things in life than your current earnings allow. Romantic encounters are foreseen. A brother or sister might introduce you to someone who could become more than a friend. Remain open to new experiences, and your dreams may come to fruition. Avoid drinking and driving this evening.

28. SATURDAY. Invigorating. Bulls should feel ardent, amorous, and sexy while Venus and Mars, the two lovers of the cosmos, challenge each other now. Recreation is an important component for relaxation as well as for stimulation of body and mind. This is a good time to enter a competition, to face a sporting challenge, or to participate in a special hobby. An intense romantic encounter could leave your head spinning with the many possibilities that could eventuate. Tell an important person in your life how much he or she means to you; do not give the impression you are taking a loved one for granted. Stick to a budget while shopping and socializing.

29. SUNDAY. Cautious. A methodical approach is essential regarding money and personal possessions. Take extra precautions when locking up your house or car. Be careful not to misplace a credit card or something else of value. Intellectual planet Mercury now moves into Scorpio, your opposite sign and your solar seventh house of relationship. Your thoughts may turn to personal and business partnerships. Time spent at home or with intimates will appeal. The transit of Mercury in Scorpio could also find you taking a more diplomatic approach in discussions and negotiations. But there will be an edge to communications if anyone tries to mess around with you.

30. MONDAY. Good. Prepare for a busy first day of the workweek and last day of the month. Get off to a fast and furious pace early in the morning. Relationships remain a focal point. Taurus in a business partnership should find that working together toward mutual aims will proceed smoothly. This is a good day to conduct a meeting about sales, profits, staffing, and general commerce matters. Plans for a getaway with a significant other should come together with a minimum of fuss; having plenty of fun is assured. A current plan concerning your home could stir up some conflict, but it shouldn't take long to resolve the issue.

OCTOBER

1. TUESDAY. Contradictory. This day of contrasts could be easy yet confusing for some Taurus folk, while for others of you, impatience and intimidation might rule. With Mars still transiting Leo, your solar fourth house of close environment, your romantic and creative life may be quite colorful but family life may be fraught with conflict and argument. The best alternative is to keep a low profile around household members because entering into disputes could work against you now. Finding the right words to back up a belief or opinion may be difficult, so wisely steer clear of controversy both in speaking and in writing. Don't even think of bending the rules in any matter right now; such attempts will backfire.

2. WEDNESDAY. Annoying. There may be a profusion of petty aggravations to deal with today. Don't let obstacles and difficult tasks bother you too much; do what you can, then delegate what you can't. The Sun is still moving through Libra, your solar sixth house of health, until October 23, so ensure that mental and physical well-being continues to be at the top of your priority list. Take plenty of time to wind down from the pressures of home and work. Take things in romance a little easier over the next few days. Taurus experiencing problems in a committed relationship might need to examine your own possessiveness or jealousy, then change tactics if this is causing issues with your partner.

3. THURSDAY. Vexing. The employment scene and your home life are in the frame today, possibly in conflict. Unforeseen circumstances may be responsible for a number of headaches, particularly when it comes to the people with whom you work. Extra duties might need to be shared due to the absence of a sick colleague or the sudden resignation of a key member of the staff. With your ruler Venus meeting Uranus head-on, expect the unexpected when it comes to money and love. A partner might be hiding the true state of your joint financial holdings, perhaps to protect you from certain goings-on in the past. If so, it would be smart and timely to do some digging of your own.

4. FRIDAY. Varied. Daily life continues to be a little hectic, with so much happening that even finding time to breathe feels difficult. Changes in priorities may be the motivation for you to question a number of your values and current lifestyle. What was important in the past may now assume more of a backstage role as your needs and desires slowly shift in a different direction. Move at a steady pace, do not rush, and take extra care of your health. Your overall energy and physical resources may be running lower than usual. You have to devise a sensible regimen, then stick to it on a daily basis. Nutritious eating, moderate exercise, and regular sleep will help keep you in balance.

5. SATURDAY. Guarded. Be careful today, Taurus. It won't take much for you to get off on the wrong foot and stay that way for longer than you would like. Although change is inevitable and adaptability is a must, you may be assailed by restlessness and a bit of helplessness. A feeling that your foundations are suddenly shaky is something that can be very hard for members of your sign to deal with. Give yourself room and space. Allow new things in, but don't rush impulsively into anything until you have time to consider all angles and options. Be on guard socializing with family members, especially in-laws, as any conflict that erupts will not be easy to dispel.

6. SUNDAY. Testing. The challenge now is to recover equilibrium and stability. You could be leaning a little too much to one side or the other. It would be wiser to move to the center in order to regain a sense of peace and comfort. As insight and understanding grow, so will your ability to handle difficult circumstances. Clarity and lucidity are gifts of the universe, promoted by today's Scorpio Moon. Rely on your ability to dig beneath the surface and find answers that will enable you to make practical and responsible decisions. A profitable exchange of ideas can be shared with others. Taurus speakers and writers are about to achieve a measure of fame.

7. MONDAY. Edgy. Mental restlessness marks this day. Flashes of brilliance could be interspersed with scattered thoughts, making it hard to concentrate. It will be a challenge to explain concepts and strategies, with the result that some people may not take your ideas seriously. Make sure what you say remains positive and free from impatience, sarcasm, or criticism. An intense, overbearing manner could drive a wedge between you and family members. As your ruler Venus leaves the sign of Scorpio and now enters Sagittarius, you may experience some edginess. Don't let petty details bog you down. Keep things as light and simple as possible.

8. TUESDAY. Diverse. It is another day when you might need to confront complex issues. However, there is an underlying practical theme now, so any decisions or choices made will more than likely be well thought out and correct. Venus transiting Sagittarius is emphasizing your passionate solar eighth house of partnership money, assets, and liabilities. Social, sexual, and relationship connections may be more intense, creating a strong learning curve in these important areas of life. If you have wandered off the path and become sidetracked in matters of love or money, you have a chance over the next few weeks to discover ways to reassert yourself and regain a foothold.

9. WEDNESDAY. Restrained. Bulls might need to reel in your spending. Discipline may be lacking when it comes to plans for a future creative project, home improvements, or a romantic retreat. Lessons about debt are being sent via the universe to those of you who indiscreetly buy first, then later think about how you will pay. Loans can be sourced if you have the means to make repayments. This is an excellent time to collect outstanding debts whether these are personal or commercial. Don't let anyone rush you on the job. Make arrangements for colleagues to take up some of the slack. Seize an opportunity to get closer to your significant other.

10. THURSDAY. Demanding. Some Taurus folk might be feeling confused, even a bit blue. Those of you engaged in athletic activities as well as individual or team sports could be upset or disappointed by today's results. But that just means you will have to try harder next time to reach your goal. Deceptive trends require care in financial dealings. It would be better to defer important negotiations and transactions unless a legal representative handles the matter for you. A tender or employment offer could be delayed. Taurus entrepreneurs might need to vigorously chase clients with overdue accounts. You can collect at least some of the outstanding debt owed to you.

11. FRIDAY. Disconcerting. Romantic trends are on a downhill spiral right now. Involvement in a love triangle could be disappointing for those of you who were unaware that a partner hasn't been truthful. Resolutions are unable to come quickly, and it could be a case of waiting for things to become a little clearer. Resist the temptation to take a chance on a long shot. Losses are indicated for Bulls who gamble or who in other ways are careless with money and possessions. Live up to your reputation for being conservative and cautious. Attend to work duties as swiftly and as silently as possible, as this is no time to make waves. Be extra discriminating if socializing.

12. SATURDAY. Challenging. Everyone has a stubborn streak, especially folk born under the fixed sign of Taurus. This might be more evident now as the Moon slips through Aquarius, another fixed sign. Giving an ultimatum or demanding that something be all or nothing will not go down well with relatives, housemates, and colleagues. But be firm if a loved one tries to cajole you into spending money foolishly; it won't take much to stretch the budget to breaking point. Your creative urges are strong, and so is your tendency to promise more than can be delivered. Restlessness could make you go to extremes. Monitor your consumption of food and alcohol.

13. SUNDAY. Tough. Good cosmic vibes assist Bulls who are up early and ready for action. But as the day progresses, planetary trends rapidly deteriorate. Be careful that you don't make a few enemies along the way, as this can be a rocky period for those of you on the job trying to advance your career. Patience is also needed in other areas of your life. Social and recreational pursuits could be fraught with problems. A good deal of energy may be expended trying to keep the peace with a business partner or an intimate. A little modesty would go a long way as well. You are not always right, and you may have to admit that when someone challenges your knowledge or your beliefs.

14. MONDAY. Useful. Progress at work could falter a little. In general, though, you should be pleased with the accomplishments you can make. A situation where you're on display will be a chance to be seen at your best, so make the most of it and show others what you can do. Some Bulls may have to meet a deadline on the job front. You will have to juggle a few things, then focus totally on the objective in order to finish to everyone's satisfaction. Interesting deals will be presented, but the first offer might not be the best one to accept. Hold out for what you really want. A new acquaintance you want to get to know better seems elusive and hard to pin down.

15. TUESDAY. Positive. Things are beginning to look up for Taurus. Mighty planet Mars enters the sign of Virgo, your solar fifth house of romance and recreation, pleasure and play, leisure and love affairs. The cosmic trend is definitely on your side, conducive for having a good time. You may be invited to an exciting or glamorous event, which will keep you happily anticipating the date and eager to enjoy it. The potential for a new romance is high. More gains come by working with a team than by going it alone. Empathy is strong within you. Committing time and energy to help others will provide a lot of emotional gratification. Friendly advice should be readily available.

16. WEDNESDAY. Beneficial. The good times continue to roll. There are new energies pushing to come through as motivational Mars in Virgo, your solar fifth house, will be accenting your creativity over the next couple of months. Efforts to get ahead will bring excellent results and a sense of happiness. Your plans and aims should begin coming to fruition as some of the recent tough times start to disappear. The chance of a new love affair is high. Good luck on the dating scene will lift your spirits and boost your self-confidence. Get to know potential mates before you settle on the one you are sure is for you. This is a positive period for generating extra income.

17. THURSDAY. Opportune. Remain alert for moneymaking opportunities and pleasant social, possibly romantic, interactions. These next two days when the Moon is in Aries, your solar twelfth house of solitary activity, will call for rest, recuperation, and contemplation. It is also a period when you should complete outstanding projects rather than begin anything fresh or new. You might have a few strange dreams if subconscious issues come to the surface. Pay attention to your intuition, and you should be led along the right pathway. Doing your own thing without having to cater to anyone else will hold the most appeal now.

18. FRIDAY. Uncertain. Uneasiness develops as an eclipsed Full Moon culminates in your Aries twelfth house of hidden issues and solitary matters. This can be a positive period to reflect on where you are now and where you hope to be this time next year. Resolve to clear away old problems and grievances. Try to take care of unfinished business, which includes emotional issues as well as physical tasks, during the next two weeks. If you do, you will have a clean slate. Those of you who have neglected your spiritual needs should try to renew your faith and remove any baggage you might be carrying. Hurting someone's feelings might be unintentional, so consciously use diplomacy and tact.

19. SATURDAY. Supportive. If a particular issue with which you have had some experience is weighing heavily on a friend, it would be right for you to get involved to the extent that you provide some ease even if you can't solve the problem. Give, and you shall receive is a karmic message from the cosmos today. The Moon entering your sign of Taurus well before dawn is showering you with helpful vibes, and you want to give back to the universe. Even if people's expectations are unreasonable, you will try to please. And you will shine in the spotlight, able to dispel any dark clouds on the horizon. Dress up, express confidently, and mingle freely. Know that you can jump over hurdles now.

20. SUNDAY. Favorable. Don't hesitate to ask for what you want now. With the Moon illuminating your sign, you have what it takes to make a good impression. Favors are indicated. There are very good chances that you will receive the tools and resources you need to move ahead. It will be easier to take an adaptable approach, something that can be quite challenging for the fixed sign of Taurus. By showing even a little bit of flexibility, you can work most things out. You or your partner could remain undecided about a purchase, so it would be wiser to either discuss the situation in-depth or defer the acquisition until you can both come to an agreement. Friends gather to celebrate a milestone.

21. MONDAY. Helpful. In the main the day ahead should be fine. Don't allow minor irritations to get you down too much. Progress both at home and on the job seems certain, albeit slower than usual. At dawn planet Mercury begins moving retrograde in Scorpio, your solar seventh house of partnership. Over the next three weeks while Mercury is retrograde, if anything can go wrong it undoubtedly will. So double-checking everything is essential. This isn't the time to hire a lawyer, make an appointment with a professional counselor, enter into a new business partnership, or launch any new project. Guard your wallet and personal possessions more carefully if you are venturing away from the house.

22. TUESDAY. Variable. A traffic snarl could be the least of your frustrations, as the day periodically serves up trivial issues to impede your progress. But you may be so active, the sheer momentum overrides any obstacles. You are apt to be very busy and constantly on the go as the Moon slides through Gemini, your house of personal monies and values. Be practical and conservative when it comes to money matters. Carefully review your financial worth. Defer major purchases for the next three weeks, especially electronic equipment, computers, and cars. Faults and problems costly to fix are likely to appear later on. An absorbing discussion could fan an unspoken romantic attraction.

23. WEDNESDAY. Diligent. An industrious attitude helps to get things done today. Taurus folk who use your hands to generate income should benefit. Supporters are now more willing to provide concrete assistance. With the Sun moving into your opposite sign of Scorpio, attention turns to the needs of a significant other, a business partner, and people who are important to your overall well-being. Matters relating to assets and possibly the division of possessions might be raised, especially for those of you heading toward the divorce court. Seek legal advice favorable to you. Thoroughly understand official correspondence and contracts before you sign off on them.

24. THURSDAY. Fine. This should be a drama-free day when most things fall smoothly into place. Good news could arrive regarding a loan, an investment, or a legacy. Be choosy where you shop, be prudent what you buy. You may be inclined to let loose with the credit cards, splashing money around without thinking of any long-term consequences. The Moon now in Cancer, you solar house of communication, makes it easier for you to talk openly about ongoing issues, worries, and feelings. An impromptu gathering with neighbors could be fun. Taurus travelers should allow plenty of time to arrive at your destination and double-check all relevant details of a journey.

25. FRIDAY. Reassuring. A touch of inspiration is in the air, and creative pastimes will appeal. Increased compassion and sensitivity could find some Taurus folk lending a shoulder for others to lean on. Communications with your nearest and dearest should flow easily, giving you a number of reasons to smile. Get to know your neighbors better; a few kind, cheerful words are always appreciated. If new people have just moved in nearby, welcoming them and providing some useful information will relieve any sense of isolation or strangeness they may be feeling. If you wish to join a new social group or political association, this is a good time to find out about the clubs in your community.

26. SATURDAY. Wary. Take a deep breath today, Taurus. Just because you don't agree with the views of certain people doesn't necessarily mean they are wrong. A strong urge to experience the goodies in life could find many of you prone to overindulgence. Be sensible if you are planning to use the credit cards whenever and wherever you stop to shop now. Try not to involve flaky friends in your private or family business. And refrain from lending money to friends right now, as a nasty situation might develop later on. Drama is sure to play out in the romantic arena if expectations are dashed.

27. SUNDAY. Comforting. This leisure day should give you the free time you need just to pamper yourself in whatever environment protects and nurtures you. Lazing around the house will be a wonderful gift of having the day off work, if you are so lucky. Enjoy extra beauty sleep, read, relax; catch up on the everyday lives of loved ones, near and far. Relatives and close companions might cater to you rather than create pressure. And don't push yourself; the obligatory chores can wait a little longer. Listening to music can be a joy and will help to soothe frayed nerves. Single Bulls can look forward to a little loving and romancing. Gentle sport or outdoor exercise will reinvigorate and reward.

28. MONDAY. Mixed. Taurus folk who work from home will find that morning trends are very beneficial. The art of creating a warm and nurturing home environment does not have to be learned by the Bull; such a talent comes naturally. Now you could discover more ways to improve your living quarters and to provide enjoyment for all in the family. Remain focused as the hours progress. Being caught up in too many tasks could see you scattering your energy and getting sidetracked. A friend might prove difficult. There may be a need to dig a little deeper, as perhaps he or she really does have an ulterior motive. Count your blessings and take pleasure in the simple things of life tonight.

29. TUESDAY. Smooth. The mood lightens now as the Moon transits Virgo, your solar fifth house of pleasure and recreational pursuits. Concentration and willpower grow stronger, making the easy things go smoothly and the hard things within your capabilities to handle. You can take in stride additional responsibilities and obligations. Agreements are easily reached with others. Communications should be clearer and more direct. All work and no play will certainly make for a dull Taurus, so be a little self-indulgent and have fun. A long lunch with a colleague or a friend would be a fitting reward for those of you who have been working long and hard on the job. Professional advice received should be acted upon.

30. WEDNESDAY. Productive. An enthusiastic atmosphere surrounds Bulls today. Self-improvement activities are in the picture. Making and selling creative products that also serve a practical purpose should prove successful. Teachers and parents can profitably tap the fertile imagination of youngsters and show them how to use their many talents and skills. As youngsters learn the basics, they will become more and more proficient. Just watch the delight on their faces when they have a eureka moment. For your own inspiration, you should incorporate a little fun into your working routine. Consider taking up a sport or other recreation. Taurus professional athletes may win a grant or sponsorship. A romantic proposal, acceptance, and commitment are foreseen.

31. THURSDAY. Promising. Knowing your own mind and what you want is key. As a Taurus you are a determined individual, some say even a stubborn one. So if getting ahead is your main focus and primary motivation, you must harness restless energy and use it on the job or at home. Past matters may resurface and once again cause concern. Unexpected visitors and surprising news might clear the air. Use caution with hazardous material and machinery, as the potential for mishaps and accidents is fairly high if you are careless. Bulls setting off on a long journey for business or pleasure can expect a few obstacles, but in the main a pleasurable trip is foreseen.

NOVEMBER

1. FRIDAY. Diverse. A bevy of planetary trends is sending a myriad of complications, good fortune, and everything in between. Fortunately, your mind should be especially sharp right now, so there will not be too many problems you cannot resolve as you work your way through the daily obstacles and challenges. This is a good time to begin a new course of study or to enter into a business alliance. An urge for more freedom could propel many Taurus individuals to rebel. A subtle transformation is in the air, but not all change will be productive. Some choices you make may have long-lasting consequences, so think twice or even three times before taking action.

2. SATURDAY. Strategic. Quick decisions can be made. If you are intent on improving the bottom line for your business, you will stay on the job today and conduct whatever negotiations are necessary no matter how complex they become. Be alert for client trickery. Thoroughly peruse intricate paperwork. An intense discussion could bring surprising considerations to light. Taurus students doing in-depth research can uncover important information. Clearing your mind as well as your physical environment of clutter is time well spent now. If your vitality is on the wane, choose low-key entertainment. Go out with a friend or a date to enjoy a movie and escape reality for a while.

3. SUNDAY. Exhilarating. Today's eclipsed New Moon culminating in the sign of Scorpio generates plenty of magic and lights up your solar seventh house of relationship. There will be a focus on the other people in your life. Creating harmony within personal and business partnerships should be a priority. If relationships are a little bumpy, strive for improvements. Some Taurus might be thinking about marriage or setting up house with a lover. Other Bulls will be perfectly happy just playing the field. The New Moon phase is a wonderful time to begin new projects, made even more so now because you are feeling confident in your abilities.

4. MONDAY. Variable. Assertiveness can be easily accessed if needed today. During the early hours, though, be careful not to mistake aggressiveness for forthright action. Avoid rubbing people the wrong way. Bulls involved in negotiations of all kinds should make steady progress because your ability to cooperate and compromise can smooth things over for everyone. Let sensitive issues be discussed without restraint. Once they are aired, new ways of feeling and of thinking will emerge. Changes in a financial situation might not sit well right now. Acceptance and trust that everything will work out to your advantage might come a little later.

5. TUESDAY. Lucrative. Taurus entrepreneurs and professionals seeking the path to career advancement and wealth creation should continue to make strong headway now. Ambitious plans can be put into action and finances rearranged to ensure that you have a good basis to work from. The chance of a windfall, a salary increase, or a bonus coming your way is quite good. Soon you will be able to buy a few luxury items. This is also a positive period to review joint assets and possessions for insurance purposes and to increase the coverage if necessary. Passionate feelings grace romantic unions. Show your mate or steady date just how much you care.

6. WEDNESDAY. Favorable. Now that your ruler Venus has entered Capricorn, your solar ninth house of education and travel, meeting a potential romantic partner while you are on vacation is a possibility. Taurus in a happy union should see it flourish while you and your mate journey together. Although you may need a vacation, the universe could have other ideas. Keep enhancing your financial security, especially if past endeavors have emptied the bank account or jeopardized your cash flow. This may be an opportune time to invest in something you've always wanted, especially if prices are within your range. With knowledge and savvy, you may be on the way to increasing your wealth.

7. THURSDAY. Stable. A sensible and practical mood should be evident, even if you are spending a little more money than the limit dictated by your conscience. The travel bug might be biting, although this urge may be productively focused on making money. You may be eager to investigate business projects and possibilities farther afield. A change of workplace waits on the horizon for some of you. You will be excited thinking about a wonderful new lifestyle coming in the near future. An unusual challenge will tap your basic creativity. If artistic flair is applied, you should come out a winner. Listening to favorite music while working will feed your soul.

8. FRIDAY. Uplifting. Your adventurous side is being stimulated by the stars, encouraging you to explore, to gain wisdom, and to see what is beyond your immediate world. The pursuit of a new field of interest is foreseen. Taurus students doing research will inevitably discover something unusual. Research itself can fulfill the goal of broadening your knowledge and perspective. Bulls enjoying a vacation abroad would benefit by booking a variety of sightseeing excursions. Your travel itinerary should ensure that the colors, cultures, and customs of the countries you visit are fully experienced. Special social events may provide an avenue to showcase your skills as a host and entertainer.

9. SATURDAY. Spirited. Effort expended equals results. Today's Aquarius Moon provides the chance to demonstrate your humanitarian side by working with the underprivileged, the lonely, or those with special needs. Your guidance and support may be highly sought, so embrace the wise person within and dispense good advice if asked. A timely financial tip could help you achieve a satisfying goal. Some Taurus individuals might win a special prize, public recognition, or an honorary award for a job well done. If the practicalities of life are getting you down, look for constructive methods to buoy the romance in your life. An intimate candlelit dinner sets the stage.

10. SUNDAY. Satisfactory. A day of topsy-turvy energy greets Taurus folk. Enjoy the luxury of bed a little longer this morning, especially if the weather is cold and your plans are flexible. Putting your own needs first isn't always selfish; giving yourself small treats can be refreshing for body and spirit. Some of you will find comfort in attending a church service with family members. Other Bulls might be fulfilled by studying an appealing new spiritual interest. Good news from the universe arrives now as messenger planet Mercury ends a retrograde and resumes direct motion in the sign of Scorpio. Mercury direct here urges you to move forward with a legal or partnership matter.

11. MONDAY. Demanding. Put aside any detailed work that requires a sustained concentration. The focus of your energy and thought would be better suited to creative and artistic pursuits because your imagination and inspiration are reaching a peak. You could suffer from bluntness, so stop and think first before you say something you will regret. Remember, there are occasions when some things are better left unsaid, especially when you know the truth will hurt a friend. A long-term understanding or enterprise might demand a high level of commitment. Think long and hard about it before you enter into any definitive agreement. Group therapy may be productive if you are willing to open up and share.

12. TUESDAY. Opportune. Luck and good fortune become today's mantra. Be alert and grasp opportunities that come your way. A great job offer or other promising assignment is foreseen for some Taurus folk. For other Bulls, money gains may arrive in different ways. Growth and expansion can occur through the support of loyal friendships, social groups, or members of an association with whom you have close ties. An unusual challenge within a business or professional project could push you to further explore your innate talents. An encounter with someone who is on the same wavelength should prove beneficial. A friendship may be developing romantic overtones.

13. WEDNESDAY. Fruitful. Although a couple of upsets could occur for the unwary Taurus, luck continues to hold for you. An unusual financial plan or goal might begin to advance. Neptune, planet of inspiration, now moves forward in the sign of Pisces, helping any of your cherished aims already in the pipeline to come to fruition or to get off the ground. For many Bulls it may be a relief to lose yourself in daily life. Performing routine tasks should seem more pleasurable now, bringing a sense of comfort and satisfaction. Although some details may be more complicated than you thought, you can tie up loose ends, complete unfinished business, and fulfill social obligations.

14. THURSDAY. Tricky. Moon in Aries could make this a stressful day for Taurus folk, so try to take it as easy as possible. Focus on urgent tasks that don't require much physical exertion. That way, insignificant duties can be placed on the back burner for a short time. With your ruler Venus challenging unpredictable Uranus, the need for freedom and space within a romantic relationship could create issues with your partner. However, the currently unattached Bull should have a wow of a time. Some encounters make your heartstrings sing. Social life hums. A fascinating person or an unusual scenario may be part of today's tantalizing picture.

15. FRIDAY. Enriching. Passionate trends create plenty of loving vibrations again today. The chance of falling in love is high. There is a strong chance of a change of status happening soon. An intimate relationship could turn a corner, which might mean new connections to enjoy as well as a number of differences to confront. Hold tight and remain grounded. If in doubt, don't rush impulsively into anything. Instead, take the time to contemplate the best course of action to follow. With the Moon now in your sign of Taurus, an image overhaul should provide a boost of confidence. Don't let anyone's negativity hold you back. If you want to change your look, go ahead and do it.

16. SATURDAY. Fair. The Taurus persistence and charm are usually enhanced when the Moon is in your sign, and that helps you move into top gear. But with today's disruptive patterns, you might need to call on all of your patience and energy. A family celebration or undertaking could be quite stressful for much of the day. Hang in there, as accolades will more than likely come and pride at what is achieved will bring rewards. Those of you chained to the job either at home or at the work site would be advised to take an occasional break to avoid a stiff neck or eyestrain. Social arrangements are likely to be disrupted. Have a backup plan so that you don't miss out on a night of fun.

17. SUNDAY. Emotional. Everyone is under more pressure now as a Full Moon culminates today. Because the Full Moon falls in your sign of Taurus, you might bear the full brunt of increased sensitivity and emotions. A tactful approach in all forms of dealings will need to be taken with partners, associates, and the general public to ensure that the day proceeds as smoothly as possible. A relationship problem could come to a touchy climax, although complete closure is unlikely to occur just yet. This isn't the time to begin anything new, even if the drive to do so is strong. Hasty decisions should be avoided. Settle for the safe haven of home, nesting with loved ones.

18. MONDAY. Good. Don't let a lack of confidence hold you back. Advancement on the various stages of life can often be hindered by a reticent approach or an uncertain attitude. With the Moon now moving through Gemini, accentuating your solar second house of personal finances, the inspiration to get plenty of work done and fill up the depleted bank balance grows stronger. Work using your hands and mind can be enjoyed to the full now. Taurus folk have a fine sense of discrimination when it comes to material goods. Your eagle eye for quality will often net you a bargain at the shops. Those of you vacationing abroad should find plenty of excellent deals and souvenirs worth bartering for.

19. TUESDAY. Resourceful. You can make giant strides forward with a new project that's been on hold for too long, and it will be an instant relief. Bulls are in high gear now. Remember, though, also use the brakes whenever it is deemed necessary. Having a winning hand can work wonders, but be wary of crossing the fine line between confidence and overconfidence. Friendly competition can be a great way for you to display your good qualities and also to strengthen ties with relatives, close companions, and teammates. Know exactly what is needed to increase the moneymaking potential when you are involved in tricky negotiations, retail sales, trading, or the stock market.

20. WEDNESDAY. Uneasy. Some uncertainty reigns today. The best way to proceed forward will be to look before you leap. Don't promise more than you can deliver. Someone near and dear to you may require more support and guidance at this time. He or she should be very appreciative of your generosity in sharing knowledge and expertise. Making the right choice of a pathway to follow may be problematic but perhaps not impossible if you remember that what you think is the best approach for now might not be the wisest decision for the longer term. Misunderstandings with a partner could occur unless you make sure that a message is imparted clearly.

21. THURSDAY. Hectic. Prepare for a busy day. Don't underestimate the power of forethought, intention, and deliberation. Some of you may be inclined to bend over backward to cultivate a connection that could make a vital difference to a loved one. Changing certain arrangements to accommodate a sudden request might take some juggling. However, a break from the usual routine of daily mundane activities may be just what you need to add a touch of diversity to your life right now. Miscommunication could create a few problems. To avoid such, remember to record all incoming messages, be concise yet precise when sending out your own messages, and be diplomatic when spelling out requests.

22. FRIDAY. Positive. This should be a good day for Taurus folk. Overnight the Sun moved into party-loving Sagittarius, just in time to take advantage of the many festive functions and gatherings on offer over the coming weeks. A multitude of experiences is foreseen as the universe urges an investigation of the many different facets and mysteries of life. As the sign of Sagittarius represents your solar eighth house of shared monies, efforts to establish a solid financial base should bring gains. Taurus individuals who share assets with another should pay more attention to these joint holdings to make sure everything is in order. A visit to your accountant, financial consultant, or tax adviser could prove helpful.

23. SATURDAY. Auspicious. The focus may be on home, family, and real estate matters today. Those of you seeking to purchase or rent a new apartment could be in luck, as excellent astrological forces help you on this quest. Financial improvement is achieved through hard work and practical thinking, which are Taurus assets. So you are on track to make excellent advances. Accept an invitation to socialize with an influential person. Enjoy good entertainment with a group of friends. An older or more mature lover could appeal to the single Bull. Partnered Taurus might decide to take the plunge and accept a marriage proposal. It's an auspicious day for getting married.

24. SUNDAY. Mixed. Logical thinking could elude many Bulls today. Rather than becoming bogged down in practical matters, use your innate artistic flair. Current energies are suited to creating something of value, and it doesn't have to be something grand to be significant. You might just be moving the furniture around to create an illusion of space. Or you can be designing a piece of jewelry or an article of clothing. Remember, not everything that shines is gold. Trust your instincts, but use your common sense to point you in the right direction. In the romance arena there may be conflict between what your heart desires and what your mind is telling you.

25. MONDAY. Productive. You may be busy tweaking, winding down, or beginning new activities. Fresh enterprises beckon. A project relating to children could be on the drawing board. The talented Bull might be preparing to wrap up a special creative venture. The Moon entering Virgo this morning impacts your solar fifth house. Your desire to interact socially on your own terms is quite strong. But so is the yearning to work alone so that you can create something meaningful. So you might hide away for part of the day in order to maximize your powers of concentration. Younger folk are likely to seek you out for a shoulder to cry on or for career guidance. A legal matter should be settled favorably.

26. TUESDAY. Challenging. Today's demands may come from an overcrowded schedule and oversensitive people. You may have too many tasks and not enough time to do all of them. Teammates as well as loved ones will test your resolve and patience. You might experience mood changes, swinging from restlessness to stability and back again. Financial hurdles will require the very best of your problem-solving ability. However, staying on the side of caution will more than likely lead to resolutions being swiftly found. The social arena should be a wonderful source of comfort, adding new perspectives and giving you the chance to meet a diverse range of folk.

27. WEDNESDAY. Reassuring. A productive atmosphere prevails. Wonderful social vibes continue unabated as the lead-up to the festive season begins. Improvements in business and personal relationships are foreseen; particularly for those of you who have experienced a bumpy ride of late. Start counting your accomplishments as you launch exciting projects. Rely on your creativity as well as your common sense to steer them forward. An ongoing health matter may call for new tactics. Intimate conversations will flow freely, so take this good chance to pour your heart out to a loved one or a trusted confidante. This is an excellent day to agree to or sign a prenuptial agreement.

28. THURSDAY. Varied. A mixture of trends is likely to test your ego and willpower today. Self-confidence is likely to soar, but taking a moderate approach in every action and situation is essential to preserve overall well-being now. A business speculation, a modest inheritance, or even a game of chance could put money in your hands. The challenge for you, though, will be to keep it there. You will encounter new opportunities to increase your financial resources and assets. Be aware that some opposition from others exists, indicating that you will have to work hard to seal the deal. Get ready to be wined and dined tonight, but stay within healthy limits.

29. FRIDAY. Empowering. Beware big ideas and grandiose schemes today and throughout the weekend. Maintaining good health will take more effort and strategizing than just sticking to a sensible diet. To achieve balance, you will have to cover all bases. Exercise and sport, fresh air and fresh food, relaxation and stimulation all count. Resist the temptation to push yourself too hard; pace yourself and have intervals of rest. Moderation in everything plays a major role in remaining fit and vital. On the job front a change of plans or tactics with a special project could require quick reorganization. Joining friends in a mutually supportive and nurturing leisure environment will give you great pleasure tonight.

30. SATURDAY. Restless. Edginess marks this day. Being spontaneous and at the same time keeping within a balanced structure won't be easy, as the urge to be on the move could impede progress. An adaptable approach is essential. If you can be flexible, you are very likely to gain the benefits of the current astrological influences. Enhanced insight and intuition will spark unique ideas, so be sure that you embrace change as it happens. As far as interacting with close companions goes, the less said the better. A sensitive discussion point with your opposite number could be a stumbling block to resolving a tricky joint issue. Choose your words carefully so that you do not step on anyone's toes.

DECEMBER

1. SUNDAY. Stable. As this last month of the year gets under way, current celestial energies focus on partnership, cooperation, investment, credit and debit, and long-range financial security. An ambitious monetary plan should power ahead over the next few weeks. To maximize the forces now operating, you should curb a tendency to spend too much money, especially during the upcoming festive period. Digging for information is indicated. Any type of research conducted now should uncover vital data, although there might be a few surprises. Watch your manner of speech; bluntness may alienate the people around you. Be sure to check on the ones you most love and depend upon.

2. MONDAY. Empowering. The approaching New Moon falls tonight in Sagittarius, your solar eighth house of shared assets and liabilities. You and your significant other could make major economic decisions with assurance that things will proceed as hoped. Success will take strategy and stamina and the ability to focus on what is before you, not what is currently out of reach. There will be plenty of time at your disposal to get where you want to go, so be patient. This is a good time to apply for a home improvement loan, credit card, or mortgage and also to investigate various investment prospects. Taurus employed to collect money from others should fare very well now.

3. TUESDAY. Smooth. If you started the workweek yesterday on a roll, keep doing what you have been doing in order to keep it up. Mental alertness aids work that requires concentration and attention to detail. Clear thinking assists all types of communication projects. If you hit a snag trying to repay a financial obligation, you can recover quickly enough as long as you are honest with the people involved. Some Bulls might need to deal with a tax issue, which should be resolved favorably. Romance is in the frame. Someone could make you aware of how attractive you are. Open up to a potential lover, and you will be pleasantly surprised by the situations that unfold.

4. WEDNESDAY. Helpful. With the Moon in Capricorn, your solar zone of travel, this can be a great time to forget many of your worries and do something different. You may be able to get away from home base and see part of the wider world. Include your mate or steady date in any plans for an extended journey, a brief vacation, or even a day excursion. Being together adds excitement and that much more pleasure to the trip. If there have been negative issues or power plays with a friend or an ally, attempts to resolve the problems should be met by cooperation on both sides. There might be plenty of social invitations arriving now. As you sort through them, be discriminating about whether to accept or decline.

5. THURSDAY. Beneficial. Bold moves pay off now that Mercury, planet of commerce and communication, has entered the fire sign of Sagittarius, your solar eighth house of jointly held funds and shared fortunes, assets and inheritances, debts and taxes. Good luck comes your way, more from your own hard work and careful strategizing than blind chance. If you intend to incur any debt over the next few weeks, make sure it is not too heavy a financial obligation, one you really cannot afford to pay. Keep your journal handy to record casual dates, formal meetings, even interesting observations you make and people you meet. Harmony on the home front spells a happy evening ahead.

6. FRIDAY. Fair. Some confusion and possible disappointment mark the day. Nevertheless, current planetary influences are encouraging Taurus folk to continue to act boldly even if you run up against a brick wall. You will feel the weight of responsibilities and obligations more strongly than usual. Discussions could be less than productive. Issues are apt to be clouded by delusion or deception. If possible, defer meetings that are aimed at settling problems or at making decisions that cannot be reversed. Teammates will tend to waffle rather than weigh in and provide concrete data. Disagreement with a friend or an associate doesn't need to create a rift. Just keep having civil conversations.

7. SATURDAY. Trying. Tricky trends descend again. Don't get ahead of yourself. Watch any inclination to exaggerate or embellish. Energetic Mars entering Libra, your solar house of daily work and well-being, may motivate you to go to the job on this weekend day. You could receive deserved kudos there, as your ability to work under pressure for a long time has been noticed by the people who count. You may not have ready cash to repair unexpected damage to a car, a computer, or other electronic equipment. This will call for a review of your financial position. Surround yourself with music to ease the stresses and strains of current demands on your time and money.

8. SUNDAY. Lively. Taurus students and researchers working alone should beware information overload. Take a break and have fun on this day meant for leisure. Friends could seek favors. An adjustment to a cherished aim might be required. A friend could change their mind about an arrangement you have both been working on. Dig deep to pin down the reason for his or her change of mind. Consider organizing a get-together with your closest companions so you all have the chance to gossip, tell tall stories, and swap ideas for future activith. Socializing in a group does little to promote your chances of romance. On your own, though, you can attract someone interesting.

9. MONDAY. Productive. Throwing money at a problem in the hope that this will solve the issue is unlikely to succeed. Working as a team to get things done is the way forward today. A group effort might be necessary to implement important changes. Humanitarian causes are favored. The more selfless your efforts, the more progress can be made. Mighty planet Mars transiting Libra, your solar house of work and service, enhances your assertiveness on the job and helps you make important career moves. Opportunities come to the bold and daring. Seek a promotion that includes better pay and an office of your own. Join a collective venture that has money-making potential so that you can share in the profits.

10. TUESDAY. Constructive. Innovative thinking combined with hard work can bring gains on the job. However, an underlying current of restlessness could hinder your advancement unless you maintain a sharp focus on the tasks at hand. This morning the Moon enters Aries, your solar twelfth house. Not knowing exactly what you want to do and whether you should slow down or speed up could hold you back for a while. Get feedback from the people around you, attend meetings, and talk with your financial adviser. A backroom deal should bring desired results. Stay home tonight and rest. Or opt for a low-key activity with a companion you has your best interests at heart.

11. WEDNESDAY. Subdued. Quiet solitude might be the best choice of activity today. Taurus folk probably won't have much inclination to cater to the desires and demands of people around you. The Moon gliding through your Aries twelfth house puts the emphasis on your personal interests and private matters. If interaction is unavoidable, your preference is likely to lean toward in-depth and intimate discussions rather than chitchat and superficial conversation. Coworkers could very well be a source of irritation and even conflict. So if the chance arises, work on projects and plans alone rather than in a team. Serenity can come if you tie up loose ends at home and on the job.

12. THURSDAY. Promising. Today's astrological influences should be good for you. Abundant planet Jupiter positively linked to structured planet Saturn bolsters your self-discipline. You will be determined to go after something of value to you. You can achieve something of significance. A special goal on which you have set your sights could come to fruition. However, be aware of the aims of the other people in your life. Don't leave them behind in your pursuit of happiness and cherished goals. This afternoon the Moon slides into your own sign of Taurus, enhancing your charm, charisma, and self-confidence. You should start to experience a boost of energy and an urge to have fun.

13. FRIDAY. Misleading. Try not to worry about superstitions surrounding this date. Just be sensible and vigilant. Be extra attentive to work processes and the needs of associates. A careless attitude or approach could damage your excellent reputation for following a task through to completion. A roommate or friend might be inclined to spin a tall story, either to make you feel guilty or as a deceptive ploy. Your judgment isn't quite up to scratch right now, so be on guard and don't believe everything you hear. Taurus folk attending a party or other event should sparkle in the limelight. Someone close who resents your popularity might try to steal your thunder.

14. SATURDAY. Slow. Taurus partygoers who stayed out late last night may be wishing for an easy day, and you will be grateful if you get it. You probably will be able to have a nice start to the day because the planetary vibes are soft and slow, urging you to linger longer in bed, lounge around through the early hours, and enjoy the comfort of a lazy morning. Later on you should find yourself in the right place at the right moment to benefit from a special opportunity. If you feel a little ill at ease at a social function, try to put discomfort aside and stay open to the possibilities. A good aspect between your ruler Venus and the Moon in your sign hints at a promising romantic encounter.

15. SUNDAY. Rewarding. Retail therapy could be tempting, especially if you are out shopping for holiday gifts and birthday presents geared for the people you like the best. It is absolutely essential to create a budget, and follow it, so that you don't go overboard on spending money this festive season. Determine who will get a gift, what entertainment supplies you need, and approximately how much the costs will be. As a Taurus you are a member of a very creative sign of the zodiac. So rely on your talent and inclination. You can make unique things that will be hugely appreciated by anyone lucky enough to be on the receiving end of your skill and expertise.

16. MONDAY. Difficult. In sharp contrast to yesterday, this is no day to buy gifts for relatives and friends. Your tendency right now is to go overboard, and you probably won't be thinking clearly or worried about the budget. So unless money is no object, stay away from the stores and online shopping sites. Some of you might receive a nasty phone call or collection letter if you have not been paying your bills on time. Respond constructively, but don't make any promises if you aren't sure you can keep your word. Gossip can be upsetting. Before you blame or accuse anyone, first talk to them and check out the facts. Some stories are likely to be grossly exaggerated.

17. TUESDAY. Distracting. Confusing influences surround Bulls now and over the next couple of days. Although negotiations should proceed amicably, there is a chance that you might either settle for too little or ask for too much. Someone you trusted implicitly might turn out to have feet of clay, but don't be too disappointed or disillusioned. Perhaps in this instance he or she swayed toward self-preservation over loyalty. This morning's Full Moon in Gemini encourages Taurus to be very serious about your values in life. Rewards can come but only after responsibilities and obligations are embraced. Defer discussions involving shared assets and liabilities.

18. WEDNESDAY. Vexing. Emotions remain charged under lingering Full Moon influences. Now, though, the Moon is moving through Cancer, bringing attention to your conversations and communications, transportation and trips. You could be close to burnout with too many errands to run and tasks to complete as the yuletide draws ever closer. Taurus drivers should be especially careful not to rush; pay heed to the other driver and to what is happening on the road. Disagreements and disputes with siblings or cousins could spoil a family celebration, so proceed with care, tact, and diplomacy. You are not the only one prone to anxiety and stress at this time of year.

19. THURSDAY. Testing. It is another day when celestial trends lean toward the cranky and the unhelpful. Expressing yourself won't be smooth or rewarding. Be satisfied with low-key conversations. Making decisions, especially regarding major purchases, may be very challenging. If the price of a desired item is cause for concern, opt for something cheaper or wait for the item to go on sale. Being in a rush can lead to errors, so pace yourself. Refuse to let anyone push you into working harder or faster just to suit their agenda, not yours. Use all the safety precautions indicated when using machinery of any kind. Social gatherings may not be the sparkling events you hoped they would be.

20. FRIDAY. Good. Cosmic trends are improving. A meeting perhaps related to finances, a wedding, or a reunion might take place at your home today. Don't feel nervous; the proceedings should go well and the desired outcome accomplished. If some friends and relatives will not be around for the big holiday, hosting a celebratory gathering for them now or tomorrow would be favored. This is also a reasonably good day to go shopping. Fun products for home and garden could be a hit for the folks on your gift list and guest list. Singles, be alert when an extended family member visits and brings along a newcomer. A sudden romantic attraction is foreseen for some of you.

21. SATURDAY. Bright. The pace of life is bound to have you hopping now. Two major transits begin. The Sun enters Capricorn, your solar ninth house of adventure, belief systems, education, politics, and travel. Venus, your life ruler, starts a retrograde in Capricorn, which will further emphasize long journeys and higher learning for many of you. While Venus is retrograde in Capricorn from now through the end of January, you may want to return to places you have visited before. They will evoke powerful and happy memories, and might be as much or more pleasurable than experiencing new vistas and adventures. If you are not already off on a trip, today is excellent for home entertaining.

22. SUNDAY. Renewing. Being part of a worship service, a spiritual practice, or a youth ceremony with family and friends could really appeal to Taurus folk today. Such a gathering will remind you of the real meaning of this festive period. It is a wonderful time to rest, relax with nearest and dearest, and reinforce or reinvent your worldview. Sun in Capricorn over the next four weeks will be accentuating your interest in study and higher learning, short and long trips, religion and philosophy. Personal growth is foreseen as you learn more about any subject that is of intellectual interest or of spiritual value to you. As a practical Taurus you will also selectively study specific topics that increase your worth in the job market.

23. MONDAY. Pleasing. Taurus folk who are on the job this first day of a new workweek can have fun as well as perform at a high level. Your efficient, perfectionist approach will help you complete a workload and also draw admiring attention from teammates. Some of you who are earning extra money from writing, broadcasting, even blogging may also earn significant praise for such work. Single Bulls may begin a lighthearted flirtation. During the next four weeks, the coupled Bull and your partner may be eagerly pursuing the goal of having children and raising a family. Right now, spending time with children can be rewarding for all of you, regardless of status or station in life.

24. TUESDAY. Uplifting. Inspiration and imagination are at a high peak, perfect timing for the Bull who will be entertaining people in this holiday period. Whether you are hosting a casual gathering or a formal event, you will be using your creativity. You community spirit is roused to help others, so you may be volunteering your services by cooking a festive meal for the homeless, playing Santa for children confined in the hospital, or distributing clothes and appliances to needy families. Share your talents with others. Raise your voice in song and laughter. Some Taurus will choose to honor this Christmas Eve in a traditional way by joining nearest and dearest in a worship service or a family ritual dinner.

25. WEDNESDAY. Merry Christmas! It will be a joyful day if everyone with whom you interact is on their best behavior, and that includes you. You might have to walk on eggshells around certain folk who become especially sensitive on this holiday. An argument does appear to be unavoidable, but you have the ability to keep things on an even keel. Just be diplomatic, tactful, and fair. Don't play favorites with family members. A brother or sister may be intent on upsetting another relative or an in-law. Be alert for any such deliberate baiting, and you will be able to foil the attempt. If you have to visit several people, don't rush or drive fast; take necessary precautions to avert mishap and accident.

26. THURSDAY. Spirited. Messenger Mercury has joined the Sun, Venus, and Pluto in the sign of Capricorn, your solar house of travel and adventure. Mercury here encourages you to experiment and to move out of your comfort zone. This is certainly a time when you can dare to be different and make a success of it, just as long as activities are not high risk or dangerous. Your intuition is sparking on all cylinders, so you are well aware that being spontaneous and having fun are very different from acting impulsively and rushing headlong into things. Unexpected visitors may bring a surprise gift and some surprising news. Taurus collectors searching for a special piece may be in luck.

27. FRIDAY. Low-key. Mental and physical fatigue could set in today. If excessive socializing has started to pall, it might be time to take a break and spend leisure hours at home with the people you love the most. Bulls who are involved in any kind of competitive undertaking should meet with some success, even though the outcome may not be entirely as you wanted it to be. Don't make unilateral decisions for a group project. To have it work out well, a team effort is essential. Encourage everyone's input and feedback. Ongoing issues of concern to you and your partner should be settled satisfactorily, which will restore some harmony and happiness to the relationship.

28. SATURDAY. Cooperative. Although energy could be a bit limited when the Moon moves through your opposite sign of Scorpio, that shouldn't be too much of a concern for most Taurus folk. If there is a social function or gathering to attend, you probably will be more than ready and willing to get up and go. A party atmosphere is sure to energize you. Be selective about doing chores today, especially strenuous ones, and insist that the people with whom you live do their fair share as well. Group meetings and activities should proceed with a minimum of fuss and with cooperation coming from all involved. Coupled Taurus may hear some promising about having children and raising a family.

29. SUNDAY. Uncertain. There is potential for chaos when the planetary forces of Mercury and Uranus are at odds, as they will be today. Too much information coming at you all at once could make it difficult for you to think clearly. Frustration quickly mounts. As a Taurus you are fortified with a placid nature. But now you might yell or throw things in anger, which would upset the people you love. Be wise and quell restless urges through constructive labor, physical exercise, or intellectual absorption. Getting into a research project online might ease edginess and anxiety. Bulls with spiritual and religious leanings can abate inner tension by attending a place of worship.

30. MONDAY. Edgy. Most Bulls are unlikely to be bored today, but that isn't necessarily a good thing. Restless energy is bound to put a few vexing people and annoying obstacles in your way. Whether you are back at work or still on vacation, let matters unfold at their own pace. Go with the flow; resisting will get you nowhere. Conflicts and power plays will more than likely arise unless you are prepared to back down and give up any desire to control others. Expect plans either to change or be canceled both on the job and at home. Taurus drivers starting a long-distance journey should have the car thoroughly checked, especially brakes and tires, for total roadworthiness.

31. TUESDAY. Intense. The Sun, Moon, Mercury, and your ruler Venus all in the sign of Capricorn today heavily accents your solar ninth house of higher learning and long journeys and will give you a penetrating intellectual focus. Searching for the truth of a matter or investigating in-depth is beautifully supported by these planetary forces. Taurus students could discover valuable information, then write about it with great clarity. This is also a good time to enter competitions that require thinking outside the box. With intensity at a high now, some Bulls could be very prickly. It won't take much to say the wrong thing and upset someone. Drive sensibly or go by taxi; have a safe and sound New Year's Eve.

TAURUS
NOVEMBER–DECEMBER 2012

November 2012

1. THURSDAY. Volatile. As the new month unfolds, Taurus folk will need to be more flexible, something that isn't one of your innate qualities. With your life ruler Venus opposing unpredictable Uranus, fluctuations in love and money are bound to occur. Expect erratic behavior from a lover. For some of you in a committed union, discontent with a significant other could grow very strong. Solo Bulls looking for romance could team up with someone who gives you the thrill of your life. However, the universe is warning you to proceed with care. Enjoy the moment but don't become too attached to this casual love affair. It is likely to disappear just as quickly as it came.

2. FRIDAY. Diverse. The changeable mood of the day could find some of you involved in clashes with a business or intimate partner over financial outlays. If possible, defer entering into serious monetary discussions; otherwise, discord and tension could linger all day. It is also wise to avoid arguments with the ones you love; this way you forestall difficulties in your love life. With your ruler Venus currently in Libra, your solar sixth house of work and health, improved relationships with coworkers are now likely. Self-nurturing and pampering should also be a major consideration, especially for Taurus individuals who are prone to neglect overall health and well-being.

3. SATURDAY. Bumpy. It is another day when conditions for lovers are not looking very bright. Planet Venus challenges fanatical Pluto, increasing the passion and sexual intensity but possibly triggering possessiveness and jealousy. Compulsive and obsessive feelings could also emerge. If you are traveling with others, make sure a lighthearted atmosphere prevails; otherwise, someone could become incensed and create issues for all. Discussions with an authority figure should go well. Taurus who are endeavoring to learn something new should not experience problems remembering important details. A potential new romantic partner, with whom you may be flirting, seems more attractive than your current lover. Be careful!

4. SUNDAY. Helpful. With the Moon sliding through nurturing Cancer, you can make progress dealing with relatives, possibly your parents or aunts and uncles. The urge to get out and about should lift your spirits. A lunch date with a neighbor, friend, or sibling should be a pleasant diversion. The afternoon hours could be very busy. A number of minor obstacles may appear out of nowhere to test your patience and resolve. Taurus folk prefer a stable and solid structure. You want a place all your own that you call home. Those of you eager to purchase a new house or apartment may spend productive hours today viewing property that has just come on the market.

5. MONDAY. Structured. Building an asset base slowly and surely is an innate characteristic of those born under the sign of Taurus. Your strong determination and persistence to make something of your life will shine through in many and varied ways. Take advantage of the quiet conditions surrounding you today in order to push your agenda forward. Success is foreseen. Such success breeds self-confidence to bring about further positive change and growth. Business opportunities related to real estate and home-based products would be perfect for the astute Taurus. Stylish possessions that add flair and appeal to your living quarters can be acquired now. Check the terms of the warranty before purchasing major appliances.

6. TUESDAY. Trying. It might be a day full of bumps and blips, but positive thinking can help you move through any madness. An awkward conversation with a partner could touch a nerve, especially if this involves careless money management. Handling the issue with tact and a gentle approach should fix the problem quickly. A power struggle for dominance or to claim your undivided attention might be something that you need to resolve. Late afternoon the speedy planet Mercury begins to slow down and go retrograde in Sagittarius. Mix-ups, misunderstandings, and mayhem are foreseen. If career pressures are creating stress and strain, take time out to appreciate home comforts and relax tonight.

7. WEDNESDAY. Constructive. Nostalgic pursuits are the flavor of the day. You will enjoy a trip down memory lane. Working harder on relations with extended family can bring future dividends, especially if petty feuds have recently created tension when the clan gathers together. Although most Bulls are patient souls who enjoy many of the simple pleasures in life, keeping your temper under control might be more difficult over the next few weeks. Matters relating to a home loan, a pension, an inheritance, taxes, or an insurance settlement could be stalled and create angst for everyone. Take the time now to review interest rates on loans and current investments to ensure that your money is working for you.

8. THURSDAY. Joyful. Mix with people who are happy and positive, and that is the way you should aim to be as well. Interacting with children and teenagers can be fun, so don't pass by the opportunity to share your wisdom or sense of adventure with youngsters in your life. Really listening to what others have to say is essential. There may be something important going on, but it isn't being spelled out. A promised delivery might not arrive in time for a special occasion, so you might need to improvise instead. Spend the leisure hours doing things that please your partner. This can be a step in the right direction, and you are sure to receive pleasant rewards.

9. FRIDAY. Fruitful. Your ruler Venus is happily linked to jolly Jupiter today, promising good things. The weekend ahead can be a joyous period of celebration for Taurus folk who are getting married, whether you are walking down the aisle in a fine wedding ceremony or standing before a justice of the peace. Plans for a special occasion should be falling neatly into place, but it can be easy to overlook the catering costs unless you are rigorous about expenditure. Satisfaction can come from turning creative ideas into something concrete, but carefully check any buy or sell contract. Weigh advice from a friend, as their own agenda might not take your wishes or best interests into account.

10. SATURDAY. Good. There is a very good chance that you will wake up feeling a little under the weather this morning. With the Moon in your Libra solar sector of health, your body is sending signals to eat right, achieve a moderate amount of exercise, and stick with a healthful sleeping regimen. Have fun by enjoying the bounty of the day without going beyond your personal and monetary limits. Large social gatherings, parties, and ceremonies can bring excitement and pleasure, but make sure you don't go overboard in your attempts to be in the spotlight. Charming new friends and acquaintances can expand and enhance your social circle. For some Taurus singles, this could also mean a blossoming new romance.

11. SUNDAY. Smooth. Surprise is the order of the day. A favorite visitor could arrive unannounced at your door, bringing loads of presents, lots of love, and tall tales of adventure. A relative or in-law may also figure in activities, which could make relaxing a bit difficult. Loosen up, be calm, and let people do their own thing. Organize early in the day; the more efficient you are, the less pressure you will be under later. Neptune, the planet of inspiration and imagination, comes out of a retrograde and now moves direct in Pisces. This will help to push ahead long-term goals that have been stalled over the past few months. Bringing a personal aim to fruition can open the door for future achievements.

12. MONDAY. Fine. Communications with clients, customers, and partners flow smoothly to start the workweek. This can be a period when business sales should increase. The Moon moving into Scorpio this morning puts the focus on significant others. Deep, intimate discussions with a lover about long-term intentions and cherished desires can be revealing. Seek understanding and agreement on the direction in which both of you wish to head. You cannot please everyone all of the time, but you should be able to please a number of folks today. A mystical aura continues to surround love and affection. Many Bulls should be lucky in the romance stakes.

13. TUESDAY. Tricky. Mixed fortunes apply today. An eclipsed New Moon in Scorpio, your solar house of partnership, can bring positive healing to important relationships that may have soured recently. Work on tricky issues. Remember that communication is vital. Talking openly about any and all concerns will maintain loving ties. Deceptive trends are strongly influencing joint finances and income obtained from professional endeavors. Taurus business owners should carefully check the references of potential new customers before allowing them to purchase goods or services on credit. Refrain from lending friends money regardless of how long you have known them; it is unlikely the debt will be repaid anytime soon.

14. WEDNESDAY. Murky. Mercury retrograde now slips back into the deep waters of Scorpio. Your ability to think clearly is below par. Mistakes in judgment could occur, so don't allow others to push you into quick decisions. If something looks too good to be true, it probably will be. Working with a partner or a group might be wise even if you would prefer to work alone. Dealing with a cranky person in authority could take skill and patience, especially if that person is a relative who is creating trouble. Contending with a power struggle or political issue will be stressful. Refrain from blaming others after something goes wrong; it may be your oversight that was at fault to begin with.

15. THURSDAY. Complex. Contradictory influences mark this period. A longing for success is at odds with the desire for freedom and autonomy. Major changes can occur now, and these may be either positive or negative. Bulls will need to guard against restlessness. The urge to tear down solid structures could become overwhelming, and quelling this energy will be rather difficult. It would be beneficial to discipline your thinking and keep physically active. There may be many times over the next few weeks when it will be essential to bite your tongue. If you do not, you might be left to deal with unhappy consequences. An evening at home within the bosom of family life should bring comfort.

16. FRIDAY. Expansive. With the Moon now in Capricorn, your solar ninth house, a desire to travel and to broaden your horizons comes to the fore. People close to you may be demanding, but you are unlikely to give in as quickly as usual. The desire to get away from it all remains high. Consider adding a dash of excitement to your life by enrolling in a new course, learning another language, or joining a choir. Enjoying a foreign cuisine either at home or at a local restaurant can be fun for those of you who delight in sampling the different foods and flavors of other countries and cultures. Dancing the night away might appeal to energetic Bulls regardless of age.

17. SATURDAY. Beneficial. Energetic planet Mars has overnight entered Capricorn, your solar ninth house of travel and education. Furthering your education to realize an ambition or to expand your academic qualifications can be undertaken. Those of you interested in recording memoirs for publication or for the benefit of family should begin the process now. It is advisable to defer instigating legal proceedings until the last week in December, as the chances of reaching a settlement in your favor are greatly reduced. Successful ceremonies are in the offing. Your plans for a graduation, reunion, or wedding should soon come to fruition.

18. SUNDAY. Inspired. Imagination is greatly enhanced, allowing the talented Taurus to create and produce. Use this period to brainstorm at home or on the job. Your ideas could be inspirational now. Those of you with time on your hands can gain emotional satisfaction by volunteering at a local religious, charitable, or community organization. Some of you will offer to teach your special field of expertise to a youth group. A travel chance of a lifetime could become available. But a spur-of-the-moment decision might need to be made so you can take advantage of the offer. A closer, happier connection with a relative or a lover who is living abroad is foreseen.

19. MONDAY. Manageable. Those of you who have been unsure about employment or career choices for some time should not rush into decisions just yet. You will need to wait a little longer, at least until clarity is gained on what you really want to pursue and what will give you emotional fulfillment. Wisely use your gentle people skills and good public relations demeanor now. Be careful around sensitive others. Communications may be forceful. So the assertive among you could be inclined to verbalize thoughts without thinking first. An intense atmosphere could color staff meetings, appointments with clients, and job interviews, so don't expect too much to come from activities today.

20. TUESDAY. Restrained. Moderation in all things should be the rule today. The inclination to overdo, to promise more than is possible, and to overindulge is enhanced now. Acting on this urge could create serious problems for the bank account, so keep the impulse in check. Defer counseling sessions, even casual discussions, intended to resolve personal issues; you are unlikely to get very far, and confusion may be the end result. News regarding professional interests might at first seem disconcerting; however, with further investigation you should discover other more favorable options. Plans might need to be canceled in order to deal with domestic concerns. A social function might not live up to your high expectations.

21. WEDNESDAY. Significant. Two important planets are on the move today. Your lifetime ruler Venus is moving forward in Scorpio, your solar seventh house of partnership. Venus in Scorpio provides a chance for solo Bulls to meet a potential partner. The Sun enters Sagittarius, your solar eighth house of shared finances and resources. You can expect to be spending more time alone in the boudoir with the love of your life. If you are headed toward the divorce courts, this is a favorable period to enter into discussions relating to property settlements and custody of children. The savvy Bull keen to learn more about trading on the stock market could enroll in a course and begin putting together a solid investment portfolio.

22. THURSDAY. Dreamy. A strange atmosphere prevails, and many of you could feel tired, confused, or out of sorts. Conversely, the urge to produce something beautiful increases and creative juices flow freely. A friend might make special plans, so allow your buddy the freedom to surprise you. Strange dreams and fantasies could occur, but don't try to analyze your visions now; instead, write your thoughts down and review them in a few days. Make the most of loving overtures from your honey, and be prepared for the possibility of a special proposal coming your way. Coupled Taurus should find that recent changes are already improving the union. Those of you single are likely to be sought after.

23. FRIDAY. Strained. Tension and restlessness are heightened today as energetic Mars challenges explosive Uranus. A sense of unease and impatience develops, and the urge to rebel comes to the fore. Taurus folk are naturally cautious and wary, which is a blessing in this time frame that poses accidents and traps. Be on the lookout for dangers as you go about your daily activities. Pace physical tasks and refrain from pushing yourself or others too hard. Whenever and wherever possible, take time out to rest and relax. If you are unable to get out of a social event, steer clear of people who rise to anger quickly. As soon and as early as possible, escape to the comfort of your own home.

24. SATURDAY. Steady. Your natural Taurus vigilance is an asset today. This is not a time for impulsive action. You are not likely to jump into things without thinking. Attention to detail is strong, making this a great period to tidy up loose ends and to complete projects before beginning new ventures. Handle hot and sharp objects with care. Drivers should slow down and diligently obey the road rules. Stay firm on decisions you have already made. Many hands make light work, so pitch in to help teammates and housemates. A long-distance romance could gather momentum. Some of you might arrange travel plans so that you can visit a relative or lover residing abroad.

25. SUNDAY. Demanding. The celestial trends are busy today, so expect to see more action than you did yesterday. Many Bulls could experience problems with a partner over the cost of purchases. Right now the temptation to spend more than the budget allows is on the increase. Tensions with friends could emerge, love affairs are unlikely to proceed smoothly, social life might disappoint, and some of you might feel smothered by a significant other. Working behind the scenes toward a cherished desire you feel passionate about can test your endurance, commitment, and self-discipline. A personal lesson might be hard to grasp at first; but once you do, you will remember it forever.

26. MONDAY. Stimulating. Excitement pervades the atmosphere today. Many of you could find that your mind is inundated with new ideas, schemes, and plans. Include plenty of variety in your daily routine in order to limit boredom and monotony. There is a chance you want to purchase something that you cannot really afford, but it would be better to resist the temptation. Mercury moves out of retrograde and goes forward now in Scorpio, accentuating your house of partnerships. And lovely Venus, your ruler, is merging with serious Saturn in Scorpio. So there is a strong emphasis on marital bliss and on money from a business partnership. This is a good time to plan an engagement party or wedding ceremony.

27. TUESDAY. Favorable. Dynamic planet Mars fuels your motivation today. Energy is up. A fiery enthusiasm can take you to new heights, as the drive to obtain successful results increases. You might feel that there is not enough time in the day to do everything that needs to be done, so tackle the big things first. If you are traveling in unfamiliar territory, steer clear of danger spots, guard precious possessions, watch out for pickpockets, and ignore con artists trying to sell you something. Taurus detectives and researchers are likely to receive good results from investigative work. Students taking exams or presenting verbal reports should also do better than expected.

28. WEDNESDAY. Chancy. An eclipsed Gemini Full Moon brings money issues to the surface. If you are seeking a line of credit or a home mortgage, your chances are not auspicious right now. Pent-up emotions and frustrations could easily boil over, and you might become quickly overwhelmed by the tense atmosphere. An insightful talk could touch an emotional spot. Your love could return for a relationship or project over which you lost enthusiasm some time ago. Intense passion sparks romance on this day. Those of you seeking a new partner might be lucky if you circulate at the usual social haunts. Expect the unusual, though, and look for a surprise opening.

29. THURSDAY. Ardent. High emotions linger from yesterday, leading you toward certain choices and decisions. An end of a cycle could be reached. Or you may give up doing something that you have done for a long time. Today is also another wonderful day for love and romance. Someone familiar could claim your attention and perhaps your heart as well. Fun encounters should leave you smiling. This is a favorable period for those of you who are one half of a couple to organize romantic getaways so that you and your intimate partner can be alone to take advantage of loving vibes. Plans for an upcoming special occasion should come together nicely.

30. FRIDAY. Auspicious. Putting in extra effort to complete a task should be worthwhile. If there are negotiations to strike a deal, you will need to be organized and clear in your presentation to ensure that a contract favorable to your interests is drawn up. Creative inspiration can be a minefield for future success, so record whatever ideas come to mind. This is a good time to learn a new skill, study an interesting topic, or write a piece for publication. Make sure that communication with a business or intimate partner is clear and concise to avoid mix-ups and misunderstandings. Take a practical approach to problem solving; there is usually more than one way to reach a goal.

December 2012

1. SATURDAY. Uncomfortable. Mixed influences mark the first day of the last month of this year. A stressful situation might be presented, and will require careful handling if a quick resolution is to be found. Unless nervous anticipation and anxiety are used constructively, it would be very easy to become overwhelmed by this task or any other burdensome circumstances that arise. Refrain from gossiping, especially among friends in your social circle, and don't allow your mouth to run off unchecked. The urge to blurt out what is better kept to yourself may be hard to resist. A loved one could be a touch cranky. So unless you are prepared to deal with discord, steer clear of controversial topics.

2. SUNDAY. Lethargic. An extra cup of coffee might be needed to fire up many Bulls this morning. Restrictions seemingly placed by another, especially when it comes to financial concerns, might be stifling. Those of you heading out to the large department stores are cautioned to take it easy with the spending; the urge to splurge is high. Arguments with your partner over money management could take a turn for the worst if you cannot stay within budgetary boundaries. Consider using your innate creative skills to make festive goods if money is stretched to the limit; handcrafted goods are always valued highly. A personal experience could be a positive test of your resourcefulness.

3. MONDAY. Supportive. Matters of property and family life are in the frame as the Moon moves through your Leo solar sector. Weighing the pros and cons of saving money versus purchasing a gift for a loved one could add extra strain. Those of you expecting guests during the holiday period might want to beautify your living quarters. This can be inexpensive if you merely add small touches, perhaps a dash of color here and there, that express your flair. Taurus business owners might be under pressure to underwrite an innovative venture or to finance new debtors. Give extra tender loving care to a family member who is experiencing some sadness or unhappiness.

4. TUESDAY. Unsteady. Home and family life could be a little rocky under current lunar vibes. However, this is a passing phase and will not linger on to upset the upcoming festive period. Maintaining the balance between employment matters and personal life might be adding stress due to the number of negotiations and business tasks requiring attention and completion. Plans for renovations are likely to keep many Bulls busy. But at this time of year some work might not be finished before year's end. You may be unsure about taking a long trip before or during the holiday vacation time. Leaving familiar territory does not appeal to you right now, but wait before you make a decision

5. WEDNESDAY. Eventful. Festive greetings and communications might be filled with emotion now, and most of it should be happy news. Coping with the daily grind can proceed smoothly as long as you maintain a respectful yet lighthearted attitude. A number of planets are about to or are currently influencing your urge to learn. So expanding your knowledge through study, travel, or hands-on training would be beneficial. Your ability to penetrate the deepest reaches of topics of interests can make study interesting, easier, and fun. This is a favorable time to conduct research in any area, ranging from math to music to money and the markets.

6. THURSDAY. Useful. The cosmos provides the opportunity to get organized either on the job or at home. Use the time wisely to make headway on pending deadlines, outstanding paperwork, and the growing clutter around your work space or living space. Set a sensible goal for completion of these tasks, then do whatever is required to reach your target. A confidence from someone who holds a special place in your heart could raise some questions. Patience will be needed until another is ready to reveal the whole story. Pleasure grows when youngsters are involved in proceedings. If children have been deprived of your company recently, make sure this imbalance is corrected.

7. FRIDAY. Pressured. Muster as much restraint as possible. It may be one of those days when you wonder if staying in bed would be a better option than getting up and facing the crowd. There is a tendency for things to be misplaced or to go missing entirely. However, slowly rising to anger followed by sudden outbursts would only make matters worse instead of better. Take into account that diminishing physical energy is a possibility now, which suggests that labor-intensive and long-enduring tasks would be better left on the back burner. Dressing to impress and putting your best foot forward should provide the confidence you need to shine in a challenging social situation.

8. SATURDAY. Persevering. Diligence and hard work always pay off in the end, and this should be your motto to abide by today.

Although a range of bumps could appear in the roadway, your innate Taurus tenacity can achieve the desired rewards and dividends. Health matters are in focus. This is a good period to make sure you are in top physical shape, ready to enjoy the pleasures of the upcoming festive parties and social gatherings. Getting yourself into debt with extravagant purchases is not a good idea. So although this is a season of giving, make sure your practical and conservative nature is to the fore. Home entertaining should be a delightful treat for all guests tonight.

9. SUNDAY. Unsettled. Deceptive trends over the next few days require more care exercised with money management, financial negotiations, and buying and selling in general. Comparison shopping is a good idea, so conduct a little research before you actually enter a store. And don't just take the word of salespeople if an item is required to perform a specific action. Joining with others in a financial deal could help the savvy Bull expand property holdings or improve a portfolio position. But any investment proposal, regardless of how solid it seems, should receive due scrutiny before a decision is made. A newcomer to whom you are introduced may become important to you down the road.

10. MONDAY. Creative. Pouring love and attention into a special creative project will bring many moments of joy. If adjustments to an original design are required, do them without worrying whether you are sacrificing artistic integrity. Your effort will be worthwhile. A potential romantic admirer could be drawn to your charm and charisma, but taking things slowly without rushing in blindly would be advisable. Quick-witted planet Mercury zooms into Sagittarius, your solar eighth house of financial security and shared resources, for a three-week stay, impacting all money matters connected with other people, notably debt of any kind. Guard against overoptimism and a tendency to waste your resources.

11. TUESDAY. Volatile. Wild imaginings can give rise to an unrealistic attitude. The tendency to project fantasies onto others could bring difficulties. If the course you are pursuing seems to be leading nowhere, adjustments will be required. Confusion is rife now, so this isn't the period to trust certain people with your hopes and dreams. Sudden setbacks could assail you. Some Taurus will be misled by the tricky maneuvers of rivals out to steal your thunder or by the insincere motives of friends who really want to take advantage of your generosity. Keeping life simple is the recommendation now. Home entertaining might be quite stressful, so give it a miss.

12. WEDNESDAY. Spirited. Daydreaming or indulging in fantasies continues to be a cause for concern. Avoid misunderstandings in financial exchanges, limit your purchases to necessary essentials, and count the change given in any transaction. The risk of taking on more debt than affordable is high. It would be wise to stick with small monetary outlays. Self-employed Taurus should consider consulting a financial expert if help is needed managing money; it is better to take this action sooner rather than later. With the Moon now in the sign of fun-loving Sagittarius, you should enjoy an hour or two outdoors getting some gentle exercise and recreation or just quietly communing with nature.

13. THURSDAY. Constructive. A New Moon culminates before dawn in the sign of Sagittarius, giving you cause for optimism. A partner's income or jointly held property may require attention. Issues concerning a tax bill or an investment property should be resolved as quickly as possible. It is time to collect debts. Taurus business owners should recoup a number of outstanding payments if you make an exerted effort now. Those of you with loans and accounts outstanding could relieve some pressure by contacting companies or creditors and arriving at a satisfactory repayment agreement. If insurance coverage on business or personal possessions hasn't been updated for some time, consider doing this important task now.

14. FRIDAY. Stabilizing. Today's advice urges Taurus individuals to go slow and steady and to focus on practical matters. You may not want to proceed this way because of an atmosphere of edginess. Scattered energy could limit progress, meaning that you might begin a number of tasks without completing any of them. So observe the advice and home in on what is important. The opportunity to express new ideas and plans and to take diverse viewpoints into consideration will help you achieve something worthwhile. Your ability to charm people with whom you come in contact is enhanced, and they should be more than willing to listen to whatever you have to impart.

15. SATURDAY. Uplifting. Pack up the family and head off for a fun-packed day. The urge for adventure hits hard now. Visiting far-flung destinations may be not in the picture, though. If the most you can afford is a trip to the local park or shopping mall, you can still make that an inexpensive treat for loved ones, especially at this festive time of year. Taurus with vacation time due and plenty of moncy to spare might consider a journey to an exotic location or luxury resort. A woman could feature strongly in your life today, particularly someone who is living at a distance or away from home. Your luck improves in the romance stakes through sheer determination and staying power.

16. SUNDAY. Sensitive. Saucy Venus, your lifetime ruler, has just entered Sagittarius, your solar eighth house of deep personal transition. Venus in Sagittarius over the next three weeks ushers in a period of intensity and passion, and emphasizes the need for intimacy and love. An overly generous approach could find you splurging more than you should. Tone down the spending on festive gift giving and holiday partying, or deal with the consequences later. Over the next few days there is a strong likelihood that many Bulls will place a significant other on a pedestal. Inevitably, when this occurs, you are setting yourself and others up for a fall. Stop yourself from doing this and avoid subsequent disappointment.

17. MONDAY. Wary. Most Taurus people will be in hot demand socially as the holiday period draws closer. With your companionship sought after, guard your reputation zealously. Don't let people influence you unwisely or let a silly act undo all your hard work. Life isn't all about dollars and cents even for the most materialistic Bull. But you should still remain alert to possible career contacts who can help you advance swiftly up the ladder of success. A troubleshooting mood applies. So focus attention on the area that might need it the most, which may be your penchant for overspending. A vulnerability to flattery suggests that this isn't the right time to become romantically involved.

18. TUESDAY. Uncertain. It is a day to tell the truth or to say nothing at all. A waiting game is likely when it comes to romance. Over the next few days unanswered questions relating to a love affair could crop up. Problems could arise with a wedding ceremony, an overdue school assignment, or a visa application. It would be painful and expensive to drag out a particular legal matter. You should consider accepting the judgment or the settlement so that you can move on. Taurus folk could feel more competitive than usual, but this will give you the advantage in a sporting event or a public relations exercise. Spend some time developing an itinerary for your next vacation.

19. WEDNESDAY. Playful. Fun and romance are priorities today. Combining business with pleasure will work wonders for the Taurus entrepreneur looking to obtain new clients. Don't reveal all your ideas and schemes; keep a few aces up your sleeve and keep the players in suspense. Devoting energy to an artistic endeavor could be therapeutic, and this is a good time to get in touch with your inner feelings. Singles should go on a mission to develop a specific relationship further. Or put yourself in a position where you can meet other unattached people. A friendship could turn into something much more. A partner may get a fat bonus or a big commission check, and you will share in the bounty.

20. THURSDAY. Revealing. Resist the temptation to buy on impulse now even though you may be richer through either a gift of money from a loved one or the rewards of your own hard work. This can be a positive time to enter negotiations of all descriptions as long as you are aware that there may be hidden clauses and secrets not divulged. Don't be afraid to talk about your feelings, especially if resentments are being internalized. It is better to reveal concerns gradually than to let off steam all at once. If past hurts or regrets continue to be a source of annoyance, the wise move would be to let go and move on. Looking back in anger and wondering what could have been are merely exercises in futility.

21. FRIDAY. Interesting. Today marks the solstice and the beginning of a new season, winter in the northern hemisphere. At dawn the Sun enters the sign of Capricorn, your solar ninth house of the higher mind and belief systems. Sun in Capricorn urges Taurus people to take more interest in cultural, religious, and educational pursuits. With the Moon in Aries, your twelfth house of personal limitations and solitude, a nostalgic mood could have you thinking pleasant thoughts of yesteryear. Getting an early night is advised. If you cannot opt out of a social function, pace yourself and refrain from overindulging on food, drink, and anything else that is bad for your health.

22. SATURDAY. Encouraging. A busy start to the weekend is assured. Fighting the crowds might be the only option for those of you determined to do last-minute shopping, even if you arrive at the stores very early in the morning. The Moon enters your sign of Taurus after midday. Moderation is still a good practice to follow. If decisions are based on realistic plans, success can be attained and problems averted. Avoid implementing major life changes. Bulls in a new or blossoming love affair should remove the rose-colored glasses and put things into perspective. Mixed influences apply to the social scene. There may be a hiccup or unexpected expense that puts a damper on your party mood.

23. SUNDAY. Happy. With the Moon in your home sign of Taurus you might still be in party mode. Most things should lighten up considerably as the countdown to the big day begins. This is an auspicious period to invite people over to share warmth, hospitality, and a generous spirit; now is a time for giving. Something that you have wanted for a long time could suddenly materialize. Celebrating a family success or a personal achievement can bring emotional satisfaction. Appreciation that comes your way and given in a meaningful manner is a wonderful confidence boost. Return the compliment and display your gratitude and humility. Romance is likely to be private, intense, and very rewarding.

24. MONDAY. Reassuring. All eyes are looking your way now, so make sure you are well groomed and at your best before heading out the door. Accept interesting invitations that fit into your schedule. Being seen and noticed positively by others is empowering. Plans for your own family gathering might experience a few adjustments at the last minute, but this will add to rather than spoil the fun and excitement. Those of you currently going solo could discover that a wonderful new romance is in the offing. If you are in an established relationship, a desire for greater intimacy will encourage you to work harder to ensure that the zip and zest spice up your love life.

25. TUESDAY. Merry Christmas! All the hard work and effort applied over the last few weeks to make this a great day will surely pay off, and the scene is set to begin festive celebrations. Differences of opinions could occur between in-laws and other relatives, so be prepared to play peacemaker at times throughout the day. Recreational activity can help to discharge the restless energy that is in play. This is best handled by keeping everyone amused or engaged in gentle physical pursuits. Not all of your guests, whether neighbors or beloved friends and family, are going to be happy and outgoing. A feeling of homesickness or missing a special loved one could put a damper on high spirits.

26. WEDNESDAY. Opportune. Motivating planet Mars now starts what can be a fruitful period for the career-minded Taurus, with several options open from which you will be able to choose pursuits. Mars is gracing your Aquarius solar tenth house of vocation, status, and destiny in life for the next six weeks. Mars in Aquarius provides an opportunity to take huge strides toward your ultimate goals. Set the wheels in motion and turn your attention to professional and business pursuits. A promotion or transfer might be offered to you. Even if the move would mean relocating, possibly even going overseas, it should be seriously considered if advancing in your current field of expertise is your aim.

27. THURSDAY. Active. Post-season sales might be calling to Bulls who regard shopping as a relaxing and therapeutic pursuit. Those of you attempting to return unwanted gifts to the stores could be in for a shock. Goods are unlikely to be refunded without the original sales receipt, and store policy might be very strict on what will be accepted. Learning something important from a loved one could be a thrill. Over the next few months changes in your life are likely to occur. The ability to take a flexible approach will be essential. New projects and situations can be successfully implemented but only for Taurus individuals who are ready to let go of the old and embrace the new.

28. FRIDAY. Stormy. A certain amount of frustration will be evident today. Be prepared, as the Cancer Full Moon is bound to raise emotional sensitivity and lower physical vitality. The accent will be on communication, so take care with the spoken word. If you have the authority, consider delegating mundane duties; you can supervise from a distance. Conflict in the workplace will be disconcerting, so endeavor to remain under the radar and out of reach of any colleagues who are prone to argue. Taurus professionals who are struggling with image and reputation are likely to take steps now to make sure you are taken more seriously by your peers as well by the people who wield power higher up the ladder.

29. SATURDAY. Moderate. On this leisure day many Taurus people should observe the advice about doing everything in moderation. If you do succumb to temptation and overindulge to a point of excess, be ready to experience a guilt trip. Dreaming big and fantasizing about a glorious future can be productive at times. But right now you need to be practical and forget those grandiose ideas and schemes that have little basis in reality. This is a positive period to organize a special New Year's Eve celebration. Let someone else take charge of the budget, as keeping within a set limit might be impossible for you. Keeping the channels of communication open will strengthen loving ties with a significant other.

30. SUNDAY. Thrilling. The universe conveys power plus today. You should feel stronger than usual and very able to cope with all forms of interruptions, hassles, or equipment breakdowns. Family secrets could be revealed, but this should work to your advantage. Your Taurus leadership qualities are highlighted, and you could assume a position of authority now. Social events, whether casual or formal, might be held in your honor or for a close loved one. This is a great day to start the research for a book on family history; you may learn something exciting about relatives from a distant land. Taurus first-time travelers abroad are about to be awed by famous sites and sightseeing in general.

31. MONDAY. Sparkling. As the year comes to an end, messenger planet Mercury moves into Capricorn, your house of travel, philosophical beliefs, and academic qualifications. Tackling a backlog of work before the new year kicks in would be worthwhile, but don't go overboard. A sense that things are about to change could find many Bulls moving out of your comfort zone, more prepared to take risks and to do something very different from your usual mode of operations. Taurus planning on celebrating at home or elsewhere should maintain a responsible and sensible attitude when it comes to having fun. Put impulsive actions aside so that you will be happy and healthy and wise this New Year's Eve.

FREE PARTY LINE

Stay connected 24/7 with interesting people that call to party!

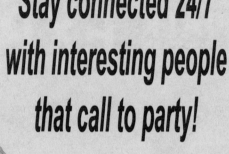

712-338-7724